Traditional Horse Husbandry

Traditional Horse Husbandry
A Practical Guide to Horsekeeping

Carl W. Gay
Edited by Kary C. Davis, Ph.D.
Foreword by Steve D. Price

THE LYONS PRESS
Guilford, Connecticut
An imprint of The Globe Pequot Press

The Lyons Press is an imprint of The Globe Pequot Press

10 9 8 7 6 5 4 3 2 1

Printed in the United States of America

ISBN 1-58574-817-X

Library of Congress Cataloging-in-Publication data
is available on file.

FOREWORD TO THE 2003 EDITION

Some two years ago the Newport, Rhode Island, Jumping Derby included among its events an auction of European warmblood dressage and jumping horses. Organized by a former world-class show jumping rider turned horse dealer, it was a no-expense-spared production. Huge tents housed the horses that, we were assured, had been specially selected and imported from the finest European breeding facilities. The day before the auction, the dressage horses were put through their paces and the jumpers shown over a small course of fences ("these horses are so uncomplicated, even girls can handle them," touted the announcer, neglecting to add that the "girls" in the saddle happened to be Olympic-caliber riders).

The auction took place in the evening, following a reception with vast quantities of champagne intended to lubricate voices for bidding and hands for wallet-reaching. The tent in which the sale was held was festooned with flowers imported from Holland. A disk jockey spun recorded music selected to underscore the dressage horses' performances and the jumpers' being free-jumped through a chute.

Glancing around at the proceedings, a colleague turned to me and said, using a popular expression of the day, "There's a lot of sizzle—let's hope there's some steak too."

The memory of that comment came to mind as I read TRADITIONAL HORSE HUSBANDRY. In an age when "sport" has eclipsed "industry" in the minds of the majority of horselovers and where the word "husbandry" sends many readers galloping to the dictionary, Dr. Gay's book provides virtually no sizzle, but a great deal of steak of the practical variety.

Several decades ago when scientific and technical advances were growing more common, the author's intent was similarly to present information on breeding, showing, and dealing in a similar fashion. To quantify as well as qualify, to treat the subject as a science, it was clearly Dr. Gay's goal, would make producing, training, buying, and selling livestock cost-, time-, and energy efficient. Which is, of course, the very definition of the word "husbandry."

Some of the book's contents are admittedly of an era. To refer to the relationship between equine and human as between horse and master, as Dr. Gay does in Chapter XIII, is light years away from our contemporary attitude of friendship and partnership. However, those were the days when horses were not pampered; the relationship was all business. Similarly, we now refer to the process of training horses to accept tack and rider as starting or gentling, certainly not as breaking.

Readers whose interest in riding includes jumping will be intrigued by the photographs of pre-World War I form over fences. At that time, the concept of the forward seat, in which the rider's weight remains over the horse's forehand from takeoff to landing, was still in its formative stage, accepted by only a handful of European cavalrymen. That riders could survive, much less prosper, by leaning backward over formidable fences seems impossible. But they did, and that's a testimony to their secure seats and sense of balance as well as their mounts' ability.

However, far from being only of historic curiosity, TRADITIONAL HORSE HUSBANDRY offers information that remains relevant today. The discussions of breeds and types of horses, breeding principles and practices, and stable management are worth considering in the light of contemporary horsekeeping.

Among the hallmarks of that era was a transition in transportation. The automobile became affordable in the decade before World War I, which meant that horsedrawn buggies and wagons were forced to share urban and rural roads with private and commercial horseless carriages. Commentators spoke and wrote with assurance that the days of the horse were limited.

They could not, of course, have been more wrong. There are now more horses in the United States than at the turn of the century. Some, such as those used for ranch work or hauling logs, still cannot be improved upon by any mechanical equivalent.

As for the horse in contemporary sport, one need look no farther than this book. Dr. Gay wrote, "Motor possibilities have left horses, except those in the commercial field, chiefly in the hands of those who want them because they are horses, with the result that they are now in their highest estate, a condition most satisfactory to them and most gratifying to those interested in their well-being."

And with regard to the commercial side, the author tells us with remarkable prescience that "Competition stimulates to best efforts. Now the consumers of horses are discriminating; demand is for horses of the highest type. It has been observed that after an experience in buying and maintaining automobiles in service one becomes more appreciative of horse values and more liberal in his allowance for cost. The result will be more intelligent and systematic breeding for a definite purpose, with consequently less failures, and, finally, a more liberal profit to him who meets the demand of those who can afford to discriminate and pay well for what they require."

The organizers of the Newport horse auction couldn't have said it better.

Steven D. Price
New York, NY

PREFACE

It has been the author's purpose to emphasize *industry* as applied to horses. If the production, marketing, and use of horses were regarded as an industry and conducted more generally along business lines, with a definite purpose in view, more uniform results could be obtained and with greater profit to those engaged.

It is quite generally conceded that the investigations of the experiment stations, as well as the instruction in the schools and colleges, have been more exhaustive in their application to cattle, hogs, sheep, and poultry than to horses. This is unrepresentative of the importance of the horse industry and inadequate to its needs. The aimless, hit or miss, haphazard system prevails in the production of horses more than in any other class of live stock; the scrub stallion is less in disrepute than the scrub bull, and most producers of market cattle, hogs, or sheep devote themselves more intelligently to their enterprise than do the breeders of horses.

Commonly the original producer receives a lower percentage of the price which a horse ultimately brings than is the case with most market products. Indifference to market demands and lack of information concerning the best means of meeting the requirements are largely responsible for the advantage of the middleman. In fact, they constitute the principal asset of a certain class of dealers who derive their profits in direct proportion to the ignorance of those from whom they buy and to whom they sell.

Notwithstanding the keen competition between the horse and the motor in some fields, the horse business in general is on a sound basis and bids fair to continue so, as far as can be foreseen. But to successfully compete requires most careful attention to detail. *Economic efficiency* is the standard by which comparisons are made. Science and system must govern in the profitable production of market horses and their subsequent service.

Economy and efficiency have, therefore, ruled in the preparation of this subject-matter. The scope of the work outlined is too broad to admit of an extended discussion of all points referred to. Duplication of other texts has been avoided, as far as possible, while those phases of the subject that have received the least mention prior to this time have been most fully developed.

This book is intended to present to students of live stock husbandry the same systematic and complete study of the horse that has been accorded the other classes of live stock. Works on the horse are legion, and many of them excellent, but the majority of writers view the proposition from an angle which does not comprehend the student's requirements so fully as is attempted here.

The author duly acknowledges much valuable information gleaned from the current literature on the subject, while he claims no authority but assumes entire responsibility for the accuracy of much that is said. He deeply appreciates the counsel and assistance of a wide acquaintance of practical horsemen in acquiring the fund of horse lore from which the material, herewith presented, is drawn.

Sectionalism and partiality to special classes or breeds have been avoided. Emphasis has been laid upon the practical side of horse husbandry. Students as well as horse breeders have been kept in mind while preparing this book. It is hoped that short-course students and college students will alike be able to use the text to advantage. The grouping of the chapters into four parts should aid in rapid reference and student work.

CARL W. GAY.

UNIVERSITY OF PENNA.,
    Nov., 1913.

CONTENTS

ILLUSTRATIONS

xi

PART I
STRUCTURE AND FUNCTION

PRODUCTIVE
HORSE HUSBANDRY

CHAPTER I

THE HORSE—A MACHINE

A horse's usefulness depends upon his power of locomotion. A clear conception of his simple mechanical features affords the best means of measuring his serviceability.

As a mechanical structure the horse consists chiefly of an arch, represented by his vertebræ, supported upon four upright columns, his legs. The balance of this arch is largely determined

by the position of the appended head and neck at one end, and the tail at the other. In the standing position all four legs have a supporting function, although greater weight is borne by the forelegs. In locomotion the hind legs are propellers, the forelegs retaining their supportive function, the degree of which is increased to the extent of constituting a lift (Fig. 1). The propulsive effort of the hindquarters is met by the forehand in such a manner as to maintain the equilibrium as the body is advanced.

Locomotion is accomplished by the supporting columns being

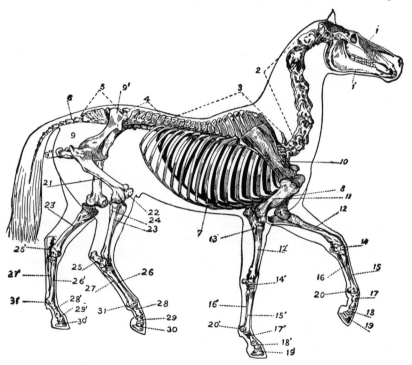

FIG. 2.—Skeleton of the horse, showing the vertebral arch and the bone columns, one pair of legs supporting, the alternate pair, partially flexed, in a stride. 1, bones of the head; 1', lower jaw; 2, cervical vertebræ; 3, dorsal vertebræ; 4, lumbar vertebræ; 5, sacral vertebræ (sacrum); 6, coccygeal vertebræ; 7, ribs; 8, sternum (breast-bone); 9, pelvis; 9', ilium; 9'', ischium; 10, scapula (shoulder-blade); 11, humerus; 12, radius; 13, ulna; 14, carpus (knee); 15, large metacarpal bone (canon); 16, rudimentary metacarpal bones (splint-bones); 17, os suffraginis (long pastern); 18, os coronæ (short pastern); 19, os pedis (hoof-bone); 20, sesamoid bones; 21, femur; 22, patella (knee-pan, stifle); 23, tibia; 24, fibula; 25, tarsus, or hock; 26, large metatarsal bone (canon); 27, rudimentary metatarsals (splint bones); 28, os suffraginis (long pastern); 29, os coronæ (short pastern); 30, os pedis (hoof-bone, "coffin-bone"); 31, sesamoid bones.

broken, and the foot elevated, by the flexion of the joints, into a position from which it is advanced by the subsequent extension of the joints. A single advance of one foot constitutes a stride, and a series of strides, which involve in turn the four feet, brings the entire structure to an advanced position (Fig. 2). Each alternate pair of legs supports the weight while the other pair is executing a stride. The primary motive for the stride is furnished by the hindquarters, the propulsive action of which displaces the centre of gravity forward, to such an extent as to necessitate locomotion in order to maintain or regain the equilibrium. There are five distinct phases of the stride:

1. A preliminary, during which the leg is undergoing flexion, but the foot has not left the ground, at which point the real stride begins.

2. The breaking over, in which the foot is raised heel first, finally leaving the ground by being rocked up and over at the toe.

Fig. 3.—Each and every phase of the stride is demonstrated by some one of the ten fore and ten hind legs shown.

3. Flight, during which the foot is describing a more or less regular arc of a perpendicular circle.

4. Contact, at which point the foot is again brought to the ground.

5. Recovery, as the weight gradually falls on the foot and the original position of the leg is momentarily established, preparatory to a repetition of the stride (Fig. 3).

Mechanical Analogy.—In order to carry out the idea of a mechanical analogy, the digestive system of the horse may be regarded as the boiler whence the energy is supplied; the muscular system as comprising the motors; the power exerted by the muscle motors at the expense of the energy derived from the digestive boilers, operating the bone columns, by the alternate flexion and extension of which locomotion is accomplished; the whole procedure being under the control of the nervous system.

Muscular Action.—In accomplishing locomotion, the part played by the muscles is fundamental. The chief characteristic of muscular tissue is its contractility. Contraction takes place on receiving a stimulus through the voluntary nerve, which terminates between the two extremities of the muscle. One end of

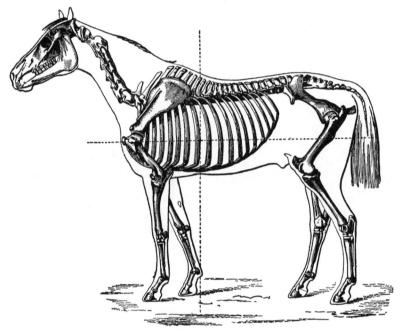

Fig. 4.—Situation of the centre of gravity in the horse.

the muscle has a fixed insertion; the other is attached to a movable bone lever. The two bones are apposed end to end, by means of a joint, the surfaces of which permit of motion of one or both bones, the degree or amount of motion depending upon the kind of articulation. When, therefore, the contracting muscle draws the movable bone to which it is attached toward the bone to which it has its fixed insertion, either flexion or extension of the joint takes place.

The centre of gravity in the horse, standing naturally, has been fixed at that point in the median vertical plane of the body where a perpendicular line from the posterior extremity of the breast-bone intersects the line of division between the lower and middle thirds of the body divided horizontally (Fig. 4). The centre of gravity is stationary only when the horse is standing

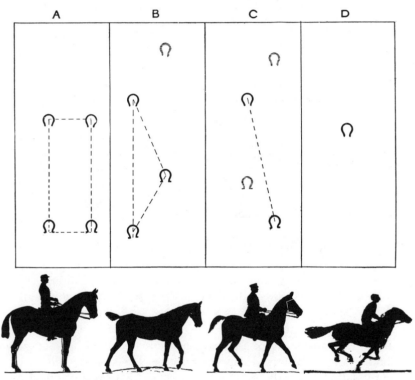

Fig. 5.—Diagram showing contact of feet in various gaits. A, standing, rectangular base of support; B, walking, triangular base of support; C, trotting, linear base of support; D, running, point base of support.

absolutely still. When moving, there is a constantly repeated displacement; ultimately in the direction taken by the leading foot, although prior to the commencement of the stride, there is a momentary displacement in the opposite direction, as the weight is shifted to the supporting leg in order to reduce the weight on the side of the foot to be advanced.

The stability of equilibrium is in direct proportion to the size and especially the width of the base of support. It is the measure of power. Power and speed are not correlated but opposite extremes. Instability of equilibrium is the measure of speed. In order, therefore, that the horse may take strides in rapid succession, the base of support must be so reduced as to permit of the ready displacement of the centre of gravity. It may then readily follow the direction of each stride in turn. Increase in the rapidity of the stride has the effect of reducing the size of the base of support, so that the faster a horse goes the more favorable are the conditions for still greater speed. This is exemplified in the fact that the base of support is a rectangle in case of the horse at rest(Fig.5). It is reduced to the general form of a triangle as the horse leads out with one foot at the walk. It takes the form of a line as the horse extends himself at the trot or pace; and finally it consists of a point only as but one foot is on the ground at the run. On the other hand, the horse at the run is not capable of any draft effort except that which comes from the momentum he has already attained; he has a better chance at the trot; can pull well at the walk, and he is capable of his greatest effort at the starting of the load, as he is practically standing on all fours (Fig. 6).

FIG. 6.—During the greatest effort the base of support is rectangular, the horse being practically on all fours.

REVIEW

1. Of what does the horse's mechanical structure consist?
2. How is locomotion accomplished?
3. What constitutes a stride and what are its phases?
4. Explain the part played by the muscles in locomotion.
5. Where is the centre of gravity in the horse standing naturally?

6. How does the centre of gravity conduct itself when the horse moves?
7. What is the relation of the size of the base of support to the stability of the equilibrium?
8. What are the changes in the size and shape of the base of support which may occur as the horse progresses from the standing position to the run?
9. How does the stability of the equilibrium measure the power of which a horse is capable?
10. How does the instability of the equilibrium measure the speed of which a horse is capable?

CHAPTER II

CONFORMATION—THE STRUCTURE

Conformation is the " putting together " of the parts which, collectively, compose the animal structure. Its study has reference to the proportions, dimensions, external contour, and internal construction of the parts and their relation in the general arrangement. Not only should the parts be well formed individually, but they must fit and blend with the other parts in order to make the whole structure symmetrical and sound. The strength of a chain is measured by the strength of its weakest link. In the same manner defection in one part of conformation may offset an otherwise perfect structure. Unlike a chain, however, the parts or units of conformation in a horse are not identical. Some are of greater relative importance than others, and interfere more with serviceability in case they prove defective. A study of conformation consists in the detection of points of superiority and inferiority of structure, and in allotting to each their proper significance.

For the purpose of studying conformation, the structure may be divided into regions and each region subdivided into its component parts, with specifications for each (Fig. 7).

Head and Neck.—*Head.*—Size proportionate to size of horse; dimensions—length, breadth, and depth—proportionate to each other; face line straight; features sharply defined; lower jaw strong with open angle between branches so as not to compress larynx when neck is flexed.

Forehead.—Broad, full and flat.

Ears.—Medium size, fine, pointed, set close, carried alert.

Eyes.—Prominently set, large, full, clear, bright, lids thin, uniform curvature, no angle caused by atrophy (Fig. 8).

Muzzle.—Not too fine, nostrils large but not dilated, lips thin, trim, teeth regular, sound.

Neck.—Long, lean, crest marked, but not too heavy, throat latch fine, head well set on.

10

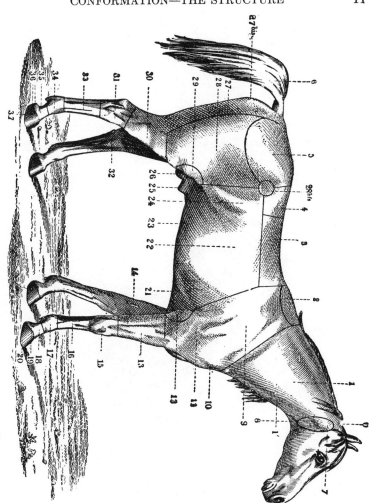

FIG. 7.—Regions of the horse seen in profile.

0. Poll or nape of the neck
1. Neck.
1'. Jugular gutter.
2. Withers.
3. Back.
4. Loins.
5. Croup.
6. Tail.
7. Parotid region.
8. Throat.
9. Shoulder.
10. Point of the shoulder.
11. Arm.
12. Elbow.
13. Forearm.
14. Chestnut.
15. Knee.
16. Canon.
17. Fetlock.
18. Pastern.
19. Coronet.
20. Foot.
21. Xiphoid region.
22. Ribs.
23. Abdomen.
24. Flank.
25. Sheath.
26. Testicles.
27. Buttock.
27 bis. Angle of buttock.
28. Thigh.
28 bis. Haunch.
29. Stifle.
30. Leg.
31. Hock.
32. Chestnut.
33. Canon.
34. Fetlock.
35. Pastern.
36. Coronet.
37. Foot.

Forehand.—*Withers.*—Well set up, extending well back, muscular but neither low nor heavy, free from scars.

Shoulders.—Long, oblique, smooth.

Arms.—Short, muscular, carried forward.

Forearms.—Broad and muscular.

Knees.—Size proportionate to the weight of the horse, straight, broad, deep, smooth, strongly supported.

Canons.—Short, broad, fluted. Tendons, smooth, well set back.

Fetlocks.—Wide, smooth, well supported.

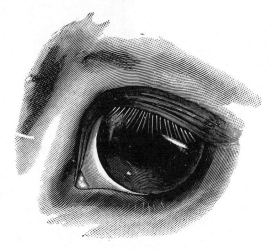

FIG. 8.—Normal eye.

Pasterns.—Long, sloping but strong.

Feet.—Size in proportion to the weight of the horse, uniform; form circular, walls straight, slope corresponding to slope of pastern; height at toe, side wall, and heel as 3 to 2 to 1. Sole concave, bars strong, frog large, elastic, heels wide, full; texture of horn dense, smooth, dark colored (Fig. 9).

Legs.—Viewed from in front, a perpendicular line dropped from the point of the shoulder should divide the leg and foot into two lateral halves (Fig. 10). Viewed from the side, a perpendicular line dropped from the tuberosity on the scapula should pass through the centre of the elbow-joint and meet the ground at the centre of the foot [1] (Fig. 11).

Body.—*Chest.*—Deep, full, large girth.

Ribs. — Long, well sprung, close.

Back.—Short, straight, strong.

Loins.—Broad, strong, coupling well back, smooth; flank, close, full, deep; top line short, level; under line long, let well down in flank.

Hindquarters.— *Hips.* —Wide, smooth, level.

Croup.—Long, level, broad, muscular.

Tail.—Set high, well carried.

Thighs.—Long, muscular, deep.

Stifles.—Wide, thick, muscular.

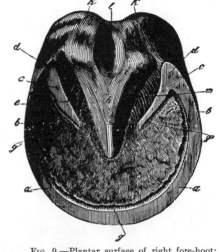

Fig. 9.—Plantar surface of right fore-hoot: *a, a,* bearing surface of the toe; *a, b,* bearing surface of the side walls or mammæ; *b, c,* bearing surface of the quarters; *d,* buttress, or angle formed by wall and bar; *e,* bar; *f,* sole; *f′,* branches of the sole; *g,* white line; it passes between the sole and bars and ends at *g′; h,* horny frog; *i,* branches of the frog; *k,* heels, bulbs, or glomes of the hoof; *l,* median lacuna of horny frog. Between the bars and the horny frog lie the lateral lacunæ of the frog.

Gaskins.—Long, broad, muscular.

Hocks.—Size in proportion to weight of horse, wide, deep, straight, flat, smooth, point prominent, well supported.

---

[1] The correct standing position of the horse at rest has formerly been determined from side view by a perpendicular line dropped from the tuberosity of the scapula, which it was claimed should divide the leg to the fetlock and meet the ground just back of the heel. It has been frequently demonstrated, however, that the best horses do not conform to this standard, but show, as a rule, a slight deviation downward and backward, which brings the fetlock posterior to the line which terminates in the centre of the foot. Recently Doctor H. Schwyter, technical secretary to the federal chief veterinarian of Switzerland, has established the direction described above as being correct. By it the centres of weight-bearing and of the base of support coincide as they should.

Canons, Fetlocks, Pasterns, Feet.—Size in proportion to weight of horse, wide, deep, straight, flat, smooth, point prominent, well supported.

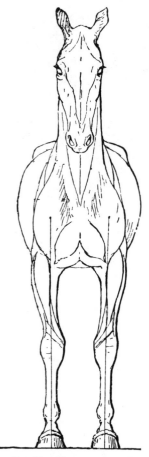

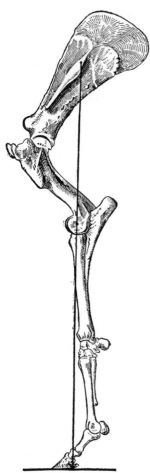

FIG. 10.—The correct standing position of the foreleg, viewed from in front, as determined by the plumb line.

FIG. 11.—The correct standing position of the foreleg, viewed from the side, as determined by the plumb line.

Legs.—Viewed from the rear, a perpendicular line dropped from the point of the buttock should divide leg and foot into lateral halves (Fig. 12); viewed from the side, this line should touch the point of the hock and meet the ground some little distance back of the heel. A perpendicular line dropped from the hip-joint should meet the ground midway between heel and toe (Fig. 13).

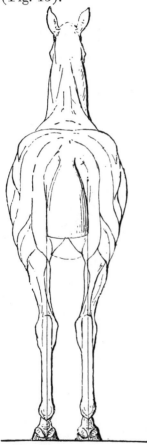

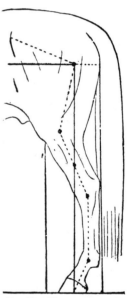

FIG. 12.—The correct standing position of the hind leg, viewed from the rear, as determined by the plumb line.

FIG. 13.—The correct standing position of the hind leg, viewed from the side, as determined by the plumb line.

REVIEW

1. What sort of an eye should be avoided in selecting a horse?
2. Where are the withers and what are their desirable features?
3. When is the foreleg in the correct standing position and of what importance is it?

4. Describe the ground surface of a normal forefoot.
5. In a horse of good conformation, how should the top line compare with the under line?
6. What are the common undesirable features of the croup?
7. What kind of stifles should a horse have?
8. What are the gaskins?
9. Describe the hock that is most likely to remain sound under stress of wear.
10. What is the importance of having the hind legs well set?

CHAPTER III

WAY OF GOING—THE FUNCTION

THE term, way of going, is self-defining. Pace refers to the rate at which the horse moves. Action implies flexion of knees and hocks.

The Stride presents for study the following features:

1. Length, the distance from the point of breaking over to the point of contact.

2. Directness, the line in which the foot is carried forward during the stride.

3. Rapidity, the time consumed in taking the stride.

4. Power, the pulling force exerted at each stride.

5. Height, the degree to which the foot is elevated in the stride, indicated by the radius of the arc described.

6. Spring, the manner in which the weight is settled upon the leg and foot at the completion of the stride.

7. Regularity, the rhythmical precision with which each stride is taken, in turn.

8. Balance, the relative degree of any of the other features of the stride manifested by fore and hind legs.

THE GAITS

A gait is a particular way of going which is characterized by definite and distinctive features regularly executed.

Walk is a slow, flat-footed, four-beat gait; one of the most useful, whether in harness or under saddle, if executed with snap and animation, as it should be.

Trot is a rapid, two-beat gait, in which the diagonal fore and hind legs act together. The fast stepping trot is characterized by the length and rapidity with which the individual strides are accomplished, and is executed with an extreme degree of extension (Fig. 14). The high stepping trot is characterized by the height and spring of the stride, the horse placing himself, going collectedly and executing each step with an extreme degree of flexion and the utmost precision (Fig. 15).

Pace is a rapid, two-beat gait, in which the lateral fore and hind legs act together (Fig. 16). It is characterized by the readiness with which pacers can get away at speed, a minimum of concussion, more or less side motion, the absence of much knee fold (although some pacers are trappy), and the necessity for smooth, hard footing and easy draft, for its execution. It is difficult for most pacers to go in deep or heavy footing, such as

FIG. 14.—The fast trot, characterized as a diagonal gait of extreme extension and rapidity of stride.

fresh snow, sand or mud, and they have a jerky, unsteady way of pulling a wagon, if any pull is necessary. The increased draft of an additional person up behind or of a rough bit of road will swing most pacers into a trot if they can trot at all. Jogging down hill will force some trotters to pace, while an up grade will set pacers to trotting. The pace is more essentially a speed than a road gait.

Amble is a lateral gait usually distinguished from the pace by being slower and more broken in cadence.

Rack is a fast, flashy, four-beat gait, more clearly defined by the discarded name " single foot." It is rarely executed voluntarily but under compulsion of hand and heel, and is characterized by quite a display of knee action, and many horses can rack very fast. While most agreeable to the rider, it is most distressing to the horse, and should therefore be called for with discretion.

Gallop is a fast, three-beat gait, in which two diagonal legs are paired, their single beat falling between the successive beats of the other two legs, the hind one of which makes the first beat of the three (Fig. 17). With the third and last beat the horse is

Fig. 15.—The high-stepping trot, showing extreme flexion of knees and hocks.

projected clear of all contact with the ground, as in a leap, and there is a period of silence, broken by the contact of the independent hind foot, in the commencement of a new series. The two legs acting independently, the fore, with which the horse leads, and its diagonal hind, naturally bear more weight and are subject to more fatigue than are the other pair which act simultaneously, and, therefore, divide or bear jointly the work. The hind leg receiving the full weight at the phase of contact at the conclusion of the leap bears more than the foreleg, which supports the weight alone just before the projection of the horse at the beginning of the leap. The gallop may become so fast as to break the simultaneous beats of the diagonal pair, the hind foot striking first and causing four beats, although following in such rapid succession as to be distinguished with difficulty.

Canter is a restrained gallop in which the weight is sustained chiefly by the hindquarters, the lightened forehand rising and falling in a high, bounding fashion, the gait being executed in a slow, collected, rhythmical way, on either lead at command. Since the canter, like the gallop, imposes a special wear on the leading forefoot and its diagonal hind, the lead should be changed frequently. When the simultaneous beat is of a lateral instead of a diagonal pair of feet, and falls between the successive beats

FIG. 16.—The pace, a lateral gait of extreme extension and rapidity of stride.

of the other lateral pair, the leading fore and hind on the same side, it constitutes a cross or *lateral canter,* and is productive of a twisting motion to one in the saddle.

Jump, whether high or broad, is accomplished by the forelegs raising the forehand at the take-off, thus bringing the body in line with the direction in which the jump is to be taken, when a strong, propulsive effort of the hindquarters carries it over or across, as the case may be (Fig. 18). In alighting, the forefeet come in contact with the ground first and almost simultaneously, the leading foot being a little in advance, after which the horse quickly gathers himself in a stride to avoid the hind feet, which follow quickly and strike the ground slightly ahead of the imprints of the forefeet.

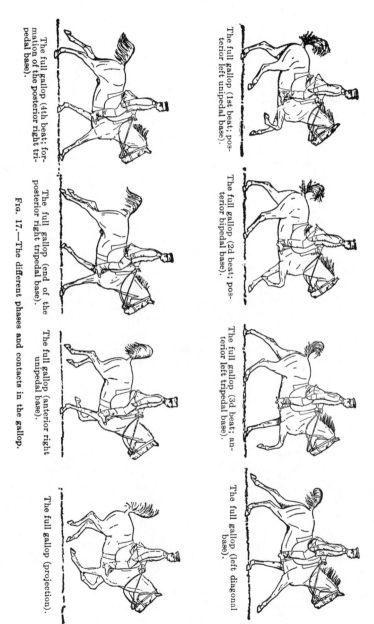

The full gallop (1st beat; posterior left unipedal base).

The full gallop (2d beat; posterior left tripedal base).

The full gallop (3d beat; anterior left tripedal base).

The full gallop (left diagonal base).

The full gallop (4th beat; formation of the posterior right tripedal base).

The full gallop (end of the posterior right tripedal base).

The full gallop (anterior right unipedal base).

The full gallop (projection).

Fig. 17.—The different phases and contacts in the gallop.

The leap (preparation).   The leap (propulsion)

The leap (passing the obstacle).

The leap (descent in front).   The leap (descent behind).

FIG. 18.—The different phases and contacts in the jump.

Running walk is a slow, single foot or four-beat gait, intermediate between the walk and rack, suggestive of a continued breaking out of a walk. It is the business gait in the South and West, where gaited horses are ridden extensively, since it can be maintained all day. It is good for six to eight miles an hour, with the greatest possible ease to both horse and rider.

The fox trot is a short, broken, nodding trot, in which the hind legs go in more or less of a lateral step. It is used as a substitute for the running walk.

The stepping pace is distinct from the ordinary pace of the harness horse, being characterized by very little if any side motion and a somewhat broken cadence in the action of the lateral pairs of legs.

The traverse is a side step, in which the forehand and hindquarters respond to both rein and heel; it is useful in opening and closing gates, when riding after cattle, also to " dress " or take position in a troop drill.

FACTORS DETERMINING WAY OF GOING

The factors determining a horse's way of going are either natural or acquired. The former consist of type, conformation, direction of leg and form of foot, and breeding. The acquired influences are schooling, handling, and mechanical appliances.

Type.—The close observer of athletic events is impressed with either the distinctiveness which exists among the winners of the different events or the similarity of type of those who excel in the same feats.

On account of the correlation between form and function, a horse must do as he is. His capabilities in the way of performance will be limited in some respects and extended in others, according to the plan of his structure. A short, thick, low set horse will have more power than speed, the reverse being equally true. A cobby horse has a trappy stride, while the stride of a tall, rangy horse is characterized by reach.

Conformation.—A horse low in the forehand is liable to forge, while one long and loosely coupled will have a tendency toward an incoördinate way of going.

Direction of Leg and Form of Foot.—The relation that the direction of the leg bears to the form of the foot is most intimate, and each is an important factor in determining the directness, especially, of the stride. The form of the foot fixes the point at which the leg breaks over; the centre of the toe, or the outer or inner quarter depending upon whether the foot is symmetrical or

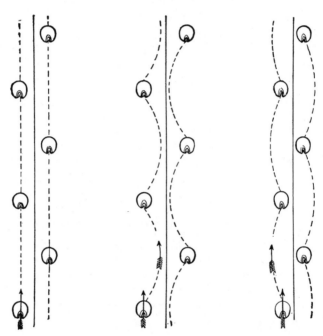

Course taken by the foot in correct standing position.

Course taken by the foot in base or toe wide direction of leg.

Course taken by the foot in base or toe narrow direction of leg.

Fig. 19.—Relation of direction of leg to course taken by foot in the stride.

the inner or outer quarter is higher. The direction of the leg determines the course taken by the foot during its stride, whether advanced in a straight line or describing the arc of a circle inward or outward, depending upon the deviation in the direction of the leg (Fig. 19). The form of the foot and the direction of the leg are correlated, usually, so that their combined influence on the way of going may be considerable.

The following are the common deviations in the direction of the leg. Foreleg viewed from the side: Figs. 20, 21 and 22. Foreleg viewed from in front: Figs. 23, 24, 25, 26, 27 and 28.

Hind leg viewed from the side: Fig. 29.

Hind leg viewed from the rear: Figs. 30 and 31.

Breeding has most to do with the particular gait at which a horse goes. One may visit a collection of foals or weanlings in a field, and upon starting them off across the field note that some

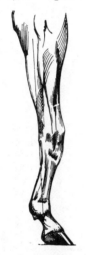 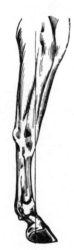 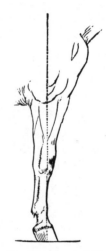

FIG. 20.—Knee-sprung or over on the knees. FIG. 21.—Calf-kneed. FIG. 22.—Too straight pastern.

square away at a long, reachy trot, others go high enough to clear the tops of the daisies, while still others break away in an easy gallop, each gait being executed with equal ease and naturalness. The reason is found in the fact that the first described lot are Trotting-bred, the second are Hackneys and the others are Thoroughbreds. In each of these the particular way of going is a matter of breed character, and the instinct to go that way is almost as strong as for either the field dog to point or the game bird to battle.

Heredity.—Type, conformation, direction of leg and form of foot are all more or less hereditary characters and are asso-

26 STRUCTURE AND FUNCTION

ciated with a corresponding instinct. A colt is not likely to be endowed by inheritance with an instinct to trot and at the same time inherit a structure which is only adapted to galloping. Horses are occasionally seen, however, which, though bred properly, manifest a disposition to do what they are physically incapable of doing. Others seem structurally qualified for superior performance of some one sort, but fall far short of doing anything remarkable, because they do not know how. Hence, we know that the highest order of performance can only be attained when the inherited instinctive tendencies are in line with the horse's inherited physical development.

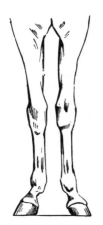 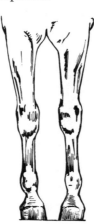 

FIG. 23.—Base narrow, toe wide; nigger-heeled or splay-footed.

FIG. 24.—Toe narrow or pigeon-toed.

FIG. 25.—Knock-kneed.

Schooling.—Horses, like men, reflect in their attainments: First, their inherent capabilities, and, second, what has been made of them. All the graduates of a given academic or gymnasium course are not equals, either in their mental or physical accomplishments. Neither are all those who have been deprived of any educational advantages destined to a common level or rank in society. Some from the latter class may even reach a higher rung on the commercial or social ladder than others from the first class. An individual may owe his proficiency to either his opportunities or what is in him, exclusively, or to a favorable combination of both. Only the highest education, in accordance with the strongest natural aptitude, can accomplish the greatest attainment. Hence, it is hardly worth while to spend time and money in educating a colt in ways to which he is not adapted. It is a difficult and unsatisfactory task to school a born trotter to an acceptable show of action. Ample proof of the accuracy of this statement, reversed, is found in the earlier days of horse shows in this country. It was common to find single-minded horsemen resorting to all sorts of ingenious ways and means of

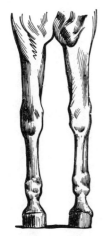  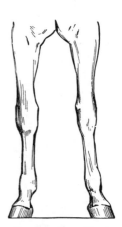

Fig. 26.—Bow-kneed.   Fig. 27.—Too close at ground.   Fig. 28.—Too wide at ground.

preventing a horse from going high in order to make a trotter of him. They often gave up in despair, and sacrificed him to the knowing buyer, who, by changing tactics and schooling him along the line of action for which he had a strong inclination, finally turned him out a show horse of note. If, on the other hand, we take a natural character and develop it by artificial means, we may expect results far in advance of what could otherwise be obtained. No race or show horse, of any class, comes to his high degree of proficiency without an education. The trotter must not only be trained to make him physically fit for the race but he must be taught to step. The same is true of actors, saddle horses, jumpers, and others. They are all given the natural aptitude to begin with, but that is not sufficient to get the best out of them.

Handling.—Handling is but the application of the schooling. It is painful to see a well-schooled saddle horse, to whom every little movement of hand or heel has a meaning, with some awkward man up who is reaping the fruits of his ignorant handling in a ride that is most distressing both to himself and his mount; or to see a horse, on whom much effort has been spent in teaching him to flex his neck, knees, and hocks in a proud, col-

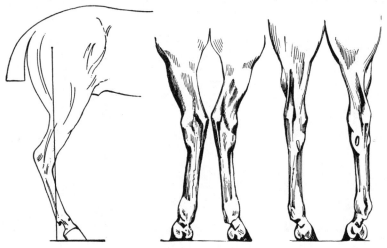

FIG. 29.—Bent, sabre, or sickle   FIG. 30.—Cow-hocked.   FIG. 31.—Bandy-legged or
          hock.   wide at the hocks.

lected, high way of going, put in light harness, with the omnipresent Kimball Jackson overdraw, and a heavy-fisted driver up who boasts of how fast the horse can step. It is as essential that the handling be in accord with the schooling as that the schooling should follow the line of natural aptitude. The handling offers the stimulus, the schooling makes possible the response; harmony is, therefore, imperative. There are individual differences in the methods of different handlers, though the same general system may be employed. Among all race and show riders or drivers, each fundamentally correct in his methods, there is always one who is capable of better results than the others.

Mechanical appliances are chiefly accessories to the handling and schooling of horses. They consist of the bit, shoes, weight, and hopples.

Bit.—The influence of the bit is strongly suggestive of one or the other ways of going, as discussed under equitation.

Shoes.—The style of the shoe and the dressing of the foot for its application have considerable influence on the way of going. By shortening or lengthening the toe, the breaking over is either facilitated or retarded, with a consequent shortening or lengthening of the stride; by raising or lowering the inner or outer quarter, the point at which breaking over takes place may be regulated, within limits.

Weight.—By either putting weight on or taking it off the foot, the stride is heightened or lowered. Weight may be secured either by permitting an abnormal growth of the foot itself or in the shoe. Weight fixed at the toe promotes extension on the principle of the pendulum, the weight coming into play toward the end of the stride to carry the foot out. On the other hand, weight well back in the shoe, toward the heel, is believed to be conducive to action by calling for extra flexion, in order to lift the foot. Whatever alterations are made in the matter of shoeing or weighting must be gradual, in order not to unbalance the horse in his stride.

Hopples.—By uniting a hind and a fore leg by means of hopples, a horse is held to his stride and prevented from breaking, mixing, or going any other gait. The straps are crossed or straight, depending upon whether the horse trots or paces. Hopples about the pasterns are sometimes put on harness horses to develop action.

Going Surface.—While not of a mechanical nature, the character of the surface on which the horse steps has a marked influence on the kind of stride he takes. As a general rule, heavy, soft, or deep going causes a high stride, while a hard, smooth surface is more conducive to speed. Of the speed horses, trotters and pacers require the hardest, smoothest track. Heavy going frequently influences double-gaited horses to trot instead of pace and seriously interferes with pacing performance. Runners do best on the turf or a dirt track that has had the surface loosened by a scratch harrow.

Defects and Peculiarities in Way of Going.—*Forging.*— Striking the ends of the branches or the under surface of the shoe of a forefoot with the toe of the hind foot.

Interfering.—Striking the supporting leg at the fetlock with the foot of the striding leg. It is predisposed in horses with base narrow, toe wide, or splay-footed standing position.

Paddling.—An outward deviation in the direction of the stride of the foreleg, the result of a toe narrow or pigeon-toed standing position.

Winging.—Exaggerated paddling, noticeable in high going horses.

Winding.—A twisting of the striding leg around in front of the supporting leg in much the same manner as in paddling. This is most commonly seen in wide-fronted draft horses at the walk.

Scalping.—Hitting the front of the hind foot above or at the line of the hair against the toe of the breaking over forefoot.

Speedy Cutting.—The spreading trotter at speed hits the hind leg above the scalping mark against the inside of the breaking over forefoot as he passes.

Cross-firing.—Essentially forging in pacers, in which they hit the inside of the near fore and off hind foot or the reverse in the air as the stride of the hind leg is about completed and the stride of the foreleg just begun.

Pointing.—A stride in which extension is much more marked than flexion. It is especially characteristic of the Thoroughbred. The same term is also used to indicate the resting of one forefoot in an advanced position to relieve the back tendons.

Dwelling.—A perceptible pause in the flight of the foot, as though the stride had been completed before the foot has reached the ground. Most noticeable in actors.

Trappy.—A quick, high, but comparatively short stride.

Pounding.—A heavy contact usually accompanying a high stride.

Rolling.—Excessive lateral shoulder motion as in wide fronted horses.

REVIEW

1. Name the features of the stride.
2. How may the pace be distinguished from the trot?
3. What are the special advantages and disadvantages under which pacers labor?
4. How may the gait of a racking horse be recognized in the dark?
5. Describe a cross canter.
6. What is the importance of changing leads at the canter or gallop?
7. How may a horse's way of going be predicted without seeing him move?
8. To what extent may the schooling determine the horse's way of going?
9. What effect does weight in the foot, also the surface over which the horse steps, have on the stride?
10. What is understood by forging, interfering, pointing, and dwelling?

PART II
TYPES AND BREEDS

CHAPTER IV

THE TYPES OF HORSES

A HORSE's usefulness depends upon his power of locomotion, and whether he moves with power, speed, show, or to carry weight will determine whether he is a draft, a race, a show, or a saddle horse. The sum total of those characteristics, by which adaptability to the different kinds of service is determined, constitutes the type.

Draft Type.—The service of the draft horse is to furnish power to move the heaviest of loads, usually over the paved surfaces of traffic-congested city streets (Fig. 32). Special efficiency in this line of service depends upon the possession of:

1. Weight sufficient (1500 to 2400 pounds) to hold the horse to a secure footing during muscular exertion, by increasing the friction between the shoe and the opposing hard, smooth surface of the roadway or pavement. Weight thrown into the collar also supplements muscular exertion.

2. Low station, to bring the centre of gravity as near the base of support as possible, thereby increasing stability of equilibrium, as stability of equilibrium is the measure of power. Length of leg is largely determined by length of canon bone, and a short canon is correlated, and therefore indicative of a short, broad, deep, and compact horse.

3. Breadth, to give a horse ample skeletal foundation for the support of great muscular development, and also to increase laterally the base of support, which affords a much more stable balance and in turn increases the power.

4. Depth, to afford heart, lung, and digestive capacity, which is a most essential asset to a horse which must expend much energy, almost continually, for long hours, and six days a week.

5. Compactness, to insure a short vertebral column, bringing the source of power, the hindquarters, nearer to the application of power at the shoulder, thereby minimizing loss in transmission, and making for strength and rigidity of the shaft, as it were.

6. Massiveness, which suggests heavy muscling with the thick, bulky power variety; therefore, a horse cannot be drafty without being massive.

7. Bone. The muscles operate the bone levers by contracting upon them through a fixed point and a movable insertion. For that reason the resisting power of the bone must be proportionate

Fig. 32.—The draft type, showing the weight, the low, wide, compact, massive form, the bone and the muscling which characterize the horse of power.

to the contracting force of the muscle. Horses have been known to fracture their own bones by the power of muscular contraction. Furthermore, a horse has the appearance of being unbalanced in his makeup if too fine in his underpinning. Hence the demand for heavy bone in draft horses is fully warranted, but should be made with a full knowledge of just what it means. The region of the canon, usually regarded as the index of bone, includes, in addition to the canon bone proper and the two rudimentary splint bones, the flexor and extensor tendons, the suspensory ligament, a variable amount of connective tissue, and the skin and hair. The total circumference may, therefore, be considerable and yet not represent real bone. The bony structure itself is made up of inorganic and organic constituents; the former are the more essential to wear and determine the texture. As a matter of fact, coarse texture of tendons, ligaments, and bones themselves, together with too much connective tissue, a thick hide, and coarse hair, tend to increase size in the canon region without increasing the wearing qualities of the bone. It is therefore real, and not apparent, bone which counts, and the eye and hand are more reliable than the tape line for determining its amount. Furthermore, the object of " big bone " is not to insure against fracture of the horse's leg but to furnish joint surface of sufficient area and durability to insure the horse remaining sound under stress of the wear to which it is subject in the course of its work. The bone of the canon region is, therefore, but an index after all.

8. Quality, not being correlated with substance, is more difficult of attainment in a draft horse, but there is an increasing favor expressed for more refined heads and necks, general finish, and better texture of bone, hoof, and hair. As much quality as is consistent with the required substance is desirable.

9. Temperament of the draft horse is generally lymphatic, but sluggishness is discriminated against. While the nature of his work requires that the draft horse be steady, patient, and readily tractable, it is, nevertheless, essential that it be performed willingly and with some snap and aggressiveness. Disposition should be good to offset frequent provocation.

10. Way of going. Most drivers, for well-regulated draft horse stables, are instructed to walk their teams both when loaded and light, and experience seems to justify such action. In the first place, a draft horse must walk at least one-half his time, and if he is never allowed to trot he acquires a rapid, snappy walk which will accomplish as many miles in the course of a day's work as can be done by the horse which is compelled to trot and allowed to walk only for the purpose of resting. The weight

of the draft horse is so great and the surface he walks over so hard that concussion is a big factor in endurance and durability, and concussion is increased immeasurably at the trot. Conditions of traffic in most city streets are such as to make trotting impracticable. However, any draft horse should be able to trot well. The trot accentuates all features of the walk, so that to be able to trot well insures a good walk (Fig. 33).

The draft horse gait, then, is the walk, a powerful, prompt, swinging stride of as much length as the short legs will allow.

Fig. 33.—The way a draft horse should be able to move. A powerful, straight, free stride, hocks sharply flexed, well under and close together, good knee action but no rolling or pounding in front.

The notion that a longer legged horse, with his longer stride, can accomplish more is not borne out in experience, except with mules. A leggy drafter lacks coördination in his movements, which counts against him in the course of the day, even though his single stride is longer. Furthermore, correlated with his length of leg is a general deficiency in draftiness.

There is a tendency in massive draft horses to roll or paddle in front and go wide behind, on account of their broad fronts and thick thighs. This is objectionable, if very marked, as it results in an unequal distribution of weight and work on the joints and foot, as well as being unsightly.

Speed Type.—When speed performance alone is considered, the minimum weight to be pulled or carried is imposed. Speed depends upon the length of the individual strides and the rapidity with which they can be repeated. Muscular contraction, therefore, must be of greatest degree and most quickly accomplished.

FIG. 34.—The speed type, representing the long, rangy, angular, narrow but deep form correlated with length and rapidity of stride.

Muscles capable of such contraction are long and band-like, compared to the short and thick muscles of power.

Form.—A horse to be fast, at whatever gait, must have the following form:

(1) Must be long and rangy in form to accommodate the length of muscles and to increase the length of the reach in extension.

(2) Must be lithe, indicating a system of muscles of the speed sort (Fig. 34).

(3) Must be angular, not having the form rounded out by bulky muscles, and carrying no excess weight in fat.

(4) Must be narrow, to permit of the greatest directness of shoulder motion and to offer the least resistance to the wind.

(5) Must be deep, to insure ample heart, lung, and digestive capacity, which it is not possible to secure by width.

Quality, denoting the finest texture of structure, to insure durability, with least weight and bulk, is necessary in a horse that is to attain great speed.

Stamina, bottom, and heartiness are most essential.

The temperament should be nervous, affording the requisite nerve force and courage to properly control and sustain the performance of which the speed horse is mechanically capable.

Their way of going serves as a basis for further classification into (1) trotters or pacers, (2) runners or jumpers.

Trotters and pacers accomplish what is asked of them by virtue of their ability to extend themselves into a long, reachy stride done rapidly. They are capable of the greatest length of stride, on account of the greater proportionate length of forearm and lower thigh which they possess. Their muscles are correspondingly long, narrow, and band-like, with the capacity for rapid contraction in an extreme degree. Pacing is differentiated as a lateral instead of a diagonal gait, and usually goes with greater length of limb in proportion to body, lower forehand, longer, steeper croup, and more bent hocks than are seen in the trotter. In double-gaited horses these differences may not be apparent.

The runner attains speed by a series of successive jumps, in which the propulsive power of the hindquarters is most marked. He is, therefore, characterized by greater development of forehand, a thicker stifle, and a straighter hind leg with less proportionate length from the hip-joint to the hock than characterizes the trotter. His characteristic way of standing easy on his front legs is shown by experience to have its influence in reducing con cussion, in the recovery at the end of each jump. As a rule, speed over the jumps is more a matter of schooling and temperament than of conformation, although there is alleged to be a certain straightness of top line, especially in the region of the loin, which is distinctive of the steeple chaser. Then, too, the characteristics associated with a runner may be somewhat accentuated in a steeple chaser.

Show Type.—So far as speed and power are concerned the show horse requirements are intermediate. It is the manner in which he moves and the appearance he makes while going, rather than the pace or the weight of the load, which count.

In order to qualify as a show horse he must possess:

Fig. 35.—The show type, representing the close and full made form, the quality and style essential to look the part, and the sort of conformation that enables a horse to be an actor.

Form, close and full made, stout enough to pull a vehicle designed after the English notion that " to drive handsomely is to drive heavily," smoothly turned and rotund enough to harmonize with the lines and proportions of the vehicle to which he is put, and to look well before it (Fig. 35).

Substance, present in a degree proportioned to the style and weight of the vehicle concerned.

Quality, general refinement and finish to enhance good looks. *Temperament,* active, stylish, proud, bold, and courageous. The actor or high going horse is such structurally and temperamentally. He must possess a general suppleness and flexibility that is found only with length of shoulder and pastern, neck and croup. But this is true in equal degree of the saddle horse. The actor, in addition, is close made in profile, full made from the end, in order that he may better fit heavy leather and

Fig. 36.—A weight carrier, illustrating the bone and muscular development which with a short back and legs render a horse "up to" two hundred pounds or more.

conform to the heavy vehicles to which he is put. Furthermore, he must not only possess joints of such angles as to permit of extreme flexion, but he must be thoroughly disposed so to go, bending himself in every joint from the ground to the tip of his chin and to the last segment of his abbreviated dock. Height of stride is his, and he must have the style and finish to properly set off the show he is to make.

Saddle Type.—The saddle horse must carry weight from 135 to 200 pounds or over, with greatest satisfaction to his rider and least distress to himself. The prescribed ways in which the weight is to be carried differentiate the classes of saddle horses.

Ability to support weight requires comparatively short, stout legs, acting as columns, and a short, strong, closely coupled back and loin, constituting the arch (Fig. 36).

The actual carrying of the weight is accomplished by the horse's placing himself in such a way as to balance his load,

Fig. 37.—The saddle type, showing the short top and long under line, sloping shoulders, the high, well-finished withers, and the long, fine, supple neck essential in the saddle horse.

going well off his hocks, and working his legs under him in such a way as to sustain the weight at all phases of the stride. There is a knack in carrying weight; the remarkable feats of the experienced baggage man in the handling of trunks can be accounted for on the same principle. Size is secondary to the way a horse is set up, and to the way he goes.

A saddle horse must be light in the forehand, possess a supple neck, a responsive mouth, and a high order of intelligence in order to qualify for the schooling which is required to make a finished mount. His form is outlined by a short top and long under line, and is characterized by the development of the forehand. Shoulders should be unusually long, sloping, and extended into high, narrow, well-finished withers, which have the effect of placing the saddle well back and holding it in that position, without suffering injury from its impingement (Fig. 37). The greatly desired "long rein" and "much horse in front of the rider" are thus secured. Such a forehand will be comparatively narrow and deep, thus permitting a secure and comfortable seat without the spread of knees and thighs occasioned by the full-made harness horse.

The chief characteristics of the saddle horse stride are spring and accuracy, both being most conducive to the comfort and security of the rider. All gaits but the gallop and run are executed in a collected manner, with only sufficient action to insure freedom of stride. A well-schooled saddle horse should be capable of a most finished performance; he should change gaits, canter on either lead or in a circle, back, traverse, or side step, and be thoroughly responsive to the hand, rein, and heel.

REVIEW

1. Why should a draft horse be low set, broad, deep, compact, and massive?
2. Explain how weight increases the power of the city draft horse.
3. Describe the ideal draft horse bone; of what importance is it?
4. How should the draft horse walk and why?
5. What is the relation of speed to draft?
6. What are the characteristics of the speed type and why?
7. How may a trotter, a pacer, and a runner be distinguished without seeing them go?
8. Describe the show type and give reasons for each feature.
9. Account for the fact that an 800 pound pony may carry a 200 pound man more easily than a 1200 pound horse can.
10. Describe the forehand of a typical saddle horse and give reasons.

CHAPTER V

THE CLASSES OF HORSES

Basis of Class Distinctions.—The characters upon the basis of which class distinctions are made are height, weight, form, quality, substance, condition, temperament, manners, and color.

Height.—The stature at the highest point of the withers, measured in hands, four inches to the hand. Fractions of the hand are expressed in inches, as 15 hands, 2 inches or 15–2.

Weight.—Height and weight combined determine scale, which is synonymous with size.

Form.—That general contour of outline which determines whether a horse is smoothly turned or angular, massive or lithe, low set or rangy.

Quality.—That which refers to the texture and finish, as determined by the character of the individual units of structure. Quality is indicated in hide and hair, bone and general refinement.

Substance.—That which refers to the amount of the structural material, as determined by the number and size of the individual units of structure.

Condition.—Not so much the state of health as that which comes as a result of fitting. In the ordinary market horse it is the difference between being fat and thin, while in the race horse it suggests the trained, as against the untrained.

Temperament.—A horse may be too hot to work or too cold for a race horse.

Manners.—It has already been stated that a horse's value is materially influenced by what he can do. It is essential that he should do all, and that as well as he can. Manners, therefore, " count " in the value to users of all horses.

Color.—Color has much to do in determining a horse's class value. A good horse is said never to have a bad color, yet certain colors are preferred or even required in some classes of horses where other colors are undesirable or even prohibited.

45

Color is the most conspicuous feature by which a horse can be described or identified, so that a uniform and comprehensive color standard is important. Colors may be generally classed as solid or broken, distinguished by the presence or absence of white spots. Solid colors are further differentiated as hard or soft. A hard color is one in which the shade is sharply pronounced, while soft colors are characterized by either a total absence of pigment, as in the case of the white horse with pink skin, or a washed-out or faded shade of some of the other colors.

Broken colors are either the piebald and skewbald, in which the amount of white is considerable and the distribution irregular; or marked, when the white is limited in amount and definitely restricted in its location.

Then there are a number of odd colors and markings which do not conform to the above distinctions nor admit of any but a group classification.

Classification of Color.—*Solid hard colors* are: Bay—Bright or cherry, blood red, mahogany or dark.

Brown—Bay, seal, mealy, black.

Chestnut—Golden, red, burnt, black.

Black—Jet, sooty.

Gray—Dappled, steel, iron, black, flea-bitten.

Roan—Blue, red, strawberry.

Solid soft colors are white (pink skin), mealy bay, and washy chestnut.

Broken colors are piebald, skewbald, and marked.

Odd colors are cream, mouse and dun. The dun may be grouped into light or Isabella and dark or buckskin.

Markings.—White—Bald face, blaze, star, snip, strip, splash, stocking, sock, fetlock, pastern, coronet, heel.

Black—Points, lines.

Odd—Tiger spots, leprous spots, wall-eyed.

The standing of different colors will depend, in the case of many of them, upon the class of the horse in question. In general the different shades of *bay* may be considered as the best all-round color. Bay has been referred to as " everyman's " color.

Brown is also a staple color like bay.

Chestnut, especially the golden and red, is one of the most attractive colors and when accompanied by white markings, as chestnut is quite liable to be, presents an extremely flashy appearance. This is one of the most popular colors in high-class harness and saddle horses.

Black, while most popular in fiction, is in fact not a good color for selling. It is objected to chiefly on the ground that it is not often fast black but fades and sunburns badly in hot weather; the sooty more so than the jet black. Black is also objectionable on account of the flecked appearance which it acquires as the horse is warmed up. No matter how carefully the coat is groomed, every hair that is turned appears as a dirty, gray fleck, as soon as the sweat dries. Black harness horses are commonly cross matched with grays. The chief specific demand for black horses comes from undertakers.

Gray is the color most in demand in the draft classes, although frequently discriminated against in horses of any other type. The preference for grays is stated, by draft horse buyers, to be due to the fact that they experience less difficulty in matching up a team of from two to six grays than in the case of any other color. This may be accounted for to some extent by the fact that gray is the predominating color in the draft breed which outnumbers all other draft breeds combined, in this country. It would seem at first thought that bays could be more easily matched than grays. But bays are most frequently marked with white, which necessitates a matching of markings as well as of shade. Grays, furthermore, appear to harmonize better with the red, green, or yellow combinations in which most commercial vehicles are finished. It is also reasonable to claim that the gray horse is less sensitive to heat than the horse of darker color, since white has the physical property of reflecting the sun's rays, while black absorbs them. This fact is borne out by one's ordinary experience with light and dark suits of the same weight. Gray horses, outside the work horse division, are generally objected to on account of the conspicuousness of their hair when shed; the degree in which they show stable stain, although this difficulty is largely overcome by the use of peat moss bedding; and the inevitable disappearance, with advancing age, of the black pigment in the hair, resulting in white color and a predisposition to melanotic tumors. On the other hand, gray horses show dandruff and body dirt less than most other colors. The darker shades are most preferred, although in the hunting field, on the race track, or even in the show ring a beautifully dappled light gray horse will invariably catch the eye. History has done much to offset the prejudice against gray horses. Grays are cross matched in pairs with blacks, chestnuts, and browns.

Roan of either shade is becoming more popular or prevalent in draft horses, due perhaps to the increasing number of Belgian grades which come to market, roan being common in that breed. In harness and saddle horses, red roan especially is a rather pleasing though not common color.

Piebalds and skewbalds are popular colors in ponies, and in sporting fours and tandems where striking colors are a feature; also for advertising wagons and the circus, where it is desirable to have them conspicuous. A piebald is a black and white combination, while any color other than black, such as bay, brown, or chestnut, combined with white, constitutes a skewbald.

Cream, dun and mouse colors are generally in disfavor except for some special purpose, although the buckskin, a darker shade of dun which is distinguished from cream by black points, has a reputation for stamina.

White markings are most desirable in horses of the show type, since they enhance the brilliancy of a flashy performance. Even here they are objectionable in ladies' classes.

Black points are, as a rule, considered indicative of greater wearing qualities, and it is a fact that the blue horn of the black foot is more dense and tough than the white. White points behind are less objectionable than in front. In fact they are generally considered to improve a horse's appearance as does some white in his countenance. White markings, wherever they may be, should be as symmetrical as possible and sharply defined. Large, irregular white patches or splashes are extremely objectionable.

Odd markings are undesirable. The leprous spots are the small, more or less regular areas, completely denuded of pigment, that are seen about the muzzle, the eyes, and under the tail.

The so-called tiger spots are the large, irregular areas of a pinkish or yellowish tint, surrounded by a zone of lighter shade, which resemble in appearance the spots on the tiger lily. They are especially common over the croup.

By classes of horses is meant the market and show ring creations. The classes should not be confused with types, which are mechanical distinctions.

Market and Show Classes

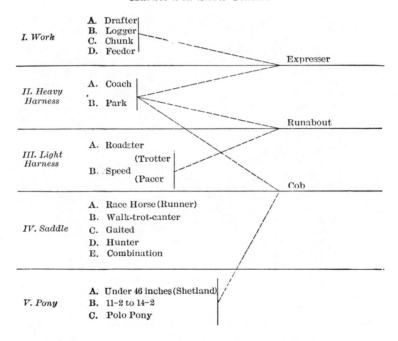

The Work Horse Division.—*Drafters* have already been described as the power type. Drafters are worked in single, pair, three-way, four-, or six-horse hitches. The demand for the highest class of draft horses comes chiefly from city business firms who make the appearance of their horses and wagons on the streets a feature of their advertising policies (Figs. 38, 39, and 40).

4

In a consideration of draft form, height is secondary to weight and station. In the selection of market draft geldings, however, height is important. While the low set, compact horse is most powerful, such chunky form is not conducive to as great size as that of more range and higher stature. This is especially true of immature draft colts. There must be considerable "stretch" to them if they are to attain the required size at maturity. An upstanding growthy two-year-old gives greater

FIG. 38.—A trey or three-way hitch of drafters to truck, showing the scale, form, and conformation of horses of this class, also the manner of hitching.

promise than the smoothly turned, mature looking chunk of the same age. Growth takes place first upward, then downward and outward.

Appearance, as well as power, counts in the service for which the highest class of draft geldings are bought, and unless a horse has stature he appears "squatty" before the big wagons or trucks to which he is put.

Loggers are up to draft horse requirements in all but quality. They are too coarse, unsymmetrical, low bred, or badly blemished to satisfy the city demand, and are therefore relegated chiefly to the lumber camps, where hard work only is required. *Chunks* represent the extreme of draft form, as their name

FIG. 39.—A draft pair of unusual quality and attractive color.

FIG. 40.—A six-horse draft team to packer's van, showing the relative balance between the lead, swing, and wheel pair, also complete appointments.

implies, but are deficient in scale, ranging in weight from 1200 to 1500 pounds (Fig. 41). They are handy work horses, taken chiefly for the hauling of heavy loads which must be delivered more rapidly than can be done with draft horses, as in the case of breweries. The lower grade of chunks meets the demand of the contractors and the farm trade.

Expressers are rapid draft horses, capable of working at the trot. They have enough of the draft form to insure the requisite size, substance, and power, at the same time departing from the draft type in that they are more rangy and less massive, in order that they may be capable of stepping away at a sharp trot (Fig. 42). They have been referred to as " drafters with coach horse finish " and as " coachers with draft horse substance." Expressers vary in weight from 1250 to 1500 pounds, and serve a wide range of uses in the numerous lines of delivery service.

Fig. 41.—A pair of chunks to truck, showing the extremely drafty form, bone, and ruggedness typical of this class.

Feeders are thin horses of any of the above classes, the demand for which comes from those who make horses the medium through which to market their corn. A feeder, to be profitable, must have class and be deficient only in condition.

Heavy Harness Horse Division.—There is a suggestiveness about the term heavy harness which is not generally comprehended. Harness horses are of two classes, heavy and light, the adjective in each case qualifying the harness and not the horse. The heavy harness horse is one of fashion, of English creation, and it is to English sentiment that he owes his name. He conforms to the Englishman's idea that " to drive handsomely one must drive heavily." Their vehicles are designed on lines of dignity and elegance, which make them in some cases almost ponderous. The harness, by which the horses are put to them, is of necessity correspondingly heavy, characterized by weight of leather, Kay collars, metal mountings, Liverpool, elbow, or Buxton bits, with side or no bearing reins. The horse, to complete this equipage and be capable of both acting and looking the part, must be close and full made with extreme finish, style, and action—the show type.

Fig. 42.—An expresser for light delivery service, showing the combination of draft horse; size and substance with coach horse form and finish.

Coach horses are big, substantial, heavy harness horses with enough size and substance to pull a brougham or coach, yet sufficiently refined to make a good appearance (Fig. 43). They must have an elegant, bold, commanding way of going about an eight-mile pace, with manners that will insure safe conveyance through city traffic, or standing in pose for long periods of waiting. Coach horses are put to the brougham, landau, or, as wheelers especially, to the brake, drag, or coach, hitched singly, in pairs, or fours.

Park horses, as the name implies, are for park driving, not

for town work. They are the show harness horses, only sufficiently close and full made to have that rotundity of form which
looks best in heavy leather, possessing a degree of refinement
equaled only by the park saddle horse and the most extravagant
flexion of knees and hocks. They should be capable of a pace
of twelve miles an hour, which greatly enhances the flashiness
and brilliancy of their action. Park horses are driven singly,
in pairs, and fours, put to the gig, the Sayler wagon, an American four-wheeler which has taken the place of the gig quite
generally (Fig. 44); demi mail, Stanhope, spider or George
IV phaeton (the latter for ladies' use), park drag or victoria.

Fig. 43.—A class of coach horses to brougham and victorias. Pair on the right to brougham
show the size and substance which distinguish the coach horse from the park horse.

Usually owners drive in all but the last instance. Park horses
are classified by height, ranging from the pony limit of 14–2 to
15–3 hands.

Runabout horses are defined by the name under which they
are classed, that is, handy little harness horses with which to
get about (Fig. 45). They are small, not over 15–1 as a rule,
in order to have the requisite handiness and combine some of the
step of the road horse with some of the shape and action of the
park horse, although extreme action is not typical of this class.
Manners must be of the best to insure them standing without
hitching, backing out of tight places, and going anywhere. Runabout horses are put to the light four-wheel wagon designated by
the same name.

FIG. 44.—A park mare to Sayler wagon, representing the extreme refinement and brilliant action which distinguish the park horse from all other harness horses.

FIG. 45.—A runabout horse, a handy, shapely, well-mannered little horse, with a fair degree of both pace and action.

Cobs are of a type readily distinguished from any of the other classes in the heavy harness division, although the term cob is loosely used in referring to any docked horse, whether of cobby build or not. The typical cob does not stand over **15.1,** is low set, extremely close and full made, has unusual bone and muscular development, and a short but trappy way of going (Fig. 46). He may be briefly described as a big little horse, of a rugged though not coarse appearance. Cobs are used to both ride and drive and are remarkable weight carriers.

Light Harness Horse Division.—Light harness horses are as distinctly American in their origin as the heavy harness are English, and it is interesting to note the reciprocal favor which each is receiving in the other country.

Fig. 46.—A cob to runabout, a big, little horse of extremely compact and rotund form.

Since maximum speed requires minimum draft, American road wagons are built of such material and in such fashion as to impose upon the horse the least weight that is consistent with the safe and comfortable conveyance of one or two people. They are, therefore, in striking contrast to the English carriages and require harness correspondingly light.

The light harness horse follows the speed type but differs from the running race horse in being somewhat lower in the forehand, longer and more sloping in the croup, longer from the hip-joint to the hock, with the hocks set further back and the leg below the hock directed more downward and forward (Fig. 47).

True pacers, as a rule, are longer in legs, lower in the forehand, with longer, steeper croups and more bent hocks than the trotter. The size of the light harness horse is too variable to be defined by any but the widest limits. If horses of this type are of good size, well made, stylish, straight gaited, even though not possessed of extreme speed, and have good manners, they are classed as gentlemen's road horses (Fig. 48). On the other hand, extremely fast horses, either at trot or pace, whether they have anything else to recommend them or not, are classed as speed horses (Fig. 49).

Road horses are hitched singly or in pairs, while speed horses are seldom used to pole. The road wagon is the typical roadster hitch, while speed horses are hooked to bike sulkies, or speed wagons, the lightest type of vehicle built to meet the amateur requirements, which call for a four-wheeled wagon. Speed horses are classified according to their record performances.

Saddle Horse Division.—The saddle horse was primarily a utility horse, as a matter of necessity, in pioneer times prior to the construction of roads and vehicles, but he has become in addition a most popular source of pleasure, with circumstances

FIG. 47.—The bent hock-joint.

attending his use so diversified as to call for a variety of types. Some horses are ridden for the ease with which they carry one, while others are used for the exercise and liver stimulation which they afford. Then, again, some are ridden in a dignified manner in the parks and on the boulevards, while others are ridden " rough " in the field and cross country. The distinction between the first two, in this country, is very largely one of schooling and trimming, although the English type of walk-trot-canter saddle horse is quite distinctive in breeding and general make-up.

The race horse is the truest exponent of the speed type, but is used essentially as a saddle horse, a galloper, and is therefore

Fig. 48.—A gentleman's road mare. Although of speed form, she is of good size, symmetrical shape, faultless conformation, and shows great refinement, style, and intelligence.

Fig. 49.—A trotter to sulky, adhering strictly to the speed type yet possessing more size and substance and better conformation than is common in horses of this class.

classed in the saddle division. Runners are distinguished from trotters and pacers by greater development of the forehand, by a shorter back, more level croup, straighter hind legs (Fig. 50), with less proportionate length from hip-joint to hock and more from hock to the ground. Their way of going is also distinctive; they have a wonderful reach and length of jump at the run, and gallop beautifully, but have a low, pointing stride at the trot (Fig. 51). They race on the flat, or over the steeple chase course of jumps, according to their own natural aptitude and the schooling which they have received. Running race horses are handicapped by the weight required to be carried, an impost of only an ounce making a considerable difference in a horse's finish.

FIG. 50.—The straight hock-joint.

Gaited saddle horses are the distinctly American saddle horses (Fig. 52), although ambling saddle horses were at one time used in England, and at present the gaited horse is apparently losing favor in some important parts of this country to the walk-trot horse of English idea. Gaited horses are required to go at least five gaits: the walk, either the running walk, fox trot, or slow pace; the trot; rack; and canter; all described under gaits. They carry full mane and tail and are the ideal of the Southern and Western saddle horse contingent.

Walk-trot-canter saddle horses do just what is enumerated in the name, are usually docked and their manes pulled (Fig. 53). Many of our best walk-trot-canter saddle horses are converted gaited horses, showing that there is no distinction in type except in their performance.

The collected, springy, weight-carrying trot of the saddle horse should be distinguished from the extended, fast trot of the speed horse on the one hand, and the high acting, sometimes pounding, trot of the heavy harness horses on the other.

Walk-trot-canter horses are referred to as hacks, and a distinction is made between park and road hacks. The former have the finish and style characteristic of all park horses, and are usually saddle bred, while road hacks are of a somewhat plainer but more serviceable stamp, capable of taking a run cross country in connection with a road ride, if desired.

There is also a tendency to differentiate between the Saddle bred walk-trot-canter saddle horse and the one of Thoroughbred breeding and type. The former is characterized by high car-

Fig. 51.—A steeple chaser, showing the speed type and saddle form of the running race horse.

riage of head and tail, alleged to resemble that of a peacock, more knee and hock action and usually less substance—the latter by a more exclusively saddle form perhaps, but too often an erratic disposition and a low going trot, that are not conducive to either a safe or satisfactory ride (Fig. 54). Some most acceptable representatives of the latter type have been brought out, however. Saddle horses are classified on the basis of height and the weight to which they are up.

Hunters are ridden to fox hounds, cross country, and, as a rule, with considerable weight up. In order to qualify they must, in addition to being able to carry weight, stay for long, hard runs, jump safely, and preferably in their stride, all common obstacles in the field, such as fences, walls, and ditches, and gallop fast enough to keep pace with the pack. They must also

Fig. 52.—A gaited saddle stallion; one of the best representatives of this class, which is the most popular of any in the South and West but has met only limited favor in the East.

have good heads in order not to become hot in company and run away through fences or into quarry holes.

In order to meet these requirements, a horse must have all the features of the weight carrier conspicuous in his make-up, especially strong, well-developed shoulders and withers, muscular quarters, and ample bone (Fig. 55). Quality is sacrificed to substance, but a hunter must show breeding and not appear cold. He is not good looking in the same sense as the park horse, but has, nevertheless, a most impressive appearance, as a horse of great resourcefulness and serviceability. Size is being more and more insistently demanded by buyers and users of

FIG. 53.—A walk-trot-canter horse, showing the mold of form, the extreme refinement of head and neck, the peacocky carriage, the style and intelligence that are representative in highest degree of the American idea of a saddle horse of this class.

hunters, and for apparently good reasons. In the first place, a five-foot jump is four inches lower for a 16-hand horse than for one of 15 hands height. Many hunting folk are in the sport to keep down their weight, so that it takes a horse of some size to be up to the weight at which they ride. Finally, the big

Fig. 54.—A class of English saddle horses, the Thoroughbred type predominating.

Fig. 55.—A light-weight hunter having strong, well-developed, sloping shoulders, high withers extending well back, muscular quarters, ample bone, and sufficient breeding to insure the requisite courage, stamina, and pace.

horse is claimed to give a safer ride on account of the momentum
of his greater weight, insuring him a better chance of breaking
through a fence in case of a blunder, instead of being tripped by
it and coming down.

Hunters are classified according to the weight they are
capable of carrying, as light weight, up to from 135 to 165
pounds; middle weight, 165 to 190 pounds; and heavy weight,
190 pounds or over. A heavy weight hunter is shown as "a

Fig. 56.—Heatherbloom, the world's record high jumper.

weight carrier" (Fig. 36). They are also classified as green
or qualified, the latter having hunted one season with a pack
recognized by the United Hunts and Steeple Chase Association.

All hunters are jumpers in some degree, but a high jumper
is by no means necessarily a hunter. A jumper may clear six
feet at one time, and at another blunder over an ordinary post
and rail fence, while to be a safe cross country horse he must
be a consistent jumper of from 4 feet 6 inches to 5 feet only.

The record high jump of Heatherbloom, over 7 feet 9 inches, in 1903 still stands (Fig. 56).

The use of hunters is not restricted to the hunting field, although the number demanded for that purpose alone is rapidly increasing with the extension of the sport. Horses of this type are preferred by many who never ride to hounds, because they are most useful horses to ride and even to drive.

The Combination Horse.—It is customary for all saddle horses, even some hunters, to go well in harness, but their forte,

FIG. 57.—A combination horse, departing somewhat from the saddle type in being of a more "harnessy" form.

nevertheless, is under " pigskin." There is, however, a combination class of horses from which an equally good performance, either to ride or to drive, is expected (Fig. 57).

Combination horses, although shown customarily in harness first, are more especially saddle horses that drive well than they are harness horses capable of giving a good ride.

They are distinguished from saddle horses by being somewhat more of a harness form and showing more speed at the trot, with good manners when driven.

A combination horse may go either the three or the five gaits under saddle, but those which walk, trot, and canter are usually driven in heavy harness, while those which are gaited are driven in light harness.

The "fine harness" horse of the Southern shows, distinct from the "light harness" horse in that he has no speed but is a "model" horse capable of going ten or twelve miles an hour in the best form, is in reality a gaited saddle horse in harness (Fig. 58).

Fig. 58.—The fine harness horse of the South, a model of conformation, quality, style, and way of going.

The Pony Division.—Generally speaking, any horse under 14–2 is a pony, but diminutive stature alone does not constitute pony type. There is a distinct pony build or form, characterized as an exaggeration, in miniature, of either the draft or heavy harness types. An undersized light harness horse, for instance, would be a runt, not a pony.

Ponies permit of classification into three groups: (1) Those conforming to the Shetland standard of a 46-inch limit, (2) those 11–2 to 14–2 hands, and (3) the polo pony.

FIG. 59.—A harness pony under 46 inches in height.

FIG. 60.—A twelve-hand ride and drive pony of exceptional merit.

Fig. 61.—A pair of twelve-hand ponies properly turned out.

Fig. 62.—A polo mount, fast, game, handy, intelligent, and up to weight.

Ponies not exceeding 46 inches should be of a miniature draft horse pattern, although a preference has been shown in American show rings for one with somewhat more refinement and action. These ponies are used almost exclusively for small children to ride and drive (Fig. 59).

Ponies 11–2 and Not Exceeding 14–2.—These ponies are pocket editions of the coach horse, as it were, or little cobs, well adapted to the use of youths and misses who may have graduated from the Shetlands (Figs. 60 and 61).

Polo mounts are race horses or hunters on a small scale, used chiefly to play the game (Fig. 62), although making very acceptable little hacks in case they are mallet shy, or for any other reason are kept out of the game. Cutting cattle and playing polo are very similar so far as the requirements of horses are concerned, and the type is practically identical, but as the cow pony seldom gets to market, class preference is given to the polo pony. A recent ruling of the Polo Association has increased the height limit of polo mounts from 14–2 to 15–1. They are henceforth, therefore, to be called polo mounts instead of ponies and some show classifications have already adopted this revision.

REVIEW

1. What is the distinction between a type and a class?
2. Name the hard, solid colors and give examples of the influence of color on the market value of horses.
3. Name the market classes of horses.
4. Describe a typical expresser and give reasons for each feature.
5. What is a cob?
6. What is required of a roadster besides speed?
7. Compare the performance of the park horse with that of a road horse.
8. What are the chief distinctions between the gaited and the walk-trot-canter saddle horse?
9. How does a hunter differ in appearance from a park saddle horse?
10. Describe what should distinguish a pony beside diminutive stature.

CHAPTER VI

THE BREEDS OF HORSES

A breed is a group of individuals possessing distinctive characteristics not common to other members of the same species, these characteristics being sufficiently well fixed to be uniformly transmitted. It is these distinctive features which give to each breed its greater or less economic importance. Curiously enough, there is scarcely a breed which does not possess at least one distinctive characteristic, in respect to which it surpasses all other breeds.

In arriving at a fair conclusion of what constitutes " the best breed," it is necessary that conditions to be met and characters required be specified, as the same breed may not be " best " for each specific case. Too much importance should not be attached to the partisan favor in which different breeds are held. The average buyer of market horses has very little consideration for the particular breeds which may be represented in his purchases, yet striking uniformity of breed character among the lot which he selects may be manifested. This is due to the fact that the characters represented in the buyer's standard or ideal happen to be more typical of one breed than another.

It has been noted recently that the accepted types of the draft breeds, for instance, are approaching more closely a common standard, as shown by show ring awards, but the desirability of such being the case is questionable. It is not well to lay too much stress on the minor features of breed type which have no utility value, but inasmuch as each breed has distinctive characteristics, rendering representatives of that breed especially well adapted to particular requirements, their distinctiveness should be retained. For instance, the Percheron breed has, from its inception, been characterized by features which could not be duplicated in any of the other breeds, and these features should not be sacrificed in favor of others which are characteristic of other breeds.

70

The inherent qualities of a breed have been put there by one or more of three general agencies, therefore the possibilities in what can be gotten out of a breed are as definitely determined as is the character of a horse's get fixed by his ancestry. The three factors determining breed characteristics and, through them, the economic importance of the different breeds are:

1. The origin in blood which constitutes the hereditary force with which the breed is endowed.

2. The environment by which these blood lines have been molded.

3. The purpose for which they have been bred, constituting the ideal to which the breeders have selected.

The study of the breeds should, therefore, resolve itself into a consideration of the following essentials:

1. Origin: (*a*) In blood. (*b*) Geographical.
2. Development: (*a*) Men. (*b*) Methods.
3. History: (*a*) Men. (*b*) Events. (*c*) Dates.
4. Characteristics: Breed types.
5. Economic importance.

Foundation Stock.—The origin in blood is of greatest historical interest, if not the most important, of the factors which determine breed characters. The modern breeds have been more or less composite in their origin, involving, to a greater or less degree, those breeds or stocks which had already attained distinction on account of merit. In some cases, the combination of blood lines was intentional, but it was more often incidental or even accidental. These historic horses can in turn be traced to a more limited group of common ancestors and so on until the blood lines focus in but a very few basic stocks.

Darwin believed all races had descended from one common ancestry, and attributed the extreme differences noted between modern breeds to environment. The more commonly accepted theory has been that all modern breeds trace their origin in blood directly or indirectly to one or all of three primordial stocks, the Wild Black Horse of Flanders, the Oriental Horse, and the native pony stock indigenous to Northern Europe and Asia. The latter has played a more or less important part.

The Flemish horse was native to what is now a part of

France, Belgium, Holland, and Germany. The country was generally low lying, and therefore conducive to a coarse, rank, luxuriant growth of vegetation. The horse developed thereon partook of the same general nature. The Flanders horse was characterized by: First, his huge size and bulk; second, his general coarseness; third, his uniformly black color; fourth, his profusion of hair, showing in heavy mane, tail, feather and even a moustache, and tufts on the anterior face of knees and points of hocks; fifth, his sluggish, lymphatic temperament.

The Oriental horse, native to the desert regions of Northern Africa and later found in Arabia and Asia Minor, was characterized by extreme refinement, beauty of form, grace of movement, speed, stamina, spirit, intelligence, and an active, nervous temperament. The so-called Oriental Group was said to consist of the Barb, Turk, and Arabian.

Recent researches of Professor J. Cossar Ewart, of the University of Edinburgh, and Professor William Ridgeway, of Cambridge, have shown that the fountain source was not reached in either the Flemish horse or the so-called Oriental Group. Ridgeway concludes that all horses can be traced to one or more of three original stocks: the Libyan horse of Northern Africa, of which pure Barbs and Arabs are typical; the common horse of Upper Asia and Europe, represented by the Mongolian pony, and the Celtic pony of Northwestern Europe.

Origin of Thoroughbred.—He traces the Thoroughbred, through his alleged Barb, Turk, and Arab ancestors, to Libya, in Northern Africa, where he establishes a definite origin, about 1000 B.C., in a horse characterized by a bay color, sometimes accompanied by body, leg and even head stripes, a dark colored skin, white markings, as a star, a blaze, and pasterns or " bracelets," a short, fine head, well-carried ears, a peculiar depression in the skull just in front of the orbits, a light, fine, high-set tail, the total absence of chestnuts on the hind legs, and either absence or small size of the ergots at the fetlocks, an unusually long hoof, extremely docile disposition, a refined, expressive voice, and great speed.

Origin of Other Horses.—Ridgeway also establishes a small, coarse, thick set, short necked, plain headed, big boned, light colored, slow but hardy pony of Upper Asia and Europe as the original progenitor of all other horses, except those which have resulted from a blending of these two, and the Black Flanders horse is shown to have such an origin.

In 1902 Professor Ewart described what he called a " Celtic pony," a true pony and not a dwarf horse. It has a small head, with prominent eyes, small ears, a heavy mane, slender legs, small joints, well-formed, small hoofs, and " tail lock."

ARABIAN

No race of horses has enjoyed a more sentimental popularity nor had its history more obscured by myth and tradition than the Arab (Fig. 63). It is only comparatively recently that any very definite information concerning them has been available. Arabs have been considered in a general way as the original source of the best blood, but this is not the case. There is every reason to believe that horses similar to the best Arabs were in Northern Africa more than one thousand years before horses were known in Arabia. Their introduction was apparently from Africa and took place some time between the first and the sixth century.

The number of good horses in Arabia is much smaller than is generally supposed, and these are chiefly in the hands of certain families or tribes in the interior desert. The rank and file of the horses in the hands of the common people are either the common bred Kurdish ponies, descendants of the original European stock or the produce of these by true Arab sires. The Arab proper, a descendant and not an antecedent of the original Libyan horse, is known as the *Kohl* breed, so named on account of the peculiar blue black or antimony tint which characterizes the skin of the body. The breed is composed of five strains which, in turn, are believed by the Bedouins to be derived from a single mare, named *Keheîlet Ajuz,* and the most prominent strain is named Keheîlan, after her. They are mostly bays, the fastest of any, and resemble most closely the English Thoroughbred. The *Darley Arabian,* the greatest foundation sire of the Thoroughbred, was of this strain. The others are

the *Seglawi,* "powerful and fast, but not particularly hand-
some"; the *Abéyan,* generally the handsomest but small, and
resembles the Thoroughbred least; the *Hamdaini;* and the *Had-
ban.* Collectively, the strains are termed *Al Khamseh* and are
extensively interbred.

There is much confusion in this country concerning the characteristic color of the Arab. Almost any odd color or marking,
such as pure white, piebald, skewbald, leprous or tiger spots, are
attributed to Arab blood. On the other hand, such significance
of any of these colors has been absolutely denied. As a matter of
fact, bay with white markings is most characteristic, and, in the

Fig. 63.—Arabian stallion, showing the general refinement characteristic of this breed.

light of recent knowledge concerning the origin of the Arab in
the Libyan horse, is most desirable. Grays are also common,
chestnuts and browns are not uncommon, while blacks and even
pure whites are found. It is true, too, that the whites usually
show the Kohl spots about the eyes, muzzle, and elsewhere.
While the odd colors referred to as suggesting Arab breeding are
never found among pure bred Arabs, they are noted among their
half breeds, the piebalds and skewbalds, especially, occurring
with a considerable degree of uniformity when the common stock
of Upper Asia and Europe is crossed with Arab sires. This is
shown in the piebald ponies of Thibet, Sumatra, Iceland, the

Faroe Islands, Java, India, and in our original American range ponies, which were not many generations removed from an Oriental foundation. The line back is another feature which is marked in the various shades of dun, cream, and mouse color of half-bred Arabians.

THE BARB

There are many horses in the Barbary States of Northern Africa which are not true Barbs. Pure bred Barbs are found only in Morocco, where there has been no introduction of foreign blood, as has been done in the other States, where horses from France and England, in Algiers especially, Arabs from Syria, and the common-bred Italian horses have been crossed with the native Barbs. It is, of course, assumed that the pure Barb is the direct descendant of the original Libyan horse.

Description.—The Barb is described as being from 14 to 15 hands in height, body comparatively short in proportion to length of legs, his whole form being conducive to speed. The head is well proportioned, with a fine ear, broad, full forehead, large, clear, prominent eye flashing fire and yet expressing intelligence, a deep jowl with open angles, a trim muzzle, and a nostril that is thin at the margin, capable of great dilation and continually in play. The head is well set on a long, high crested neck, well cut out in the throttle, and giving the head a lofty carriage; shoulders well laid in and sloping, well set up at the withers; a round, deep rib; a somewhat drooping croup but high-set tail; straight hind legs, long pasterns, and rather deep, narrow feet of the most superior texture of horn. The characteristic bay with white markings indicates the pure Barb, an out-cross introducing browns, chestnuts, blacks, and grays.

THE TURK

The significance of this name applies, generally, to the horses of Turkey in Asia, there being but few horses in European Turkey. Originally, these consisted of Turcoman and Kurdistan ponies, representatives of the common Northern Asia and European stock. These were later, however, extensively interbred and improved with Arabs, so that it is probable that the

Turks referred to in Thoroughbred history were of this breeding.

The influence of the so-called Oriental blood has been well extended. The Darley Arabian, Byerly Turk, and Godolphin Barb, with the Barb or Royal mares, are considered the real foundation of the Thoroughbred.

The Percheron owes much to the Oriental sires with which the native French mares were mated. Gallipoli and Godolphin were two of the most important of these sires.

The Norfolk trotter was the result of mating Barbs with the black trotters of Friesland. The Cleveland Bay represents a Barb-Yorkshire cart horse cross.

Bars I, progenitor of the Russian Orloff, was three generations removed from Smetanxa, a gray Arabian imported into Russia. The Prussian Trakehner is derived from an admixture of Oriental and Thoroughbred blood with the native stock of the country.

In America, imported Grand Bashaw, a Barb brought from Tripoli, founded through his immediate descendants the Clay, Patchen and Bashaw families. Leopard, an Arab, and Linden Tree, a Barb, presented to General Grant, were used by Randolph Huntingdon in his creation of the Clay Arabian. Zilcaadi, an Arab from Turkey, sired the dam of Golddust, the founder of the Morgan family of that name.

THE THOROUGHBRED

Thoroughbred is the proper name of the English running race horse breed, and any other application of the term to horses is incorrect. It should not be confused nor used synonymously with " pure bred," the adjective employed to denote the absence of any alien blood in the ancestry.

It is not probable, in view of what we know of the history of horses in Great Britain, that the origin of the Thoroughbred was of Oriental blood exclusively, although their lineage has been carefully guarded for so long that all trace of the common stock of the country, if any ever existed, has long since been bred out, and they are therefore truly " thoroughbred."

The principal foundation to which the Thoroughbred traces consists of the Barb or Royal mares, imported by Charles Second (1660 to 1685), and the Darley Arabian, a pure Anazah, imported in 1706; the Byerly Turk, imported in 1689, and Godolphin Barb, brought from Paris in 1724. The latter had been working in a water cart, a discard, no doubt, from the stable of some member of the nobility to whom he had been presented, as was commonly the custom.

There are prominent families in the Thoroughbred and derived breeds which can be traced direct to each of these sires. Eclipse, the most conspicuous individual in the history of the English turf; Blaze, the foundation Hackney sire, and Messenger, the progenitor of the American Standardbred, were respectively four, three and six generations removed from the Darley Arabian. King Herod, a great race horse, was a line descendant of the Byerly Turk, and Matchem, a noted race horse and sire, was a grandson of Godolphin Barb. It has been stated that the American bred Thoroughbreds are, as a rule, closer to their Oriental ancestry than the English Thoroughbreds and that they follow their type more closely.

Early Racing.—While the real era of Thoroughbred breeding is usually considered to have begun with the importation by Charles Second, horse racing of a primitive character was reported in the latter half of the twelfth century. The first real race was run in 1377, between Richard Second and the Earl of Arundel. Henry the Eighth was the first king to maintain a racing stable of his own, and the English sovereigns since that time have been enthusiastic patrons of the turf.

Through these centuries of breeding the most rigid selection has been practised, turf performance alone being the standard. Customs of conducting races and the types of horses that could win have undergone considerable modification within recent generations, however. Prior to 1880 it was customary to run four mile heats and carry top weight, while the present system is to sprint short distances under close handicaps, starting as two-year-olds and campaigning for entire seasons.

Thoroughbreds were introduced into this country by the English colonists in Old Dominion, and the Thoroughbred sentiment is still strongest there, especially in Virginia. The first Thoroughbred of note to be imported was Diomed, the winner of the first English Derby, the classic race in England. He was brought over in 1797. In a straight line of descent from Diomed came Sir Archy, the first truly American Thoroughbred; Boston his grandson, conceded to have been the greatest American race horse, and his son Lexington, a scarcely less remarkable performer than Boston and a most influential sire, figuring in American Standardbred and Saddle families as well as in the Thoroughbred.

FIG. 64.—A Thoroughbred stallion, the sire of race horses.

Description.—The Thoroughbred represents the speed type in the extreme, and, having been the first breed improved, their distinctive characters are well marked . (Fig. 64). Most characteristic are the extreme refinement; the small, well proportioned head; clearly defined features; straight face line; neat ear; fine throttle; sloping shoulders; well-made withers, muscular thighs and quarters; straight hind legs; usually slightly bucked knees; oblique pasterns; and a rather small foot of dense horn. Their way of going is especially characterized by being low and pointing at the walk and trot, but perfection at the gallop or run. Their temperament is naturally racy, of such a highly nervous organization as to cause them to become " hot " and erratic.

Bay and chestnut with more or less white markings are the common colors, although black, gray, and white were frequent among the early Thoroughbreds. Typical Thoroughbred weight is about 1000 pounds, and they stand from 15 to 16 hands high. Sir Walter Gilbey estimates an average increase of 1 hand $2\frac{1}{2}$ inches from 1700 to 1900, 15–$2\frac{1}{2}$ being the average at the present time.

Relation to Other Breeds.—This breed is of the greatest historic importance. It was the first breed improved, and barring the Oriental from which it is derived it has the purest blood lines. For it the first studbook was established. Having been the first breed improved, the blood of the Thoroughbred has been most freely used in the improvement of other breeds and types. In all but the draft breeds the influence of the Thoroughbred may be demonstrated. In the heavy harness division the foundation blood lines are significant. The Hackney descends from Shales, the son of Blaze, a Thoroughbred, out of a common mare of Norfolk. The French *demi sang* refers to the cross of the Thoroughbred on French mares. Thoroughbreds are used extensively in German studs, the Prussian Trakehner being produced from both Thoroughbred and Oriental sires. The Yorkshire Coach horse represents a Thoroughbred–Cleveland Bay cross. The three most important foundation sires of American horses, Messenger, Justin Morgan, and Denmark, are credited with Thoroughbred pedigrees. In addition, the majority of hunters and polo ponies, as well as a great many saddle horses, are clean or part bred.

The greatest value of the Thoroughbred as foundation stock has no doubt passed, as the breeds which have been evolved from a Thoroughbred foundation have been improved along their respective lines to a point where an out-cross to the Thoroughbred might be a step backward, although Thoroughbred ancestors are within a very few generations of some of the most noted and successful Hackney, French Coach, Saddle and even Standardbred sires.

There is a strong prejudice against the Thoroughbred in some parts of this country, where he is looked upon merely as a racing machine. But any one familiar with the stamp of horse bred in Virginia, for instance, will recognize in the blood of the Thoroughbred a breeding leaven, which judiciously and intelligently used produces most desirable results.

When breeders of the Thoroughbred practice selection to saddle rather than to race horse requirements, with good dispo-

Fig. 65.—A Thoroughbred stallion suitable to get saddle horses and hunters.

sition, size, shape, and substance as the features sought, this breed will not be so exclusively dependent on the status of the racing game for patronage.

" Blood " is a term frequently used to indicate Thoroughbred breeding; " of the blood," " blood like," and " blood horse," all refer to the Thoroughbred. This being *the* blood and this breed being altogether of it, horses carrying but a fractional percentage are designated as part bred and the number of parts are specified as two, or half bred, in the case of the get of a Thoroughbred sire, out of a common bred mare; three parts or three-quarters being used to designate the get of a Thoroughbred out of a half bred mare. The blood is accounted for in this way even up to seven-eighths.

Record of Best Performances on the Running Turf.

DISTANCE.	Name, Age, and Weight.	Place.	Date.	Time.
¼ mile.....	Bob Wade, 4................	Butte, Mont........	Aug. 20, 1890.	0.21¼
⅜ mile.....	Atoka, aged, 103 lbs..........	Butte, Mont........	Sept. 7, 1906.	0.33½
3½ furlongs.	Colisse, 2, 123 lbs............	Juarez, Mexico......	Jan. 17, 1911.	0.39 2-5
½ mile.....	Geraldine, 4, 122 lbs..........	Morris Park (st. c.)..	Aug. 30, 1889.	0.46
4½ furlongs.	Preceptor, 2, 112 lbs........	Belmont Park (st. c.).	May 19, 1908.	0.51
	Joe Morris, 2, 103 lbs.......	Louisville (C.Downs).	May 8, 1909.	0.52 4-5
⅝ mile.....	Maid Marian, 4, 111 lbs......	Morris Park (st. c.)..	Oct. 9, 1894.	0.56¾
5½ furlongs.	Plater, 2, 107 lbs...........	Morris Park (st. c.)..	Oct. 21, 1902.	1.02½
	Fern L., 3, 92 lbs..........	Seattle, Wash'n......	Aug. 8, 1908.	1.05
*Futurity c..	Kingston, aged, 139 lbs.......	Sheeps'd B.(C.I.J.C.)	June 22, 1891.	1.08
6 furlongs...	Artful, 2, 130 lbs...........	Morris Park (st. c.)..	Oct. 15, 1904.	1.08
	Prince Ahmed, 5, 117 lbs....	Empire City, N. Y...	July 29, 1909.	1.11
6½ furlongs.	Priscillian, 5, 113 lbs........	Hamilton, Ont......	June 19, 1911.	1.11
	Lady Vera, 2, 90 lbs........	Belm't P., L. I. (st. c.)	Oct. 19, 1906.	1.16 3-5
	Brookdale Nymph, 4, 124 lbs.	Belmont Park, L. I...	Oct. 14, 1907.	1.17 2-5
7 furlongs...	Roseben, 5, 126 lbs.........	Belmont Park, L. I...	Oct. 16, 1906.	1.22
	Colin, 2, 122 lbs...........	Belm't P., L. I. (st. c.)	Oct. 16, 1907.	1.23
7½ furlongs.	Restigouche, 3, 107 lbs........	Belmont Park, L. I...	May 29, 1908.	1.31 1-5
1 mile......	Salvator, 4, 110 lbs†........	Monmouth P. (st. c.)	Aug. 28, 1890.	1.35½
	Kildeer, 4, 91 lbs...........	Monmouth P. (st. c.)	Aug. 13, 1892.	1.37½
	Kiamesha, 3, 104 lbs.......	Belmont Park, L. I...	Oct. 9, 1905.	1.37 2-5
	Dick Welles, 3, 112 lbs......	Chicago (Harlem)....	Aug. 14, 1903.	1.37 2-5
	Fern L., 3, 80 lbs..........	Seattle, Wash'n......	Aug. 15, 1908.	1.37 2-5
	Bourbon Beau, 3, 112 lbs....	Juarez, Mexico......	Feb. 14, 1912.	1.37 2-5
1 m. 20 yds.	Macy, 4, 107 lbs...........	Chicago (Wash. Park)	July 2, 1898.	1.40
	Maid Marian, 4, 106 lbs....	Chicago (Wash. Park)	July 19, 1903.	1.40
	Six Shooter, 5, 111 lbs.......	Chicago (Wash. Park)	June 27, 1903.	1.40
1 m. 40 yds.	Preen, 4, 104 lbs...........	Buffalo, N. Y........	June 16, 1906.	1.42
	Main Chance, 3, 114 lbs....	Buffalo, N. Y.......	June 29, 1907.	1.42
1 m. 50 yds.	Vox Populi, 4, 104 lbs........	Seattle, Wash'n......	Sept. 5, 1908.	1.40 4-5
1 m. 70 yds.	Bubbling Water, 4, 121 lbs....	Oakland, Cal........	Nov. 30, 1910.	1.42 1-5
1 m.100 yds.	Rapid Water, 6, 114 lbs.......	Oakland (Cal. J. C.)..	Nov. 30, 1907.	1.44 1-5
1 1-16 miles.	Royal Tourist, 3, 104 lbs....	Oakland, Cal........	Nov. 11, 1908.	1.44 1-5
	Green Seal, 4, 109 lbs.......	Seattle, Wash'n......	Sept. 12, 1908.	1.44 2-5
	Gretna Green, 5, 100 lbs....	Fort Erie, Ont.......	Aug. 28, 1909.	1.43 3-5
1⅛ miles.	Charles Edward, 3, 126 lbs..	Brighton Beach......	July 16, 1907.	1.50 3-5
	Green Seal, 4, 107 lbs.......	Seattle, Wash'n......	Aug. 20, 1908.	1.50 3-5
1 3-16 miles.	Scintillant II., 6, 109 lbs......	Chicago (Harlem)....	Sept. 1, 1902.	1.57 2-5
1¼ miles.	Broomstick, 3, 104 lbs......	Brighton Beach......	July 9, 1904.	2.02 4-5
	Olambala, 4, 122 lbs........	Sheepsh'd Bay (C.I.)	July 2, 1910.	2.02 4-5
1 5-16 miles.	Ballot, 4, 126 lbs.............	Sheepsh'd Bay (C.I.)	July 1, 1908.	2.09 3-5
1 m. 500 yds.	Swift Wing, 5, 100 lbs........	Latonia, Ky.........	July 8, 1905.	2.10 1-5
1⅜ miles.	Irish Lad, 4, 125 lbs..........	Sheepsh'd Bay (C.I.)	June 25, 1904.	2.17 3-5
1½ miles.	Goodrich, 3, 102 lbs..........	Chicago (Wash. Park)	July 16, 1898.	2.30¼
1⅝ miles.	Fitz Herbert, 3, 122 lbs.......	Sheepsh'd Bay (C.I.)	July 13, 1909.	2.45
1¾ miles.	Major Daingerfield, 4, 120 lbs..	Morris Park, N. Y...	Oct. 3, 1903.	2.57
1⅞ miles.	Orcagna, 4, 96 lbs...........	Oakland, Cal........	Mar. 2, 1909.	3.17 3-5
2 miles.	Everett, 4, 107 lbs...........	Pimlico, Md.........	Oct. 31, 1910.	3.25 3-5
2 1-16 miles.	War Whoop, 4, 96 lbs........	Ontario (Tor'to J. C.).	Sept 23, 1905.	3.34½
2⅛ miles.	Joe Murphy, 4, 99 lbs........	Chicago (Harlem)....	Aug. 30, 1894.	3.42
2¼ miles.	Ethelbert, 4, 124 lbs..........	Brighton Beach, N.Y.	Aug. 4, 1900.	3.49 1-5
2½ miles.	Kyrat, 3, 88 lbs.............	Newport, Ky........	Nov. 18, 1899.	4.24½
2⅝ miles.	Ten Broeck, 4, 104 lbs........	Lexington, Ky.......	Sept. 16, 1876.	4.58½
2¾ miles.	Hubbard, 4, 107 lbs..........	Saratoga, N. Y......	Aug. 9, 1873.	4.58¾
3 miles.	Mamie Algol, 5, 108 lbs.......	New Orleans (City P.)	Feb. 16, 1907.	5.19
4 miles.	Lucrezia Borgia, 4, 85 lbs.†..	Oakland (Cal. J. C.)..	May 20, 1897.	7.11
	Messenger Boy, 5, 106 lbs...	Louisville, Ky.......	Oct. 7, 1911.	7.14 1-5

*170 feet less than ¾ mile. † Races against time. St. c., straight course.

Heat Races.

Dist.	Name, Age, and Weight.	Place.	Date.	Time.
¼ mile.	Sleepy Dick, aged	Kiowa, Kan	Oct. 19, 1888.	0.21½ –0.22¼
⅜ mile.	Bob Wade, 4	Butte, Mont	Aug. 16, 1890.	0.36¼ –0.36¼
½ mile.	Eclipse, Jr., 4	Dallas, Tex	Nov. 1, 1890.	0.48–0.48–0.4
	Bogus, aged, 113 lbs	Helena, Mont	Aug. 22, 1888.	0.48 –0.48
	Bill Howard, 5, 122 lbs	Anaconda, Mont	Aug. 17, 1895.	0.47½ –0.48½
⅝ mile.	Kittie Pease, 4, 82 lbs	Dallas, Tex	Nov. 2, 1887.	1.00 –1.00
	Fox, 4, 113 lbs	San Francisco, Cal.	Oct. 31, 1891.	1.00 3-5–1.01 1-5
¾ mile.	Tom Hayes, 4, 107 lbs	Morris Park (st. c.).	June 17, 1892.	1.10½ –1.12¾
	Lizzie S., 5, 118 lbs,	Louisville	Sept. 28, 1883.	1.13¼ –1.13¼
1 mile.	Guido, 4, 117 lbs	Chicago (Wash.Pk.)	July 11, 1891.	1.41½ –1.41
1 (3 in 5)	L'Argentine, 5, 115 lbs	St. Louis	June 14, 1879.	1.43–1.44–1.47¾
1 1-16 m.	Slipalong, 5, 115 lbs	Chicago (Wash.Pk.)	Sept. 2, 1885.	1.51½ –1.48½
1⅛ miles.	What-er-Lou, 5, 119 lbs	San Fran. (Ingleside)	Feb. 18, 1889.	1.56 –1.54¾
1¼ miles.	Glenmore, 5, 114 lbs	Sheepshead Bay	Sept. 25, 1880.	2.10 –2.14
1½ miles.	Patsy Duffy, aged, 115 lbs	Sacramento, Cal	Sept. 17, 1884.	2.41¾ –2.41
2 miles.	Miss Woodford, 4, 107½ lbs	Sheepshead Bay	Sept. 20, 1884.	3.33 –3.33¼
3 miles.	Norfolk, 4, 100 lbs	Sacramento, Cal	Sept. 23, 1865.	5.27½ –5.29¼
4 miles.	Glenmore, 4, 108 lbs	Baltimore, Pimlico	Oct. 25, 1879.	7.30¼ –7.31

The English Derby, Epsom Downs—(English Turf.)

(Distance, about 1½ miles, run since 1788.)

Year.	Owner and Winner.	Sire.	Time.	Second.
1904	Leopold de Rothschild's St. Amant	St. Frusquin	2.45 4–5	John O'Gaunt.
1905	Lord Rosebery's Cicero	Satire	2.39 3–5	Jardy.
1906	Maj. Loeder's Spearmint	Carbine	2.36 4–5	Picton.
1907	Richard Croker's Orby	Orme	2.44	Slieve Gallion.
1908	E. Ginistrelli's Signorinetta	Chaleureux	2.39 4–5	Primer.
1909	King Edward's Minoru	Cyllene	2.42 2–5	Louviers.
1910	Mr. Fairie's Lemberg*	Cyllene	2.35 1–5	Greenback.
1911	J. B. Joel's Sunstar	Sunbridge	2.36 4–5	Steadfast.
1912	W. Raphael's Pagalie	Cyllene	2.38 4–5	Jaegar.

On June 28, 1913, Whisk Broom 2d, owned by Harry Payne Whitney, established a new turf record when he won the Suburban handicap at a mile and a quarter in two minutes flat, carrying the heavy impost of 139 pounds. He was ridden by Notter.

It is a noteworthy fact that the record price for which any horse has ever been sold was paid for a Thoroughbred. A French racing man, Edmund Blanc, gave $200,000 for the ten-year-old English Thoroughbred stallion, White Knight. Previous record prices were $196,875 for Flying Fox, $157,500 each for Cyllene and Diamond Jubilee, and $156,250 for Ormonde. Rocksand has recently been exported from this country at a price of $150,000.

THE BREEDS OF HORSES 83

CLASSIFICATION OF BREEDS

Breeds may be classified according to the type to which their representatives conform, as:

Draft Breeds.—Percheron, Belgian, Clydesdale, Shire, and Suffolk.

Heavy Harness Breeds.—Hackney, Yorkshire Coach, Cleveland Bay, French Coach, German Coach, and Russian Orloff.

Light Harness Breed.—American Standardbred.

Saddle Breeds.—Thoroughbred, American Saddle Horse and Arabian.

Ponies.—Shetland, Welsh, and Hackney.

REVIEW

1. What is a breed? And of what importance are breeds?
2. What are the three factors that determine breed characteristics?
3. What are the essential things to consider in a study of the breeds?
4. What have been considered as the foundation stocks from which all breeds have had their origin?
5. What additional light have the investigations of Ewart and Ridgeway thrown on this subject?
6. What are the most important facts concerning the horses in Arabia?
7. To what extent may color indicate Arab blood?
8. Review the important facts in the history of the Thoroughbred.
9. Discuss the Thoroughbred in its relation to other breeds.
10. What are the possibilities of the Thoroughbred at the present time?

CHAPTER VII

DRAFT BREEDS

The breeds of draft horses here considered are the Percheron, the Belgian, the Clydesdale, the Shire, and the Suffolk.

THE PERCHERON

France affords an example of the community system of breeding. While the production of the different types of horses is extensively practiced in the country at large, the breeders of different districts are devoting themselves to the production of one type more or less exclusively, with the result that many a horse breeding section is noted for a class of horses distinctive of and bearing the name of that community. Thus, we have the *Percheron* of LaPerche, the *Boulonnaise* from that part of the country contiguous to Boulogne, the *Nivernais* of Niévre, the *Ardennaise* of Ardennes, and others.

In America, by common consideration and studbook registration the Percheron is distinguished from the other French draft breeds collectively. In France, both the Percheron and Boulonnaise are represented by studbook associations.

LaPerche is a district comprising about three thousand square miles, situated in the northern or inland part of Normandy. It has a country-wide reputation for its grass land and the horses produced thereon.

Flemish blood predominated in what may be regarded as the native stock of France. On this cold blood base, repeated top crosses of Oriental blood were made, the relative proportions of hot and cold blood varying in the case of the different French breeds.

The foundation of the Percheron was composed of the Norman descendants of the original Flemish stock, mated with Oriental stallions, these crosses being either incidental to current events or made with a definite purpose in view. They had a most important significance in determining the type of horse

84

which the Percheron was to be. When the Saracens invaded France in 732 and were defeated by Charles Martel, the Oriental horses upon which they were mounted, mostly stallions, fell into the hands of the Franks and were eventually, by this means, distributed throughout the different parts of the country. The successful Crusaders also brought back with them entire horses, as the spoils of war, and here was a direct though unintentional infusion of Oriental blood.

Later when the desirable effect of this Oriental top cross was manifested, there were more or less systematic importations of Oriental sires, the most notable of which was Gallipoli, a gray horse, introduced from the Orient in 1820, whose impress on the horses of the country, especially through his grandson Jean Le Blanc, was most marked.

Good grass and selection are the other factors chiefly responsible for the Percherons we have to-day. LaPerche is world-famed as a grazing district.

Early Service.—The service in which the Percheron first attained distinction was as a stage-coach horse, in the ante-railroad days, when all freight and express as well as passengers were moved in this way (Figs. 66 and 67). It was a rapid draft job, hauling loads at an eight mile clip for long and hard stages. An ordinary road horse could not pull the load, while an ordinary draft horse could not stand the pace nor the distance. The breeders of LaPerche specialized in the production of this type of horse, and their success marked the beginning of Percheron popularity (Fig. 68).

The advent of railroads in the nineteenth century struck a telling blow at the diligence or stage-coach horse. At this crisis the French breeders displayed a foresight that might well be emulated by horse breeders of the present motor period. Instead of howling calamity and defaming the locomotive, they had foresight enough to perceive a new era of agricultural production on the one hand and of commercial traffic on the other, which had never before been possible, and which would require horses in greater numbers than ever. But the nature of service in the new field created essentially by the locomotive and railway train would require horses of quite a different stamp than had pre-

Fig. 66.—A French post coach for the horsing of which the antecedents of Percherons were used early in the nineteenth century.

Fig. 67.—A diligence still in use in Switzerland, that is fairly representative of that which was common in France during the first epoch of Percheron history.

viously been produced in LaPerche; the loads to be moved would be greater, the distance less, and time allowance more liberal. The true draft horse was to supersede the old " diligence " type, but even in their efforts to meet the demand for a horse of greater weight and power, the LaPerche breeders did not lose sight of the desirable characteristics of hot blood derivation, and so far as they were correlated with the increase in size and draftiness, attributes of the cold parent stock, they were retained. To this

Fig. 68.—An old-fashioned Percheron, a rapid draft horse of a type evolved in the diligence service.

may be attributed the most distinctive features of the present Percheron.

Distinctive Features.—He may attain ton weight and yet possess a refinement of head and neck, a general suppleness of form, a texture of bone and hoof, a degree of quality and finish throughout, together with an energetic, yet perfectly tractable, temperament and disposition, not equalled in any of the other draft breeds. Furthermore, the typical Percheron bears his great weight with an airiness and boldness that is unusual.

But to the same source may be charged some of his deficiencies. He is sometimes too fine, not sufficiently drafty in scale or form, and too hot in disposition to qualify, acceptably, for the heaviest draft work.

The features by which the Percherons (Fig. 69) may be most readily distinguished from representatives of other draft breeds, reckoned on the basis of averages, are size, fully up to draft requirements but hardly equal to that of the Shire and

Fig. 69.—A Percheron stallion, showing the breed character, the form, and the color that are most typically Percheron.

Belgian; form, that is somewhat more up-standing, more rounded in contour, less square ended and blocky, at all events not as squatty as in the Belgian, although he is not a leggy, light quartered horse; head of good proportions, sharply defined features, prominent, full, bright eyes, rather neat ear, a fair length of neck, well finished in crest and throttle; bone of good texture but in some cases too fine, as determined by popular standard; canons devoid of feather; well-formed feet, of medium size and of the very best texture of blue horn.

Color is gray or black most commonly, the former more typical and growing in favor, as expressed in the demand, although bays, browns, chestnuts, and even roans are encountered.

Way of going is not more accurate, but manifests a snap and boldness not displayed by draft horses as a rule.

Respects in which some Percherons are not strong and to the correction of which conscientious and intelligent breeders are giving their attention are the set of the hind legs, the conformation of the hocks, and the slope of the pasterns.

Economic Importance.—Percherons outnumber in this country all other draft breeds combined, and their popularity seems to be increasing proportionately. This is no doubt due, in part, to the good start given the breed by the pioneer breeders and importers. From the time of their introduction into Union and Pickaway counties, Ohio, in 1851, through their period of development in Ohio, Illinois, and Iowa, especially, they have been given every opportunity to make good. But more important than this, perhaps, has been their general adaptability to meet the conditions of the average American farmer. Even though the demand for the highest class of draft horses is from the cities, their production must, of necessity, involve the farmer. It is useless to attempt to interest the practical farmer in a proposition which does not appeal to him in a practical sense. From the very first the Percheron has made a strong bid for his favor. The adaptability which characterizes the Percheron as a breed may also be noticed in his use as a pure-bred sire. From a patronage of the most miscellaneous sort of mares, a Percheron will average a large percentage of marketable colts, varying, it is true, from weight-carrying saddle horses and hunters, and even harness horses, to the draftiest of draft horses, but each good in his class. The fact that most native American mares have some degree, if not a preponderance, of hot blood in their ancestry and may, therefore, be expected to nick better with Percheron stallions, may account for the manifest excellence of the latter in this respect.

THE BELGIAN

Belgium is a part of the original territory to which the old Flanders horse was indigenous, and as the history of the breed records no other stock, we conclude that this breed is, directly and exclusively, descended from the old Flemish stock. There are two respects, however, in which the Flemish ancestry is not indicated, namely, the absence of much hair and the infrequency of the black color. Selection may account for these modifications, however.

Belgium is essentially an agricultural country, flat and low-lying for the most part, and horse breeding in a limited way is followed by most farmers. Each one has a colt or two to turn off each year. The Belgian Draft Horse Society has done much in the way of conducting shows, offering prizes, and providing subsidies to promote the interests of the breed.

Three Original Types.—There were originally, according to Herr Van Schelle, who had charge of the Belgian Government horse exhibit at the St. Louis Exposition, three types of draft horses in Belgium: The Flemish, the largest, produced nearest the coast; the Brabaçon, an intermediate type, bred farther in-land; and the Ardennaise, a small, rapid draft horse similar and akin to the French horse of that name, bred in the border dis-tricts. There has been more or less amalgamation of these three originally distinct types in the evolution of the present-day Belgian cart horses.

The American Type of Belgian.—It is claimed that the type has been considerably modified in accordance with the demand of American buyers. The old fashioned, more massive, but much less refined stamp still receives most favor in Belgium. The accepted type of Belgian horse in America is perhaps the most uniformly drafty of any of the breeds, short legs, a compact body (Fig. 70), wide, muscular ends, and deep, wide, spreading ribs being the rule. The head is square and medium sized, the neck short and heavy crested. Roans and chestnuts predominate, though bays, browns, and occasionally grays and blacks appear. Hoofs deficient in circumference, bone that is not sufficiently flat, and necks that are too short and heavy, with a general absence of refinement, are features in which average representa-tives of this breed are still subject to improvement. They show an interesting conformation of the hamstring, the muscles being apparently inserted directly upon the point of the hock, without the usual tendinous continuation. The extreme width of the

Belgian may cause him to roll or paddle somewhat at the walk, but it is surprising how well many of them trot.

The Belgians have made wonderful progress in this country, considering that they have been attracting much attention here only since about 1900. The improvement noted in this time has been equally remarkable. The Belgian sire has the effect of most consistently improving the draft form of his get, especially those

FIG. 70.—A Belgian stallion of most acceptable stamp, embodying the desirable features of draftiness and good middle, and subject to little criticism of head and neck or legs and feet.

from leggy, light-waisted mares, and mares of this stamp are most likely to have the degree of quality requisite to offset the deficiency, in this respect, sometimes shown by the pure-bred Belgian. Belgian grades are especially popular among feeders, it being characteristic of the breed to be good doers. They also ship unusually well. Belgians have probably shown, in this country, greater percentage increase in numbers and in merit than any other draft breed.

Horse history in Great Britain dates back to 55 B.C., the date of the Roman Conquest. Cæsar's description of the chariot manœuvres, by which his advance was opposed, would indicate the existence at that time of a horse, diminutive in stature, but drafty in build, whose feats of handiness were remarkable. British coins, issued in the first century, confirm this opinion by the powerful type of horse struck on the metal.

During the seventh century horses came into use for riding. The chief demand was for the mounting of infantry forces, as a means of transportation only, the idea of cavalry or any form of fighting from horseback being suggested later by the Normans. As the soldier's chain armor at this period was heavy and the marches were hard, a large, stout horse was required.

Later (1300) when plate armor began to replace chain, and the horses themselves were protected, the effectiveness of weapons having been increased, the weight imposed upon them became still greater and size more essential. Horse breeding was given most careful consideration by the Throne. The use of small stallions was discouraged and even prohibited by royal edict. The condition existed until modified methods of conducting warfare, incidental to the invention of gunpowder (1650), led to the discarding of armor and consequently of war horses of this type.

Advent of Draft Horses.—Up to the eighteenth century draft work had been done principally by oxen or by inferior horses, not fit for service in war. After the beginning of that century, with its relegation of the war horse from the battlefield to become a humble beast of burden, the real era of the draft horse began. In the latter part of the eighteenth century two distinct types of cart horses are mentioned by Young, the Large Black Old English horse and the Suffolk Punch.

Thus the British draft breeds have had a long period of development, the primary motive of which was war, not work. During, or even before, the first century, horses possessed some of the same characters which are now dominant in these breeds.

THE CLYDESDALE

This breed takes its name from the Clyde River in Scotland, in the valley of which, especially the counties of Ayr and Lanark, it has been developed. The Clydesdale district is characterized by a rather broken surface and a stiff clay soil. The earliest history of horses in Britain describes a horse akin to the Scandinavian ponies, the size of which was systematically increased, by royal edict, after the importance of greater size in war horses was impressed upon the Britons by the Roman conquest. While the original British stock was more or less composite, there is no evidence to contradict that the blood of the British draft breeds was derived, essentially, from the Flanders source.

The importation of Flemish stallions into both Scotland and England in numbers as great as one hundred at a time, as in the case of King John, is a matter of record. Furthermore, the interchange of horses across the border is acknowledged, even up to comparatively recent times, so that the distinguishing differences between the three British draft breeds must be accounted for in other ways than by their origin in blood, which it must be granted had much in common. The conditions of life surrounding these breeds during their formative period, and especially the variance in the notion of what constitutes a draft horse, as expressed by the Scotchman and the Englishman, are ample to account for whatever differences in type there may be.

The Scotchman's standard attaches especial importance to the locomotory apparatus, legs, pasterns, and feet, and the way a horse moves. A free, springy stride executed with a wonderful degree of trueness and as much flash as is consistent with power have received primary consideration. As a consequence of the inevitable law of correlation, there has come to be associated with this character of stride more length of leg and back, less width and massiveness, and a somewhat shorter rib than is characteristic of the extreme draft type.

Characteristics of Clydesdales.—While Clydesdale and Shire grades, and even pure breds, which depart somewhat from the true type, may have much in common, there is no difficulty in distinguishing typical representatives of the two breeds. In contrast with representatives of most other breeds, the Clydesdale is recognized as a horse standing over more ground, with a toppy carriage, lacking somewhat in width and compactness, but well set up on legs, the direction of which, viewed from either the side or the end, is most accurate (Fig. 71). The quality of the

Fig. 71.—A Clydesdale stallion of most impressive character, showing the form, setting of hind legs, slope of pasterns, quality of bone, feather, and distribution of white most desirable in this breed.

bone is ideal; the conformation of the hocks the most perfect of any of the draft breeds; the slope of the pasterns offers the greatest relief to concussion, and at the same time affords an angle of greatest degree through which to lift. In size and form the feet reflect the great care that has been exerted in selection, although the texture of horn, especially in white points, is not as dense and tough as in the case of the Percheron. The amount of feather has been materially reduced in compliance with American demand, its quality being of the finest. The Scotchman still holds to the presence of feather, even stimulating its growth by artificial means in some instances. The superiority of the Clydesdale in action is a point quite generally conceded. The direction and conformation of his legs are such as to insure the straightest, springiest stride of which a draft horse is capable.

Color.—Gray Clydesdales have been common at times in the history of the breed, but are now discriminated against in favor of bays and browns, with occasional blacks, chestnuts, and roans. White markings are characteristic, to the extent of splashes of white on the body or an even distribution of white hair throughout the coat, in addition to white in the face and on all four legs.

Judged by the standards of other breeds, the Clydesdale has been criticised as deficient in scale and draftiness, and as being plain in the head, low in the back, short in the rib, with a shelly foot, and too much white, with no regularity of distribution.

Although introduced at a comparatively early date, the Clydesdale has not received the consideration in this country which he seems to merit.

THE SHIRE

It has already been pointed out, in reviewing the history of the Clydesdale, that from essentially the same original material the Scotchman has evolved the Clydesdale and the Englishman the Shire, in accordance with their own divergent conceptions of what a draft horse should be, and that, while they have much in common, the characters which distinguish them are extremely unlike. To be sure, the low-lying fenn country of Cambridge and Lincolnshire is more conducive to massive growth than is Scotland, it being also the home of the largest breed of sheep. Here the Shire and his antecedent, the black Lincolnshire cart horse, have been chiefly bred, but this environment has only seconded the English breeder in the attainment of his ideal.

Characteristics.—The typical Shire will weigh more on the average than any other draft horse, although he is scarcely as blocky in form as the Belgian (Fig. 72). He possesses the most substance, such as it is, but there is an absence of quality, marked

in size and contour of head, texture of hair, bone, and hoof—
the hair showing an inclination to be coarse and kinky, especially in the feather, the bone to be round and meaty, and the
hoof to be of a loose, spongy, or shelly texture. His temperament is extremely lymphatic, rendering him slower than is
desired by many. On the basis of the scales and tape line stand-

FIG. 72.—A Shire stallion of most approved type, combining an unusual degree of quality
and character with the size, substance, and draftiness typical of this breed.

ard, the Shire measures up well, but analyzed in minute detail
he is subject to some criticism, especially in so far as his materials
of construction are concerned.

Color.—The range of color in the Shire is greater than in
any other draft breed. Originally of sooty black, with white
points, he may now be found of any color, from black through
the different shades of bay, brown, and chestnut to roan and

gray. A considerable amount of white, frequently too much, on face and legs is common.

The popularity of the Shire in this country has been restricted rather than general. There are some parts where he is bred almost exclusively, others in which he is almost unknown. His grossness, abundant feather, and sluggish movements prevent him from making a strong bid for general favor in competition with the other breeds.

Crosses.—A percentage of Shire blood, especially in the dams from which market geldings are produced, is acknowledged to be a valuable asset. Attention has been called to the fact that much credit which belongs to the Shire has been assigned to other breeds through just this sort of mating, the sires usually being most conspicuous and the dams obscure. Size and substance can be derived with greater certainty from Shire blood than from any other line of breeding.

SUFFOLK

The Suffolks are characterized as being of the purest lineage, most uniform color, and are bred more exclusively for farm work than any of the draft breeds.

Their origin is untraced, but horses of this stamp are known to have been bred in Suffolk for over two centuries. So carefully has their lineage been guarded that practically all of the pure-bred representatives of the breed trace back to a common ancestor, The Crisp Horse of Ufford, foaled in 1768. They are produced almost exclusively in Suffolk and adjoining Essex, in eastern England, by farmers and for farming purposes.

Their especial adaptability for farm service is found in their good dispositions, which render them so easy of control as to make it possible to work them in tandem hitches without lines; their easy keeping quality, working long hours between feeds; and their persistence at the collar, pulling true under all circumstances.

Their distinguishing characteristics are the invariable chestnut color of varying shades (Fig. 73), with little if any white, but often with flaxen manes and tails; their smooth, rotund form;

and a clean boned leg, devoid of feather. The old-fashioned exaggerated punch form is no longer common.

Suffolks have been alleged to be under draft weight, too light in bone, unbalanced in the proportion of body to legs, and with a foot inclining to be flat and shelly. These points have all been materially strengthened in the most approved type of the present-day Suffolk.

Fig. 73.—A Suffolk stallion of the punch form, the clean bone and the chestnut color characteristic of this breed.

Distribution.—Suffolks have never been imported or bred in any considerable numbers in this country, although in some sections there is an unaccountable prejudice in their favor, especially among farmers, and in many instances they have been enthusiastically received when shown. It is claimed they are not available in large numbers, the area devoted to their production being limited and there being an active demand for them at home and in South America, Africa, Russia, New Zealand, Australia, and Canada.

Crosses.—So far as their grades have been seen, they have been of a rich chestnut color, making it easy to match up a team, smooth turned, well formed of body, of good size, and set upon feet and legs not subject to serious criticism. The prepotency of the Suffolk sire on grade mares is well marked in other respects than color. Grade Suffolk mares are said to make most acceptable dams from which to breed mules on account of their smooth form.

REVIEW

1. Name the draft breeds and the country to which each is native.
2. How are the most distinctive characters of the Percheron accounted for?
3. To what is the general popularity of the Percheron in this country due?
4. What characteristics of the Belgian are responsible for the increasing favor shown them in this country?
5. What improvement has been marked in this breed since its introduction into America?
6. Review the early horse history of Great Britain.
7. Compare a typical Clydesdale and a typical Shire and give reasons for the differences noted.
8. Describe a representative Clydesdale stallion.
9. Of what value is Shire blood in the production of grade geldings?
10. To what kind of work is the Suffolk, as a breed, claimed to be best adapted and why?

CHAPTER VIII

THE HEAVY HARNESS BREEDS

Six breeds are here included. They are discussed in the following order: The Hackney, the French Coach, the German Coach, the Cleveland Bay, the Yorkshire Coach, and the Russian Orloff. The American Carriage Horse, now being bred by the U. S. Government, is of this type.

THE HACKNEY

Curiously enough, this horse, which is preëminently a show-harness horse today and more generally criticised as deficient in stamina than in any other one respect, was originally a road horse of most unusual endurance, used chiefly under saddle and carrying great weight. The very name " Hack " to which Hackney was contracted is suggestive of this type of horse. The term Hackney is adapted from the French *Haquenée,* originally derived from the Latin *Equus.*

Early Hackney history was set in Norfolk and adjacent counties where there existed a remarkable family of distance trotters as early as the latter part of the eighteenth century. This was in the primitive days of roads and vehicles, so that these Norfolk trotters, as they were called, were used chiefly under saddle. Well-authenticated records of seventeen miles an hour over ordinary roads exist. The fact that this was the first line of trotters is most significant. England had already developed the running race horse, and there had existed at one time ambling riding horses, but this was the first horse in the world to trot fast. This fact is emphasized, as it has a bearing on the later evolution of our own Standardbred trotter. This trotting instinct in the prototype of the modern Hackney has been accounted for in various ways. Since these horses were originally stoutly made, blocky, and heavy-fronted and have remained so until comparatively recently, it is reasonable to suppose that they carried, in addition to the Thoroughbred blood which predominated at that time, some degree of cold blood.

101

Dutch stock has been suggested as a possible source of this. There were big black trotters in Friesland, but they showed no such speed at this gait as did the Norfolk Cob. Perhaps the speed, courage, and stamina of the Thoroughbred, coupled with the natural inclination to trot of the colder blooded Friesland " hart-draver," resulted in the square-gaited, fast, enduring, and rather high going Norfolk trotter.

The real beginning of the Hackney breed is fixed at the original Shales horse, foaled 1760, by Blaze, Thoroughbred race horse, three generations removed from the Darley Arabian, out of a stout, common, probably hunting mare of Norfolk.

Families conspicuous in the history of the breed have been the Fireaways, the Denmarks, the Danegelts and the Purick-willows. Leading sires at the present time are Polonius, Mathias, Royal Danegelt, and His Majesty.

With the improvement in roads and vehicles, Hackneys were used more in harness, and their naturally high, trappy step was cultivated. They have eventually become the harness horse *par excellence* in America as in England.

Description.—Typical Hackneys are comparatively short legged horses, rarely standing over 15–3, although they weigh well for their stature. They are of true harness form most uniformly of any of the breeds (Fig. 74). Their heads are square in outline, deep in the jowl; necks well crested, but frequently too strong, lacking finish at the throttle, and giving a heavy forehand.

Natural action, especially in hocks, is perhaps their most distinguishing feature; but it must not be a labored action that hits the ground hard.

Color.—Chestnut color, with flashy white markings all 'round, has been most common, although bays, browns, roans, and blacks are all acceptable. Originally, hard, solid colors predominated in the breed.

Popularity.—The Hackney's premier position in the show ring in this country is only occasionally contested by representatives of any other breed, and they contribute largely to the ranks of the park harness horse. The Hackney stallion is strong in the impress of his shape and action, and nicks most satisfactorily with either Standardbred or Thoroughbred mares in the production of a high class of harness or saddle horses.

Registration.—The American Hackney Horse Society maintains, in addition to the full registration in its studbook, a half registry, to which the filly foals of registered Hackney stallions, out of mares of Standardbred or Thoroughbred breeding that

Fig. 74.—A Hackney stallion, showing in high degree the distinctly harness form, the finish, the bold carriage, and the flash markings which have, together with their natural action, enabled them to win premier rank in the show ring.

have been approved by an authorized representative of the Society, are eligible. The filly foals of half-registered Hackney mares are eligible to full registration.

FRENCH COACH

Origin.—Since the seventeenth century, when the Government studs or " haras " were established, the French have been systematically breeding horses for army service. Their method up to 1840 was to mate Thoroughbred stallions with the native French mares of Normandy, where much of this breeding was done. These mares being of Flemish descent, the mating constituted practically a hot top cross on a cold base. Horses so bred were called, most appropriately, *demi sang* (half blood). Since 1840 the half-breds have been inter-bred, although Thoroughbred blood is still close up to many of the French coachers that have come to this country.

Fig. 75.—A French coach stallion of the more refined sort.

One of the imported stallions, Young Rattler, brought to France in 1820, gave rise to the side line of coach horses, whose production was originally incidental to the breeding of cavalry mounts. The get of Young Rattler for succeeding generations were notable for their heavy harness form, style, and action. Some of the *demi sang* horses show considerable speed. Trotting races, on the turf under saddle for distances from two to three miles, are common events.

There are really three types of *demi sang:* The cavalry horse, the trotter, and the so-called coacher. The latter have been most extensively imported to this country, although there have been some record trotters among them.

The correct type of French Coach horse as we know him in this country (Fig. 75) is a good-sized, rather up-standing individual, close and full made, but quite bloodlike in head and neck, withers, feet and legs. The big, drafty coacher is not

FIG. 76.—A French Coach sire which, mated to trotting bred mares, has produced high-class harness horses with remarkable regularity.

typical of this breed. As a class, they do not flex their hocks so sharply as do the Hackneys, and are not always faultless in knee action.

Color.—Bays, browns and chestnuts, with occasional blacks and roans, are the usual colors, with one or two but rarely more white points.

The French Coach as a Breeder.—Some almost perfect individuals are found in this breed, yet they have never proven a great success in the stud in this country. There are two possible reasons for this: Having had a cross-bred origin not so many generations back, the type is not always fixed, as is exemplified among the breed representatives themselves, hence they may not breed true; they have been largely mismated, being stood along with draft stallions and getting only those common bred mares that were considered too small to raise a draft colt. Bred to trotting-bred mares, results have proven very satisfactory in many instances, in the production of good-sized, well-shaped, and high-going harness horses (Fig. 76).

GERMAN COACH

Origin.—The different States of Germany have been producing big, stout horses for mounting the German cavalry for so long a time that their origin is obscure. Some Thoroughbred crosses have been made, no doubt, more especially in certain States, but as a rule the German horse shows very little of the refining influence of this blood. It is probable that some Oriental crosses have also been made, but cold blood dominates in their veins.

They have been bred more or less under government supervision, although the system is not so complete as in France. Each State has been, to a certain extent, a law unto itself, and has developed a type somewhat distinctive. Size and substance requisite to carry the heavy weight of the fully equipped German trooper have been sought more regularly than the pace and action of the harness horse.

The type of German coacher which has been brought forward in this country is derived chiefly from Oldenburg and East Friesland. It is the largest of any of the heavy harness breeds (Fig. 77), weighing 1500 pounds in some instances, with an ideal harness form, if not too drafty, as may be the case, but quite generally deficient in quality, finish, style, pace, and action—in short, too cold. The more refined individuals present a most imposing stamp of coach horse, and some go very well.

Color.—Hard, solid colors are so prevalent that importers will sell a stallion under a guarantee to get a high percentage of colts that will be bay, brown or black, with very little if any white.

Influence when Mated.—The finer sort of German horses, mated with mares of trotting or Thoroughbred breeding, possessing the quality and snap which the sire lacks, have produced with a fair degree of uniformity high class harness horses of the

Fig. 77.—A German Coach stallion, showing the size, shape, and color typical of this breed.

brougham type. Their long line of pure breeding has made the German Coach horse more prepotent than his French contemporary. Mated with drafty mares, the result is not satisfactory. The coach horse is strongly of cold blood extraction, and coupled with a mare of like inheritance the produce is neither one thing nor the other. A good rule is never to mate a coach stallion with mares larger than he is.

CLEVELAND BAY

The Cleveland Bay was an old-fashioned stagecoach horse, occupying much the same position in England as the diligence Percheron did in France, although never so popular nor so extensively bred. Like the latter, too, he was largely put out of business by the locomotive. Unlike the Percheron, however, the line of breeding of the Cleveland Bay, following the advent of the railroad, resulted in such a dissipation of the blood as to practically exterminate the breed. The original Cleveland Bay could not qualify as a harness or saddle horse, so the mares were bred to Thoroughbred sires. In turn the best half-breds were inter-bred, or remated with the Thoroughbred, and produced either good hunters or carriage horses.

YORKSHIRE COACH

The Yorkshire Coach horse is the result of such breeding. The Cleveland Bay takes its name from the Vale of Cleveland in Yorkshire, the coach horse from the county itself.

THE ORLOFF

The Russian Orloff is not of much economic importance in America, but is of interest in that it is the only other light harness breed beside our own, and from the fact that there is a decided interest in American trotters in Russia. The breed was developed solely by Count Alexis Orloff Tschismensky, from whom it takes its name.

The Orloff foundation was laid in a quarter-bred Arab stallion called Bars I, whose dam was a Dutch mare (another instance of the trotting instinct tracing to the black trotter of Friesland). The sire's dam was a Danish mare. The grandsire was the gray Arab Smetanxa. This breeding was begun early in the last quarter of the eighteenth century.

Fig. 78.—The lead pair in this road four are pure-bred Orloffs.

Fig. 79.—Carmon, at the head of the government stud of American carriage horses.

What few Orloffs have come to this country have been considered as heavy harness horses, and the breed is therefore classed
in this division, leaving the Standardbred supreme in the light
harness division (Fig. 78).

AMERICAN CARRIAGE HORSE

The United States Government has taken advantage of the
fact that it is not unusual to find a trotting-bred horse conforming to heavy harness specifications and that certain blood lines
are most uniformly productive of this type (Fig. 79), to as-

Fig. 80.—Pair of trotting-bred heavy harness horses to George IV phaeton. Undefeated
in their day, either single, as a pair, or tandem, by representatives of any other heavy harness
breed.

semble such representatives as are available, for the foundation
of an American Carriage Horse breed. It will apparently yet
require many generations of selective breeding before these
horses can fulfil the requirements of a breed.

Trotting-bred heavy harness horses are better qualified to
meet " pace and action " requirements than they are those of the
high stepping classes (Fig. 80). Their action is frequently unbalanced, being deficient in hocks, but they can step away.

REVIEW

1. Describe the Norfolk trotter and show his relation to the Hackney and the Standardbred.
2. What breed characteristics have enabled the Hackney to win supremacy in the show ring?
3. Name a noted Hackney sire.
4. Explain fully the meaning of the term " demi sang."
5. Account for the lack of uniformity in the representatives of the French Coach breed imported to this country, also among their get.
6. What are the most commendable features of the German Coach horse?
7. To what sort of mares should coach stallions be mated?
8. What was the original parentage of the Yorkshire Coach horse?
9. Describe the origin of the Orloff.
10. What is the so-called American Carriage Horse?

CHAPTER IX

AMERICAN BREEDS

Native American Horses.—Conditions in this country have proven most congenial for the production of horses, yet there were none inhabiting this continent when it was discovered by Columbus. This is all the more remarkable in view of the fact that fossil remains of a prehistoric horse have been found in abundance in different parts of this country. It is believed that the horses originally on this continent passed over what is now Behring Straits, into Asia, during the early ages.

The restocking of America was coincident with its exploration and colonization. Columbus landed horses on his second expedition, but it is not known whether or not they ever reached the mainland. The horses brought by Cortez, in his conquest of Mexico, in 1519, are credited with being the first to gain American soil. In 1527, Cabeza de Vaca brought horses to St. Augustine, Florida, which were afterward liberated. De Soto's expedition was equipped with horses when he discovered the Mississippi in 1541, although the majority of them were killed for their flesh after De Soto's death. These Spanish horses were derivatives from a Barb foundation with which Spain was originally stocked.

Horses, presumably of the old Norman and Breton stock, were taken by the French into Nova Scotia in 1604, and four years later were introduced into Canada. One stallion and six mares, Thoroughbred, reached Virginia with the English in 1607. In 1625 Dutch horses, possibly the black trotter of Friesland, arrived at New Netherlands. In 1629 the first horses to inhabit New England came with the English to Boston. This was the composite origin of the American horse stock, out of which our breeds have been evolved.

As early as 1678 the descendants of horses that had escaped from, or were liberated by, the early Spanish expeditions, were ranging wild in great bands over the prairies of this continent.

The American breeds of horses are the Standardbred, includ-

112

ing the Morgan, and the Saddle horse. The first pure breed to gain a foothold here was the Thoroughbred, and naturally the Thoroughbred has been the chief contributor in the foundation of the American breeds.

STANDARDBRED

This breed is so named because the members are bred to a standard of speed performance, that is, one mile in 2.30 or better

FIG. 81.—A Standardbred stallion, a leading sire of the breed.

trotting, 2.25 or better pacing. In fact, the question has been raised whether or not the Standardbred fulfils the requirements which constitute a breed, as long as individuals may become standard by performance, though not by breeding. It is probable that in the very near future the rule admitting horses to registry by standard performance alone will be rescinded.

Origin.—Orange County, New York, was the original seat of this breed; then Kentucky, and eventually the States in general, California in particular. The chief interest in trotters centered about New York City, where the improvement in the construction of roads gave a great stimulus to road driving. Their foundation blood lines were laid in Orange County.

The two most notable foundation sires in America were imported Messenger and Justin Morgan.

Messenger was a gray Thoroughbred, six generations removed from the Darley Arabian, imported from England, as an eight-year-old in 1788. He stood most of his life about New York and Philadelphia, where he left numerous progeny. Although himself a running race horse, brought to this country for the improvement of runners, he soon became noted as a sire of trotters, and upon his trotting sons and grandsons, daughters and granddaughters, the Standardbred is based. It has been suggested that the fact that the horse stock about New York was descended from the horses brought over by the Dutch, and that a family of trotters were native to Friesland, would account for so many of the get of Messenger being trotters. The inference is that Messenger imparted the speed and stamina, while his get derived their instinct to trot from their Dutch-bred dams. The most notable of Messenger's sons was Mambrino, the sire of Mambrino Paymaster and Abdallah. Mambrino Paymaster in turn sired Mambrino Chief, from whom the Mambrino family of trotters and the Chief family of Saddle horses of Kentucky are descended. Abdallah sired Hambletonian 10, the most conspicuous sire of the Standardbred.

Hambletonian 10, or Rysdyk's Hambletonian, is regarded as the progenitor of the Standardbred, so far as one individual can claim that distinction (Fig. 82). He was foaled the property of Jonas Seeley near Chester, Orange County, New York, in 1849, but soon passed into the hands of the man he made famous, Wm. M. Rysdyk. Notwithstanding the fact that his stud fees later amounted to $184,725.00, Rysdyk dickered a long time before the purchase price of $125.00 for the mare and foal was agreed upon. This would indicate that neither party to the transaction had any conception of the ultimate value and importance of this colt. Attention was first directed to Hambletonian by his gelded son Dexter, who in 1864, 1865, 1866, and 1867 defeated the best horses of the day, George Wilkes, George M. Patchen, Goldsmith Maid, Lady Thorne, Flora Temple, and others. The year that Dexter began his sensational performances Hambletonian bred 217 mares and got 148 colts; subsequently he was so extensively patronized that

FIG. 82.—Hambletonian 10, at 23 years of age.

he commanded a service fee of $500.00. It need not necessarily detract from his name and fame to state that no horse ever had such an opportunity in the stud. It was thus that he became the founder of the breed, being the sire of 1321 colts. He died in 1876, and a monument was erected to his memory (Fig. 83).

Hambletonian's best son was George Wilkes, a small but powerfully made brown horse, foaled 1856, out of Dolly Spanker, a good road mare of untraced ancestry. George Wilkes was both a race horse and a sire; after a most remarkable racing career he was retired to the stud, first in New York, later in Kentucky. His prepotency was marvelous and is still breeding on. To designate a horse as of Wilkes' breeding means little in view of the numerous ramifications of this family.

George Wilkes' best sons were Brown Wilkes, Alcantara, Alcyone, Bourbon Wilkes, Baron Wilkes, Jaybird, Kentucky Wilkes, Onward, Patchen Wilkes, Red Wilkes, Simmons, Wilkes Boy, and Gambetta Wilkes.

Fig. 83.—Monument over grave of Hambletonian 10 at Chester, N. Y., located on a lot in outskirts of town with a house on either side.

Other sons of Hambletonian were Alexander's Abdallah, Messenger Duroc, Belmont, Electioneer, Almont, Volunteer, Aberdeen, Happy Medium (sire of Nancy Hanks), Harold (sire of Maud S.), Dictator, and Strathmore.

The dam of Hambletonian 10 was the Charles Kent mare of ordinary road ability, sired by Bellfounder, called at that time a Norfolk trotter, but in the light of present knowledge a Hackney.

The Blood Line.—The following arrangement of blood lines is interesting, in view, first, of the prevalence of the trotting instinct in both, and second, of the successful manner in which Standardbreds and Hackneys nick.

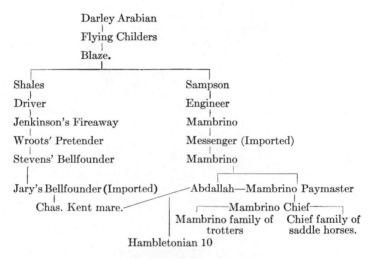

Darley Arabian
|
Flying Childers
|
Blaze.

Shales	Sampson
Driver	Engineer
Jenkinson's Fireaway	Mambrino
Wroots' Pretender	Messenger (Imported)
Stevens' Bellfounder	Mambrino

Jary's Bellfounder (Imported) — Abdallah—Mambrino Paymaster
Chas. Kent mare.

Mambrino Chief
Mambrino family of trotters   Chief family of saddle horses.

Hambletonian 10

Other families that have been interwoven into the fabric, as it were, of the Standardbred are:

The Clays, descended from Henry Clay, whose ancestry is shown below.

Imported Grand Bashaw (Barb from Tripoli 1820)
Young Bashaw
Andrew Jackson
Henry Clay

The Mambrinos descended from Mambrino Chief, who sired Mambrino Patchen, and he in turn sired Mambrino King.

The Pilots descended from Pilot, Jr., the son of a Canadian pacer, so-called, and noted as a brood mare sire. His best daughter was Miss Russell, the dam of Maud S., Nutwood, Lord Russell, and many others.

The Hals, the most distinguished and exclusively pacing family, descended from Kittrel's Tom Hal, a roan stallion brought from Canada. His get, in Tennessee, founded this

Fig. 84.—Green Mountain Maid in 1873.

Fig. 85.—Inscription on monument of Green Mountain Maid at Stony Ford.

pacing family through Tom Hal, Jr., or Gibson's Tom Hal, the sire of Brown Hal, who begot Star Pointer and a numerous progeny of Hals, all very fast pacers. In Kentucky the Hals are identified with the foundation of the Saddle breed. **The greatest brood mare** in the foundation of the Standard-bred was Green Mountain Maid (Figs. 84 and 85), daughter of Harry Clay, and dam of Electioneer, one of the most conspicuous sires of the breed. The greatest pacing dam was Sweepstakes.

FIG. 86.—An "ideal representative" of the Standardbred. In addition to 2.10 speed, he possesses beauty of form, finish, style, and intelligence.

Demand for Standardbred Horses.—The popularity of harness racing and road driving has enabled this breed to make remarkable progress in a half century. They are now the recognized exponents of the light harness type, and are exported in large numbers, especially to Russia and Austria. In fact, the rate at which some of the best stallions and mares are being taken abroad indicates a lack of the true constructive breeder's spirit, and forebodes ill for the future of the breed. Unfortunately, speed performance alone has been the standard of selection, and while attainments in this line have been great, there is a woeful lack of uniformity among trotters. They come in all shapes, sizes, and colors. Among the representatives of the breed are many ideal individuals with a wide range of adaptability (Fig. 86) to almost any kind of service, but too many are otherwise.

FIG. 87.—A 16-hand, 1200-pound standard performer, whose get are the general-purpose horses on the majority of farms within a wide radius of his home.

The show ring has served a commendable purpose wherein the race track has failed in this connection, and it is gratifying to see a uniform standard of excellence gradually being evolved.

The versatility of the Standardbred is demonstrated by the fact that the champion heavy harness horse of this country, Nala, and the champion saddle mare of a few years back, Miss Anne, were both of this breeding, while in many parts of the East, big, stout, good-headed trotters are doing the farm work (Fig. 87). Many hunters are all or part Standardbred, and this blood seems to be most favored for the production of army remounts by those who are well informed. There are great possibilities in the breed which have been overlooked in an ill-advised effort to raise race horses and race horses only.

Rules of Eligibility.—The significance of the name Standardbred is made clear by a consideration of the rules of eligibility to registry in the American Trotting Register.

The Trotting Standard.—When an animal meets these requirements and is duly registered it shall be accepted as a Standardbred trotter:

1. The progeny of a registered standard trotting horse and a registered standard trotting mare.

2. A stallion sired by a registered standard trotting horse, provided his dam and grandam were sired by registered standard trotting horses, and he himself has a trotting record of 2.30 and is the sire of three trotters with records of 2.30, from different mares.

3. A mare whose sire is a registered standard trotting horse, and whose dam and grandam were sired by registered standard trotting horses, provided she herself has a trotting record of 2.30 or is the dam of one trotter with a record of 2.30.

4. A mare sired by a registered standard trotting horse, provided she is the dam of two trotters with records of 2.30.

5. A mare sired by a registered standard trotting horse, provided her first, second, and third dams are each sired by a registered standard trotting horse.

The Pacing Standard.—When an animal meets these requirements and is duly registered, it shall be accepted as a Standardbred pacer:

1. The progeny of a registered standard pacing horse and a registered standard pacing mare.

2. A stallion sired by a registered standard pacing horse, provided his dam and grandam were sired by registered standard pacing horses, and he himself has a pacing record of 2.25, and is the sire of three pacers with records of 2.25, from different mares.

3. A mare whose sire is a registered standard pacing horse and whose dam and grandam were sired by registered standard

pacing horses, provided she herself has a pacing record of 2.25, or is the dam of one pacer with a record of 2.25.

4. A mare sired by a registered standard pacing horse, provided she is the dam of two pacers with records of 2.25.

5. A mare sired by a registered standard pacing horse, provided her first, second, and third dams are each sired by a registered standard pacing horse.

6. The progeny of a registered standard trotting horse out of a registered standard pacing mare, or of a registered standard pacing horse out of a registered standard trotting mare.

Speed Records.—The following are the record performances to date for one mile (from " Horseman's Annual ") :

Gelding,	trotter	"Uhlan"	1.58¾
Gelding,	pacer	"Prince Albert"	1.59½
Stallion,	trotter	"The Harvester"	2.01
Stallion,	pacer	"Dan Patch"	1.55¼
Mare,	trotter	"Lou Dillon"	1.58½
Mare,	pacer	"Dariel" ⎱ honors even	
Mare,	pacer	"Lady Maud C" ⎰	2.00½
Yearling,	trotter	"Miss Stokes" filly	2.19¼
Yearling,	trotter	"Wilbur Lou" colt	2.19½
Yearling,	pacer	"Present Queen" filly	2.20¼
Yearling,	pacer	"Frank Perry" colt	2.15
Yearling,	pacer	"Rollo" gelding	2.28½
Stallion,	trotting to wagon	"John A. McKerron"	2.10
Stallion,	pacing to wagon	"Dan Patch"	1.57¼
Mare,	trotting to wagon	"Lou Dillon"	2.00
Mare,	pacing to wagon	"Aileen Wilson"	2.04¼
Gelding,	trotting to wagon	"Uhlan"	2.00
Gelding,	pacing to wagon	"Little Boy"	2.01½
Team,	trotting	{ "The Monk" ⎱ "Equity" ⎰	2.07¾
Team,	pacing	{ "Hedgewood Boy" ⎱ "Lady Maud C" ⎰	2.02¾

The Light Harness Type.—The Standardbred (Fig. 81) represents so truly the light harness type that his detailed description would be a duplication of that already given under the light harness division, in the classification of horses (see Chapter V).

THE MORGANS

The propriety of designating the Morgan a breed is questionable. To be sure, there is a studbook maintained which has been duly recognized, but the requirements for registry are so open as to include many individuals that could not fulfil the specifications of a breed. The important part played by the Morgan horse in the establishment and development of the Standardbred and the American Saddle horse is sufficiently important, however, and his characteristics distinctive enough, to justify his being considered apart from the other breeds with which he has been closely identified.

Justin Morgan shares honors with Messenger as a foundation sire of the Standardbred, and the correction and verification of pedigrees of noted sires and dams have increased the credit due him. He was a remarkable individual foaled at Springfield, Mass., in 1789, and lived to be thirty-two years old. He was a small horse, about 14–2 hands high and 950 pounds weight. Of him wonderful performances of endurance, speed, pulling power, and intelligence are recorded. His individuality was no more striking than the prepotency with which he impressed his get. Had the Morgan blood been kept pure, there can be little question of its having ultimately fulfilled all the requirements for recognition as a breed. Even the wide dissemination of the blood has not resulted in the complete obliteration of the Morgan character, which may be discerned though but a fractional part of Morgan inheritance is represented.

The breeding of the original Morgan horse has never been satisfactorily established, as the horse himself and those who knew of him were dead before any effort was made to trace his ancestry. Colonel Joseph Battell, who has devoted much time to an investigation of this matter, has given the sire as a Thoroughbred called Beautiful Bay and the dam as a member of the Wildair family of Thoroughbreds. Such breeding is not indicated, however, by the descriptions of the horse with which we are furnished, although the Thoroughbreds of his time were more like him than are the Thoroughbreds of the present. A Dutch origin similar to that of the Norfolk trotter has been suggested and does not seem unreasonable, since Dutch blood was available at the time of his breeding and he more closely resembles in type the old-fashioned Hackney than any other breed. The Thoroughbred ancestry, however, is the one usually accepted, though not altogether satisfactory.

Sons of Justin Morgan.—The three most notable sons of Justin Morgan were: (1) Bullrush Morgan, the descendants of whom are especially noted for their size, substance, and soundness, and represented by the Morrill family; (2) Woodbury Morgan, who is described as possessing attractive action and spirit and who was the progenitor of the Gifford and Morgan Eagle branches; and (3) Sherman Morgan, from whom came, in

Fig. 88.—Original photo of Ethan Allen made in 1859. It shows the inaccuracy of some of the old cuts alleged to be true likenesses of this horse.

successive generations, the three greatest horses of their days, Black Hawk (Vermont or Hill's), Ethan Allen (Fig. 88), and Daniel Lambert. In Daniel Lambert the type underwent some alteration, as the blood lines of the two foundation American sires were brought together, Fanny Cook, the dam of Lambert, being by Abdallah, grandson of Messenger and sire of Hambletonian.

Morgan Blood in Other Breeds.—With the development of trotting speed and the increasing popularity of the Hambletonians, the prestige which the Morgans had enjoyed as road horses was shattered. Morgan mares were mated with sons and grandsons of Hambletonian, and later those of Denmark, to such an extent that for years the breed, in its original purity and type, has been threatened with extinction. To this very fact, however, may be attributed, in some part at least, the merit that has been attained in the Standardbred and the American Saddle horse. A study of the blood lines of a great many of the most conspicu-

Fig. 89.—A Morgan stallion, showing the size, form, and character typical of this family of horses.

ous representatives of the two breeds reveals to what extent the Morgan has been incorporated, especially through foundation mares. The blood has, therefore, been spent rather than lost.

A description of Justin Morgan is typical of his descendants (Fig. 89). He was brown, slightly over 14 hands in height, 950 pounds in weight, very compactly made, with a short, strong back, round, deep rib, broad loin, and strong coupling; a breedy head, proudly carried, rather heavy neck, with prominent crest, short legs well set and of unusual substance; and an airy, busy, but not high way of going. Bay, brown, and black colors prevail in the breed outside the Lambert family, where chestnut with a light sprinkling of white predominates.

Improving the Breed.—The United States Department of Agriculture has undertaken to assemble enough representative Morgans to form the nucleus of a stud, the object of which shall be the preservation of the stock and improvement in the line of a more approved type, better calculated to meet modern demand,

Fig. 90.—General Gates, at the head of the government Morgan stud.

especially in the matter of size (Fig. 90). We are reminded, in this connection, of the statement that when an Arab exceeds 14–2 he ceases to be an Arab. There is reason to believe that it may be necessary to sacrifice some of the most distinctly Morgan characters in order to attain the desired size, and in view of the active demand for cobs, which old-fashioned Morgans are, the wisdom of such a course is not altogether apparent.

The Morgan Horse Club, recently organized, has inaugurated an active campaign in the interest of the Morgan horse.

At recent Vermont State fairs and National horse shows some very creditable classes of Morgans have been exhibited under the auspices of this club.

THE AMERICAN SADDLE HORSE

The development of this breed has been parallel in many respects with that of the American trotter. Both are the result of a Thoroughbred top cross on what might be termed a native mare foundation, and in each case the descendants of one individual have constituted a family which has dominated the breed. Their respective histories are also more or less contemporaneous. Denmark, the Thoroughbred whose progeny founded the Saddle breed, was foaled in 1839, while Messenger reached this country in 1788 and his great grandson Hambletonian was foaled in 1849.

Evolution of the Saddle Horse.—The chief differences which influenced the evolution of the Saddle horse and the trotter are those which concerned the native mares and the ends in view of the breeders. The original American Saddle horse was born, of necessity, on the frontier where horses' backs afforded the chief means of transportation. The easy, lateral, ambling gait was cultivated, and those horses which showed greatest aptitude in this direction were selected for breeding. On the other hand, road and vehicle construction progressed most rapidly in the vicinity of the large Eastern cities, hence the breeding of the trotter or road horses centered around New York City and Philadelphia, and the foundation was laid in mares which had proven themselves best adapted to trotting in harness. While horses were more extensively used for riding than for driving purposes in this country during the earlier period, the Saddle breed, in its present degree of development, is of more recent origin than the Standardbred. Furthermore, selection in the case of the Saddle bred horse has not been to a standard of performance alone, but ideals in type, conformation, and quality as well have been sought and are as clearly marked in the prepotency of the foundation families as is performance.

Foundation Stock.—In order to establish a definite beginning, the American Saddle Horse Breeders' Association originally accepted these sires as constituting foundation stock:

Denmark (Thoroughbred) by Imported Hedgeford.
John Dillard, by Indian Chief (Canadian).
Tom Hal (Imported from Canada).
Cabell's Lexington, by Gist's Black Hawk (Morgan).
Coleman's Eureka (Thoroughbred and Morgan).
Van Meter's Waxy (Thoroughbred).
Stump-The-Dealer (Thoroughbred).
Peter's Halcorn.
Davy Crockett.
Pat Cleburne, by Benton's Gray Diomed.

Influence of the Thoroughbred.—The extent to which the Thoroughbred has been involved in the origin and development of the Saddle breed is shown by the following census of the breeding of all individuals registered in Vol. I of the studbook:

Thoroughbred	3
50 per cent. Thoroughbred blood............	50
25 per cent. Thoroughbred blood............	296
12½ per cent. Thoroughbred blood............	343
6¼ per cent. Thoroughbred blood............	152
3 per cent. Thoroughbred blood............	36
Uncertain	203

Denmark was a Thoroughbred, by Imported Hedgeford, of whom little else is recorded, foaled in Fayette County, Kentucky, in 1839. He never achieved great fame as a race horse, although it is claimed that his races were characterized by unusual gameness and stamina. He had a numerous progeny, the most notable of which was Gaines' Denmark, whose dam, the Stevenson mare, was a great natural ambler, representing the then common stock of the country and believed, by some, to be of greater foundation importance than Denmark himself.

Gaines' Denmark is considered the founder of the breed, although other lines have since been developed from which good results have been secured, either independently or in combination with the line of Denmark. These blood lines are shown below.

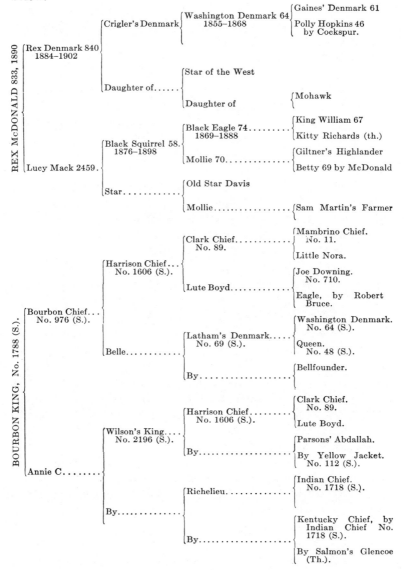

The above pedigrees of two of the greatest sires of the breed represent the two lines of breeding, the former being a strongly bred Denmark, while the latter has a combination of the blood of Mambrino Chief, Gaines' Denmark, Edwin Forrest, and Black Hawk through Harrison Chief, Latham's Denmark (grandson of Gaines' Denmark) and Indian Chief. The pedigree of Bourbon King also shows a degree of close breeding which is rather typical. The Chief family which Bourbon King represents are the principal contemporaries of the Denmarks.

Other prominent sires are Highland Denmark and Chester Dare, both by Black Squirrel and out of daughters of Dave Akin, Montgomery Chief, by Bourbon Chief, Wilson's King, by Harrison Chief, and Wyatt's Red Cloud, by Indian Chief, the latter two being more particularly the sires of harness horses.

Three of the greatest producing mares are (1) Nannie Garret, by Dave Akin, (2) Annie C., by Wilson's King, and (3) Little Kate, the dam of four of the best horses shown in 1913— Kentucky's Choice, Kentucky's Best, Kentucky's Selection, and Undulata Queen, all by My Own Kentucky.

The chief centres of Saddle horse breeding are the central counties of Kentucky and the region about Columbia and Mexico, Missouri.

The War a Setback.—The Civil War caused a serious setback to the progress of the Saddle horse breed, all available mounts being pressed into service, many of which were sacrificed, while others were kept out of breeding for a considerable period. Some of the most noted stallions of the breed served as officers' mounts during the Civil War. This breed also suffered from the increased popularity of the Standardbred during the period subsequent to the war. Many of the best Saddle bred mares were mated with Standardbred stallions. The present popularity of the Saddle horse has brought this breed into a more conspicuous position than it has ever before occupied.

Characteristics.—The Saddle horse is characterized by being rather up-standing, possessed of a most beautifully molded and set head and neck, a very smoothly turned form, short back, level croup, and high set tail (Fig. 91). From an artistic point of view, he is perhaps the most beautiful of all horses, being the extreme embodiment of quality and finish, an ideal which has been fostered by the so-called " model " classes of Southern shows. Some have been bred so very fine, however, as to be markedly deficient in substance. His flashy way of going, with head and tail carried high, has led to his being rather contemptuously dubbed a " peacock " by advocates of the plainer but perhaps more substantial part-bred hack.

Fig. 91.—An American Saddle stallion, showing the beautifully molded form, the stylish carriage of head and tail, and the extreme refinement characteristic of this breed.

Colors of the Saddle horse are not confined within any limit, although certain families are very uniform in the transmission of color, especially black in the Denmarks and chestnut in the Chiefs and Kings. Bay is also common.

Gaits.—Saddle horses were previously required to go the five gaits in order to qualify, but the increased demand for walk-trot-canter horses has led to their being given more consideration by Saddle horse breeders.

Uses.—The American Saddle horse is not used exclusively for saddle purposes. Not only are all representatives schooled to go in harness, but some of our best American bred harness show horses have been produced by Saddle breeding. Also some of the best harness horses in Kentucky and Missouri have eventually become winners in the saddle classes of the greatest American shows. Horses of this breed meet the present demand for combination horses more naturally than those of any other breed. Their intelligence, instinctively good manners, beautiful conformation, style, and finish, as well as their dual usefulness, enable them to command the admiration especially of those who use horses for the horse's sake. Their ability to go the slow gaits has also led to their being used for riding after cattle and for general business saddle purposes, while much has been claimed for them as cavalry mounts and officers' chargers. Saddle-bred horses make most acceptable models for artists and sculptors.

REVIEW

1. Review the original stocking of this continent with horses.
2. Why is the foundation of the Standardbred laid in New York, that of the Saddle horse in Kentucky?
3. Explain the relation of Messenger to the Standardbred.
4. Identify Hambletonian 10, George Wilkes, Mambrino Chief, Green Mountain Maid, Henry Clay.
5. Of what economic importance is the Standardbred?
6. In what respects were the foundations of the Standardbred and the American Saddle horse similar and in what respects did they differ?
7. Describe the Denmark branch of the American Saddle breed.
8. What of the outlook for the American Saddle horse, and why?
9. Who are Bourbon King, Rex McDonald, Cabell's Lexington, Harrison Chief, Little Kate?
10. Describe Justin Morgan and explain his work as a foundation American sire.

CHAPTER X

PONY BREEDS

HERE are discussed the Shetland ponies, the Welsh ponies, and the Hackney ponies.

THE SHETLAND PONY

Environment has had more to do in determining the characteristics of the Shetland than any other breed of horses. It has not, however, been the only factor, as suggested by Darwin, there having been a separate pony race indigenous to this part of the world, the *Equus celticus* of Ewart. The Shetland Islands, situated about 200 miles off the north coast of Scotland and within 350 miles of the Arctic circle, are rough and unproductive, and the people poor. Only a few of the large group of islands are inhabited.

This breed of ponies has developed under the most adverse conditions, being close companions in adversity with the native crofters, even to the extent of sharing their huts and provisions. Their most characteristic diminutive size, hardiness, good dispositions, and meagre requirements may be thus accounted for. Their chief occupation in the islands is to carry peat for the use of the crofters, the customary load consisting of from 120 to 140 pounds, which is packed and carried over the roughest and hardest of trails.

The first real impetus to their systematic breeding came from Scotland and England, where they were found to be of service in working out the shallow veins of coal. They were bred most extensively for mine use by the Marquis of Londonderry. It was later that there arose an active demand for Shetlands as children's ponies, and it is claimed this call came chiefly from America.

The type of the old country Shetland is that of a draft horse (Fig. 92) in miniature, the maximum of horse power in the smallest compass. In this country more refinement, in keeping

133

with saddle and harness use, is desired (Fig. 93). A slightly less blocky pony not so low down is better shaped for riding and will have more stride.

FIG. 92.—The old country idea of Shetland type is a miniature draft horse.

FIG. 93.—A Shetland stallion, American bred, and representative of the type most in favor in this country.

This breed's chief asset for their work in this country is their patient, docile, and demonstrative disposition. They are generally fearless and thoroughly reliable under all circumstances. They do not have an ideal saddle conformation nor

heads and necks that make for light mouths, but the notion enter-
tained by some that they are bullish and wilful is largely due to
the fact that, being naturally tractable, they receive but the most
elementary schooling.

A standard height of 42 inches has been fixed in this country, with a proportionate discount up to 46 inches. If in excess
of this they are disqualified.

Colors.—Solid colors, black or a cinnamon brown being most
typical, are preferred by breeders, while buyers of ponies to use
generally express a preference for the skewbalds and piebalds.
The widest range of oddest colors is permissible, but broken
colors are suggestive of some Iceland or Faroe Island foundation
in the remote ancestry.

Too Little Discrimination.—While the demand for children's ponies is strong and they meet with ready sale, there is not
sufficient discrimination among buyers to stimulate much improvement in the breed. All ponies look alike to the majority,
it seems, and so long as they are clever and safe, no further ques-
tions are asked. The result is that the average pony falls short
of ordinary horse standards, leggy, coarse-headed, flat-ribbed,
steep-rumped, cat-hammed, and crooked-legged individuals, with
no step, being all too common. On the other hand, some wonder-
fully typical, good-going ponies have been brought out by those
who have given time and study to their production.

THE WELSH PONY

The Welsh pony is native to the rough mountain districts of
Wales, but has long been bred for actual road work. Their open
life, ranging in bands, has made them extremely rugged and
thrifty. Some improvement in their way of going has been
secured by the use of small Norfolk trotting stallions from time
to time, although not enough crossing has been done to destroy
the original integrity of the breed.

The true type of Welsh pony is comparable to a miniature
coach horse (Fig. 94), pony built, yet with a good head, neck,
and forehand, well formed legs, and considerable speed and action
at the trot, with unusual endurance. They are snappy and free,

all horse for their size, and are, therefore, better adapted to the use of junior equestrians than as playmates for little children, the field of the Shetland pony.

The foreign Welsh Pony and Cob Studbook gives this classification according to height:

A. Ponies not exceeding 12 hands, 2 inches.
B. Ponies 12 hands, 2 inches to 13 hands, 2 inches.
C. Ponies 13 hands, 2 inches to 14 hands, 2 inches.
D. Ponies 14 hands, 2 inches to 15 hands, 2 inches.

FIG. 94.—A Welsh pony stallion, showing the size and form characteristic of the breed.

The last three show an increasing percentage of the Norfolk cob blood. Those of class D are in excess of the pony limit and are therefore cobs proper.

Colors are chiefly bay, although brown, chestnut, gray, and roan occur.

Importance of Size.—The frequency with which motors are met on the road and the consequent danger in sending children out unattended make a pony of more size than the typical Shetland in greater demand than formerly. Furthermore, Welsh ponies are really useful and need not be confined to children's use. A smart pair, properly appointed, is well adapted to ladies' use.

THE HACKNEY PONY

The Hackney pony is a representative Hackney under 14 hands, 2 inches (Fig. 95), eligible to the same registration and

FIG. 95.—A Hackney pony stallion; a typical representative of the Hackney breed, under the pony limit of stature.

frequently bred in similar lines on one side as are full-sized Hackneys. As Hackneys have been used in the improvement of the gait and action of the Welsh breed, there has no doubt been a reciprocal cross in the making of Hackney ponies. Some Welsh breeding in the dams of registered Hackney ponies is not uncommon nor prohibited by the rules of registry.

Show Ponies.—Hackney ponies are the smartest thing in horse form, possessing all the flash and excessive action of their larger namesakes in an exaggerated degree. A distinction should be drawn, however, between a child's pony and a show pony, and few of the sensational Hackney ponies of the show ring inspire much confidence in their trustworthiness for children. On the other hand, there is a well-marked preference expressed for the larger ponies, if thoroughly reliable, as mounts for juvenile equestrians, the number of which is increasing.

OTHER PONY BREEDS

Other pony types or strains to which reference is sometimes made but for which no studbooks exist, in this country at least, are the Exmoor, Dartmoor, New Forest, Cumberland, and West-moreland of England; the Connemara of Ireland; the Galloway and Highland ponies of Scotland; and Arabs under 14 hands, 2 inches, as many of them are.

REVIEW

1. What is believed to be the foundation stock from which all pony breeds are derived?
2. Which of the pony breeds has been most influenced by environment and how?
3. What is the difference in the accepted type of Shetlands in America and Great Britain and how is it accounted for?
4. To what breed characteristics does the Shetland owe its universal popularity?
5. Describe the origin of the Welsh pony.
6. What out-crosses have been made and why?
7. What larger type is the typical Welsh pony the miniature of?
8. What classification of Welsh ponies and cobs is made?
9. What is the Hackney pony; to what purpose are they chiefly devoted?
10. Name the other pony stocks.

CHAPTER XI

JUDGING HORSES

Purpose.—Judging is selection; the means by which the breeder molds forms by mating the approved and culling out the undesirable individuals. It should not be understood to mean the placing of awards in the show ring only, although that is a most important function of the judge, imposing upon him the responsibility of establishing ideals and standards which are to lead or mislead the rank and file of breeders. The successful buyer or breeder must be a competent judge, whether he has ever placed a ribbon in a show ring or not.

What Judging Involves.—Judging is more than measuring to a standard or the analysis of the individuals under consideration; the element of comparison must figure in the observations, from which definite conclusions can be drawn. It is the balancing of the sum total of merit and deficiency of one individual against that of another, after the same fashion that a judge on the bench weighs all the evidence before returning a verdict. There are capable buyers of market horses, who, in car load after car load, will not have a poor one, yet they would not essay the task of designating the first, second, third, and fourth choice in any one car lot. They have a definite standard in mind by which they can accept or reject, with unerring accuracy, but when it becomes necessary to arraign an especially good head and neck but rather defective hocks of one against a good back but poor feet of another, they fail. Yet selection in breeding and buying most frequently involves the choice of one from among several, as does the ranking of show entries.

Accuracy and Rapidity.—The dispatch with which decisions are arrived at is second only to the accuracy of the decisions themselves. The man who stands at the sales ring side and buys at the rate of a horse a minute must have rapid, accurate decision; so must he who picks his short leet and ultimate winners from a class of half a hundred stallions. The expert is able to place an

139

entire class of show horses or to pick out a car load in the time required by the novice to score one individual. The former has a fixed standard and a trained eye, which enable him to discern instantly any deviations from his standard.

Furthermore, he recognizes the law of correlation and goes by indices, largely, without delaying to consider each detail minutely. One feature or part is correlated with another, while to a third it may be extremely opposed. Dimensions of the same class are correlated, for instance, while those of opposite classes are related as extreme. A long legged horse is also long in neck, body, and stride, but is proportionately narrow and shallow bodied; a horse in which width is marked will be short and deep bodied, with a short, thick neck, low set on his legs, and having a short but perhaps trappy stride.

A systematic method of making observations contributes both to accuracy and dispatch in judging. By this means each look is made to count, repetitions or omissions are avoided, the proportions and relations of the parts are kept in mind, and a more comprehensive conception of the whole is obtained.

System of Examining.—The most logical system of examination begins with a view of the horse from in front, noting the temperament and disposition as indicated by the expression of the countenance, all features of the head, the width and depth of chest, the station, the direction and conformation of the forelegs and feet. Then passing to the side, near side usually, consider the stature and scale, length or compactness, station, depth (especially in the flank), the carriage and shape of head and neck, the shortness and levelness of the top line, the length and straightness of under line, height and shape of the withers, the slope of shoulder, direction and conformation of forelegs and feet, the back, rib, loin, flank, coupling, croup, tail, stifle, thigh, direction and conformation of hind legs and feet. From the rear the symmetry, levelness, width and rotundity of hips, fulness of thighs and quarters, direction and conformation of hind legs and feet may be determined. Viewing from the opposite side to confirm the original side view would complete the examination of the horse standing.

He should then be moved away from the observer, in order

that the directness and rapidity of his stride, especially behind, may be seen. Then as he comes back, or " meets you," note the directness, rapidity, and freedom of the stride in front, the boldness, courage, and manners displayed. As he is led past determine the length, the height, spring, regularity, and balance of the stride, together with the placing or set of the horse in action. An expert judge may seem careless of and indifferent to any system, yet this very manner may have been acquired from long practice, in a systematic way.

A show ring judge should not act without good and sufficient reasons. He should have the courage of his convictions and be able to give a full account of the whys and wherefores of his work. The wisdom of an award appears very different to onlookers at the ring side many times, with the light of the judge's reasons thrown upon it.

Features to Consider in Judging Horses.—The features to which the judge should give special consideration in making his observations may be summarized as follows:

1. General Appearance: (*a*) Height, (*b*) weight, (*c*) style, (*d*) symmetry, (*e*) color and markings.

2. Form: (*a*) Station (setting on legs), (*b*) width, (*c*) depth, (*d*) compactness, (*e*) contour.

3. Conformation. (As outlined in Chapter II.)

4. Quality: (*a*) Hide and hair, (*b*) bone, (*c*) finish, (*d*) general refinement.

5. Substance: (*a*) Proportion of weight to height, (*b*) bone, (*c*) muscling.

6. Constitution: (*a*) Chest and abdominal capacity, (*b*) evidence of thrift and vigor.

7. Condition: (*a*) Degree of fatness, (*b*) fitness for work.

8. Way of Going. (As outlined in Chapter III.)

9. Age: (*a*) Determination of, (*b*) significance of.

10. Soundness: (*a*) Examination for, (*b*) importance of.

11. Temperament and Disposition.

SCORE CARD

The score card consists of a word picture of the ideal horse in which a numerical value is attached to each part for the purpose of indicating its relative importance. The hock is a no more essential part of the horse's anatomy than the forearm, yet the defects to which the hock is subject are so much more numerous, and their effect on the serviceability of the horse of so much more importance, that it is deserving of more careful consideration. On this basis the hock is allotted six units or counts, the forearm two.

Scoring is the application of the score card as a standard of merit to the individual, for the purpose of determining and expressing numerically his degree of perfection. Applied successively to a number of individuals, it affords a means of determining their relative merits. However, this system is not applicable to show ring judging or sales ring selection. The chief use of the score card is in the classroom, where continued practice in scoring affords the best means of training the eye in making accurate observations, while there is being acquired, at the same time, a mind picture of the ideal. Once the ideal expressed on the score card is indelibly fixed in the mind, the card may be given up and the mental picture take its place as a standard of judgment. In the development of good judgment the score card is indispensable, but for the practice of judging it is of little use. Condensed or summarized score cards have been arranged which facilitate scoring for such objects as the advanced registry of dairy cattle and other purposes, but for students' use the full, detailed accounting of every part is essential.

The Draft Horse Score Card.—Following is the scale of points and standard of excellence for the draft horse:

General Appearance.—16.   Counts
   1. Weight . . . .
   2. Height . . . .
   3. Form—low station, wide, deep, compact, massive   4
   4. Substance—bone ample, joints broad, proportioned to scale   4
   5. Quality—bone dense and clean, tendons and joints sharply defined,
      leg broad and flat, hide and hair fine, refinement of head,
      finish   4
   6. Temperament—energetic, disposition good, intelligent   4

Head and Neck.—7.
   7. Head—size and dimensions, in proportion, clear cut features,
      straight face line, wide angle in lower jaw   1

JUDGING HORSES 143

8. Muzzle—broad, nostrils large but not dilated, lips thin, even, trim 1
9. Eyes—prominent orbit; large, full, bright, clear; lid thin, even curvature 1
10. Forehead—broad, full 1
11. Ears—medium size, fine, pointed, set close, carried alert 1
12. Neck—long, muscular but not thick, well crested, throttle well cut out, head well set on 2

Forehand.—24.

13. Shoulders—long, sloping, smooth, muscular 2
14. Arm—short, muscular, elbow in 2
15. Forearm—wide, muscular 2
16. Knees—straight, wide, deep, strongly supported 2
17. Canons—short, broad, flat, tendons sharply defined, set well back 2
18. Fetlocks—wide, tendons well back, straight, well supported 2
19. Pasterns—long, oblique (45 degrees), smooth, strong 2
20. Feet—large, round, uniform, straight, slope of wall parallel to slope of pastern, sole concave, bars strong, frogs large and elastic; heels wide, full, one-third height of toe; horn dense, smooth, dark color 6
21. Legs—direction viewed from in front, a perpendicular line dropped from the point of the shoulder should divide the leg and foot into two lateral halves. Viewed from the side, a perpendicular line dropped from the tuberosity of the scapula should pass through the centre of the elbow-joint and meet the ground at the centre of the foot 4

Body.—11.

22. Withers—well defined but muscular 2
23. Chest—wide, deep 2
24. Ribs—well sprung, long, close 2
25. Back—short, straight, strong, broad 2
26. Loin—short, broad, strongly coupled 2
27. Flank—deep, full, long, low under line 1

Hindquarters.—32.

28. Hips—wide, level, muscular 2
29. Croup—long, level, muscular 2
30. Tail—attached high, well carried 1
31. Thighs—deep, muscular 2
32. Stifles—broad, thick, muscular 2
33. Gaskins—wide, muscular 2
34. Hocks—straight, wide, point prominent, deep, clean cut, smooth, well supported 6
35. Canons—short, broad, flat, tendons sharply defined, set well back 2
36. Fetlocks—wide, tendons well set back, straight, well supported .. 2
37. Pasterns—long, oblique (50 degrees), smooth, strong 3
38. Feet—large, round (slightly less than in front), uniform, straight, slope of wall parallel to slope of pastern, sole concave, bars strong, frog large, elastic; heels wide, full, one-third height of toe; horn dense, smooth, dark color 4

39. Legs—direction viewed from the rear, a perpendicular line dropped from the point of the buttock should divide the leg and foot into lateral halves; viewed from the side, this same line should touch the point of the hock and meet the ground some little distance back of the heel. A perpendicular line dropped from the hip-joint should meet the ground near the centre of the foot 4

Way of Going.—10.

40. Walk—straight, strong, active 6
41. Trot—powerful, free, moderate action 4

Total 100

The Heavy Harness Horse Score Card.—The following is the standard of excellence and scale of points for the heavy harness horse:

General Appearance.—12.   Counts

1. Height . . . .
2. Weight . . . .
3. Form—close, full made, smooth turned, symmetrical 4
4. Quality—bone clean, dense, fine, yet indicating substance, tendons and joints sharply defined, hide and hair fine, general refinement, finish 4
5. Temperament—proud, bold, stylish, disposition good, intelligent. 4

Head and Neck.—7.

6. Head—size and dimensions in proportion, clear cut features, straight face line, wide angle in lower jaw 1
7. Muzzle—fine, nostrils large, lips thin, trim, even 1
8. Eyes—prominent orbit; large, full, bright, clear; lid thin, even curvature 1
9. Forehead—broad, full 1
10. Ears—medium size, fine, pointed, set close, carried alert 1
11. Neck—long, lofty carriage, high crest, throttle well cut out, head well set on. 2

Forehand.—22.

12. Shoulders—long, oblique, smooth 2
13. Arms—short, muscular, carried well forward 1
14. Forearm—broad, muscular. 1
15. Knees—straight, wide, deep, strongly supported 2
16. Canons—short, broad, flat, tendons sharply defined, set well back. 2
17. Fetlocks—wide, tendons well back, straight, well supported 2
18. Pasterns—long, oblique (45 degrees), smooth, strong 2
19. Feet—large, round, uniform, straight, slope of wall parallel to slope of pastern, sole concave, bars strong, frog large, elastic, heels wide, full, one-third height of toe, horn dense, smooth, dark color 6

20. Legs—direction viewed from in front, a perpendicular line dropped
from the point of the shoulder should divide the leg and foot
into two lateral halves; viewed from the side, a perpendicular
line dropped from the tuberosity of the scapula should pass
through the centre of the elbow-joint and meet the ground at
the centre of the foot 4

Body.—11.
21. Withers—well set up, narrow, extending well back............. 2
22. Chest—wide, deep 2
23. Ribs—well sprung, long, close............................. 2
24. Back—short, straight, strong, broad....................... 2
25. Loin—short, broad, strongly coupled....................... 2
26. Flank—deep, full, long, low under line.................... 1

Hindquarters.—32
27. Hips—broad, round, smooth................................ 2
28. Croup—long, level, round, smooth......................... 2
29. Tail—set high, well carried.............................. 2
30. Thighs—full, muscular.................................... 2
31. Stifles—broad, full, muscular............................ 2
32. Gaskins—broad, muscular.................................. 2
33. Hocks—straight, wide, point prominent, deep, clean cut, smooth,
well supported 6
34. Canons—short, broad, flat, tendons sharply defined, set well back 2
35. Fetlocks—wide, tendons well back, straight, well supported.... 2
36. Pasterns—long, oblique (50 degrees), smooth, strong........... 2
37. Feet—large, round (slightly less than in front), uniform, straight,
slope of wall parallel to slope of pastern, sole concave, bars
strong, frog large and elastic, heels wide, full one-third height of
toe, horn dense, smooth, dark color...................... 4
38. Legs—direction viewed from the rear, a perpendicular line
dropped from the point of the buttock should divide the leg and
foot into lateral halves; viewed from the side, this same line
should touch the point of the hock and meet the ground some
little distance back of the heel. A perpendicular line dropped
from the hip-joint should meet the ground near the centre of
the foot 4

Way of Going.—16.
39. Walk—straight, snappy, springy, proud, stylish............... 6
40. Trot—in line, bold, flashy, extreme flexion of knees and hocks,
balanced, regular.. 10
                                                          ———
   Total... 100

The Light Harness Horse Score Card.—Following is the scale of points for the light harness horse:

General Appearance.—12.   Counts
1. Height...
2. Weight...
3. Form—rangy, deep, lithe, angular.......................... 4
4. Quality—bone clean, dense, fine, yet indicating substance, tendons and joints sharply defined, hide and hair fine, general
   refinement... 4
5. Temperament—nervous, active, disposition good, intelligent..... 4

Head and Neck.—7.

6. Head—size and dimensions in proportion, clear cut features, straight face line, wide angle in lower jaw 1
7. Muzzle—fine, nostrils large, lips thin, trim, even 1
8. Eyes—prominent orbit; large, full, bright, clear; lid thin, even curvature 1
9. Forehead—broad, full 1
10. Ears—medium sized, fine, pointed, set close, carried alert 1
11. Neck—long, lean, crest well defined, extended carriage, well cut out in the throttle, head well set on 2

Forehand.—23.

12. Shoulders—long, oblique, smooth 2
13. Arms—short, muscular, carried well forward.................. 1
14. Forearm—long, broad, muscular 2
15. Knees—straight, wide, deep, strongly supported 2
16. Canons—short, broad, flat, tendons sharply defined, set well back 2
17. Fetlocks—wide, tendons well back, straight, well supported 2
18. Pasterns—long, oblique (45 degrees), smooth, strong........... 2
19. Feet—large, round, uniform, straight, slope of wall parallel to slope of pastern, sole concave, bars strong, frog large, elastic, heels wide, full, one-third height of toe, horn dense, smooth, dark color... 6
20. Legs—direction viewed from in front, a perpendicular line dropped from the point of the shoulder should divide the leg and foot into two lateral halves. Viewed from the side, a perpendicular line dropped from the tuberosity of the scapula should pass through the centre of the elbow-joint and meet the ground at the centre of the foot 4

Body.—11.

21. Withers—well set up, narrow, extending well back 2
22. Chest—medium width, deep 2
23. Ribs—well sprung, long, close 2
24. Back—short, straight, strong, broad......................... 2
25. Loins—short, broad, strongly coupled........................ 2
26. Flank—deep, full, long, low under line 1

Hindquarters.—31.

27. Hips—broad, round, smooth................................. 2
28. Croup—long, level, smooth................................. 2
29. Tail—set high, well carried................................. 1
30. Thighs—full, muscular..................................... 2
31. Stifles—broad, full, muscular 2
32. Gaskins—broad, muscular................................... 2
33. Hocks—straight, wide, point prominent, deep, clean cut, smooth, well supported... 6
34. Canons—short, broad, flat, tendons sharply defined, set well back.. 2
35. Fetlocks—wide, tendons well back, straight, well supported 2
36. Pasterns—long, oblique (50 degrees), smooth, strong........... 2
37. Feet—large, round (slightly less than in front), uniform, straight, slope of wall parallel to slope of pastern, sole concave, bars strong, frog large and elastic, heels wide, full, one-third height of toe, horn dense, smooth, dark color..................... 4

38. Legs—direction viewed from the rear, a perpendicular line dropped from the point of the buttock should divide the leg and foot into lateral halves; viewed from the side, this same line should touch the point of the hock and meet the ground some little distance back of the heel. A perpendicular line dropped from the hip-joint should meet the ground near the centre of the foot... 4

Way of Going.—16.
39. Walk—long, free stride..................................... 6
40. Trot—long, rapid, straight, reachy stride.................... 10

      Total.. 100

The Saddle Horse Score Card.—Following is the scale of points and standard of excellence for the saddle horse:

General Appearance.—12.   Counts
1. Height..
2. Weight..
3. Form—close but not full made, deep but not broad, symmetrical. 4
4. Quality—bone clean, dense, fine, yet indicating substance, tendons and joints sharply defined, hide and hair fine, general refinement, finish... 4
5. Temperament—active, disposition good, intelligent............. 4

Head and Neck.—8.
6. Head—size and dimensions in proportion, clear cut features, straight face line, wide angle in lower jaw.................. 1
7. Muzzle—fine, nostrils large, lips thin, trim, even............... 1
8. Eyes—prominent orbit; large, full, bright, clear; lid thin, even curvature... 1
9. Forehead—broad, full.. 1
10. Ears—medium size, pointed, set close, carried alert............. 1
11. Neck—long, supple, well crested, not carried too high, throttle well cut out, head well set on............................... 3

Forehand.—22.
12. Shoulders—very long, sloping yet muscular..................... 3
13. Arms—short, muscular, carried well forward................... 1
14. Forearm—long, broad, muscular.............................. 1
15. Knees—straight, wide, deep, strongly supported............... 2
16. Canons—short, broad, flat, tendons sharply defined, set well back.. 2
17. Fetlocks—wide, tendons well back, straight, well supported..... 2
18. Pasterns—long, oblique (45 degrees), smooth, strong........... 2
19. Feet—large, round, uniform, straight, slope of wall parallel to slope of pastern, sole concave, bars strong, frog large, elastic, heels wide, full, one-third height of toe, horn dense, smooth, dark color...... 5
20. Legs—direction viewed from in front, a perpendicular line dropped from the point of the shoulder should divide the leg and foot into two lateral halves. Viewed from the side, a perpendicular line dropped from the tuberosity of the scapula should pass through the centre of the elbow-joint and meet the ground at the centre of the foot.................................... 4

Body.—12.

21. Withers—high, muscular, well finished at top, extending well into
    back.. 3
22. Chest—medium wide, deep..................................... 2
23. Ribs—well sprung, long, close................................ 2
24. Back—short, straight, strong, broad.......................... 2
25. Loin—short, broad, muscular, strongly coupled............... 2
26. Flank—deep, full, long, low under line....................... 1

Hindquarters.—31.

27. Hips—broad, round, smooth................................... 2
28. Croup—long, level, round, smooth............................ 2
29. Tail—set high, well carried.................................. 2
30. Thighs—full, muscular....................................... 2
31. Stifles—broad, full, muscular................................ 2
32. Gaskins—broad, muscular.................................... 2
33. Hocks—straight, wide, point prominent, deep, clean cut, smooth,
    well supported.. 5
34. Canons—short, broad, flat, tendons sharply defined, set well back. 2
35. Fetlocks—wide, tendons well back, straight, well supported...... 2
36. Pasterns—long, oblique (50 degrees), smooth, strong........... 2
37. Feet—large, round (slightly less than in front), uniform, straight,
    slope of wall parallel to slope of pastern, sole concave, bars
    strong, frog large and elastic, heels wide, full, one-third height
    of toe, horn dense, smooth, dark color....................... 4
38. Legs—direction viewed from the rear, a perpendicular line
    dropped from the point of the buttock should divide the leg and
    foot into lateral halves; viewed from the side, this same line
    should touch the point of the hock and meet the ground some
    little distance back of the heel. A perpendicular line dropped
    from the hip-joint should meet the ground near the centre of
    the foot... 4

Way of Going.—15.

39. Walk—rapid, flat footed, in line............................. 5
40. Trot—free, straight, smooth, springy, going well off hocks, not
    extreme knee fold.. 5
41. Canter—slow, collected, either lead, no cross canter.......... 5

Total... 100

SOUNDNESS

A horse is sound provided there be not a partial or total loss
of function, preventing or likely to prevent him from performing the ordinary duties of his class.

The real significance of soundness is quite generally misun-
derstood by the users of horses, much to their own disadvantage
and to the misfortune of many an unsound horse. The importance of an existing unsoundness is directly proportionate to the
extent to which it incapacitates a horse for the service to which
he is otherwise best adapted. If it causes him little or no incon-

venience, and is not liable to, it is of little or no consequence. The technically sound horse is an exceptional individual and has less actual additional value over the serviceably sound horse than is generally credited to him.

On the other hand, the nature or extent of an unsoundness may be such as to cause the total disability of a horse either at present or in the future. Serviceable soundness is all that it is practical to seek or require; and just what constitutes serviceable soundness is arbitrarily determined by the nature of the work which the horse is expected to do. If more thought were given to the real causes of unsoundness, present and prospective, and less to its technical existence, it would probably give less annoyance.

The durability of any machine is a matter of construction, covering the grade of materials used, the assembling of all parts, the alignment and adjustment of all bearings and wearing parts in order to minimize friction, distribute wear, and to facilitate operation in general. Allow any little cog to slip or an adjustment to become displaced, and either the whole machine is rendered useless or its operation is greatly impaired.

The Equine Machine.—It is so with the equine mechanism. Most unsoundnesses have their origin in structural defects or imperfections. The spavin and the curb make their appearance on the crooked hind leg as a result of the cuneiform bone and curb ligament being called upon to do more than their normal share of the work of the leg, on account of the deflection in the line in which weight is borne and power applied.

Side bones are most common on the outer quarters of wide-fronted draft horses, because such horses are inclined to be " toe narrow," which brings the outer quarter nearer to the centre of weight bearing, thereby imposing weight and wear which should be borne by the other quarter. As a consequence the cartilage ossifies or changes to bone.

If an existing unsoundness has apparently developed, independent of predisposing causes of conformation, and does not impair the horse's usefulness, it is of less account than when the causative defect in conformation is apparent but no actual unsoundness exists yet. In the first place, a repetition of the unusual condition to which the unsoundness is due is not likely; while in the second case, the predisposing cause is continually operative, and the ultimate development of actual unsoundness is well nigh inevitable. Once developed, its condition is repeatedly aggravated by the same means which originally induced it.

Rejecting for Unsoundness.—It is not consistent to reject a horse, in all other respects suitable for one's purpose, because he cannot be certified absolutely sound, only to finally accept on the strength of a certificate of soundness a horse woefully deficient in regard to most other requirements. Counsel of the veterinarian should be on the true importance of the unsoundness, if it exists, rather than for its mere detection.

Soundness is but one of the attributes which render a horse of service. Horses unsound in some degree are giving perfectly satisfactory service in all fields in which horses are engaged, and, so long as that is the case, it is unjust to the horses and detrimental to the owners to discard them for a mere technicality. Provided a horse goes sound in spite of some unsoundness to which he is subject, and promises to continue so to go, the unsoundness should not outweigh in importance the other essentials of a good horse, as type, conformation, and performance.

Age.—*The Determination of Age.*—There is nothing mysterious nor empirical about the determination of the age by the teeth. Up to five years, it is simply a matter of the eruption of the teeth, which in the normal individual follows the same regular course that characterizes all other physiological processes. After the permanent teeth are all in, the indications are the result of wear, which is uniformly accomplished in the normal mouth on account of the extreme durability of the individual teeth and their arrangement.

Certain general features must be understood before any attempt is made to differentiate the appearance of the mouth at various years. The permanent teeth may be distinguished, after their eruption, from the milk teeth, which are shed as the permanent teeth come through, by greater size, a broader neck showing no constriction, perpendicular, parallel grooves and ridges on their face, and a whiter color.

The incisor teeth, which are the ones depended upon because

they are most easily exposed to view, are originally oval-shaped at the table or wearing end, gradually becoming triangular toward the root. The longitudinal dimensions of the teeth are curved, with the convexity forward, toward the lips, the concavity toward the mouth. The table itself is cupped out in the centre by a depression, into which the enamel of the tooth dips. As wear commences, the surface enamel is worn off, leaving two distinct enamel rings, one around the margin of the table and the other around the cup. This cup itself becomes gradually more shallow until it is finally worn almost completely away. As wear on the table removes more and more of the end of the tooth, the level of the pulp cavity in the centre of the tooth is finally reached, and the exposed tip of this canal appears between what is left of the cup and the front of the tooth. Other sequences of the continued wearing away of the tooth are the changes in outline of its transverse diameter, becoming, first, more oval from side to side, then more distinctly triangular as wear continues toward the root. Also, as the mouth end of the tooth is worn away the level of the tables and their contact is maintained by the tissues closing in behind the root and forcing the tooth forward. This gives the angle of the arch of the incisors less curve and more slant, at the same time rendering the margin and outline of the jaw sharper and flatter. As the arch becomes more slanting, the surfaces of the teeth meet at a different angle, and, in the case of the corners, the lower teeth do not wear clear to the back margins of the uppers, so that a hook or notch is gradually formed, worn away, and formed again at different years. These, with the eruption of the canines, which occurs in males at from five to six years, are the principal changes upon which the age is reckoned. It remains now to indicate just what changes are characteristic of the different yearly periods (Figs. 96–116).

The Importance of Age.—Age plays an important part in determining a horse's market value. Statistics show the best selling age to be from five to eight years, while, on the contrary, experience has demonstrated that the best wearing and most serviceable age is from eight to twelve. After a horse passes eight and has had some city wear, the market classes him as second-handed and discounts his value accordingly.

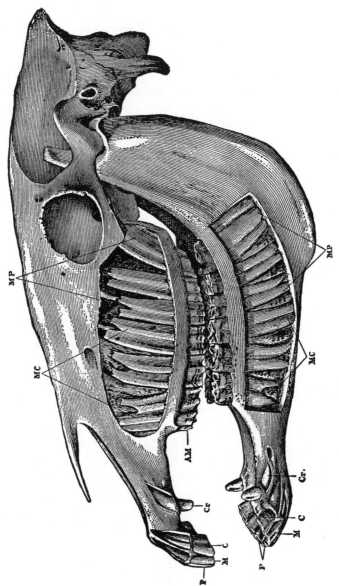

Fig. 96.—Dentition of the horse, as a whole. *P*, pincers; *M*, intermediates; *C*, corners; *Cr*, canines; *AM*, supplementary premolars; *MC*, deciduous molars or premolars; *MP*, permanent molars.

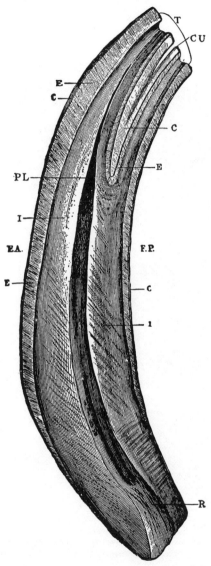

Fig. 97.—Longitudinal and median section of a permanent inferior pincer (enlarged). *FA*, anterior face; *FP*, posterior face; *C*, cement; *E*, enamel; *I*, ivory; *PL*, pulp cavity; *CU*, cup; *T*, table; *R*, root.

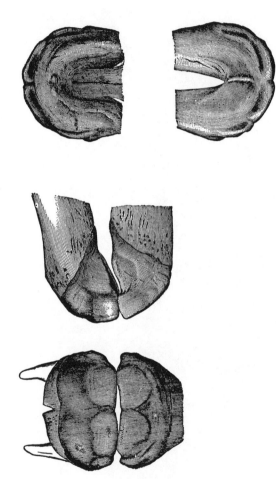

Fig. 98.—Birth: None of the incisor teeth has penetrated the gums. The buccal mucous membrane still covers those which are to appear first. In *front*, under the gums, the two pincers are perceived above and below. In *profile*, we distinguish the intermediates, less developed than the pincers. The jaws are very round at their extremity and but little separated from each other. The *dental tables* show, on each side of the median line, the prominence formed by the anterior border of the pincers and, external to these, but less developed, the borders of the intermediates. The internal side of these teeth is the more prominent, and it is this side which will first pierce the mucous membrane.

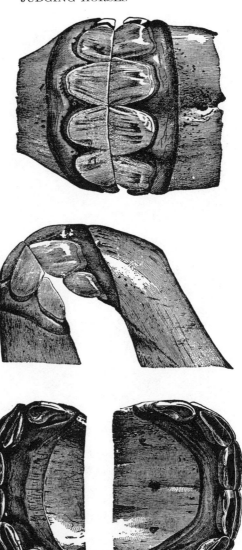

Fig. 99.—One Year: Viewed in *front*, all the milk incisors are visible; the pincers and the intermediates are well penetrated through the gums. In *profile*, the superior corners are not yet in contact with the inferior. The *tables* show that the posterior border of the pincers and the intermediates is worn more. Nevertheless, this character is liable to vary, from the fact of the unequal height of this border, according to the mouths which are examined. However, it will be easy to avoid too great errors by recognizing the degree of wear of the anterior border. The latter presents, ordinarily, at this period, a yellow line, elongated transversely, which is surrounded by the remainder of the dentin; this is the dental star. Besides, we must compare the degree of wear of the pincers and the intermediates. If the latter are the most worn off, it will tend to make the young animal older rather than younger. The corners are still virgin. The incisive arcades are wider transversely and less round in their middle.

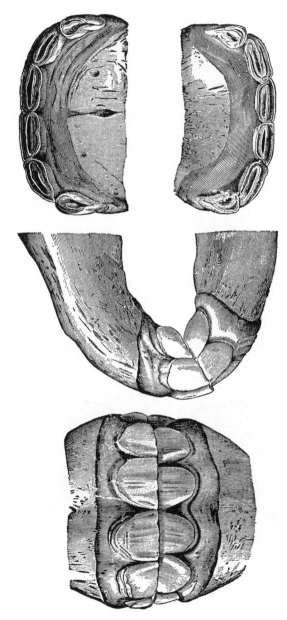

Fig. 100.—Two Years: Contrary to the preceding, these jaws belonged to a colt of a lymphatic race, having, since the period of his weaning, been fed almost entirely on forage. Also, to judge of the age from the pure and simple state of the dental tables would be to make this animal only about twenty months old. The subject, nevertheless, was two years and twenty-six days old. The mouth, however, presents some special characters which tend to modify the inferences that would be formed at first sight. Viewed in *front*, the pincers and the intermediates are quite free from the gums at their base, the superior pincers especially. This fact indicates that the permanent teeth should have accomplished their eruption in seven or eight months. In *profile*, the neck of the corners is visible. The *tables* of the latter show decided wear; the dental star is distinctly visible in these teeth, and the wear slightly involves their external border. The central enamel of the superior intermediates forms a complete circle. Finally, the incisive arcades, much elongated transversely, are greatly depressed in the region of the pincers and the intermediates. If to these signs be added the information obtained from the nature of the ailment, the period of the year, the general development, etc., one will be able to arrive easily at an accurate determination.

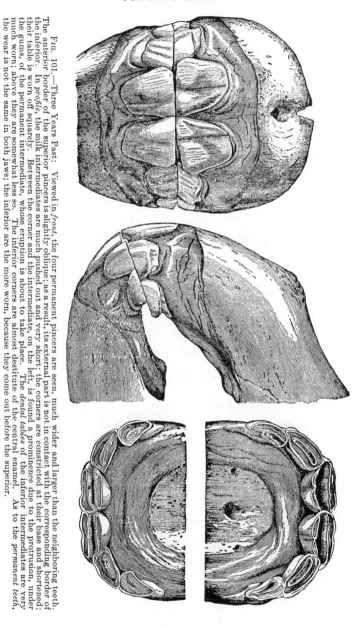

Fig. 101.—Three Years Past: Viewed in *front*, the four permanent pincers are seen, much wider and larger than the neighboring teeth. The anterior border of the superior pincers is slightly oblique; as a result, its external part is not in contact with the corresponding border of the inferior. In *profile*, the milk intermediates are much pushed out and very short; the corners are constricted at their base and shortened; their table is worn off squarely. Between the corner and the intermediate, on the left, is found a prominence due to the protrusion, under the gums, of the permanent intermediate, whose eruption is about to take place. The *dental tables* of the inferior intermediates are very much worn; above they are somewhat less so. The inferior corners are almost destitute of the central enamel. As to the *permanent teeth*, the wear is not the same in both jaws; the inferior are the more worn, because they come out before the superior.

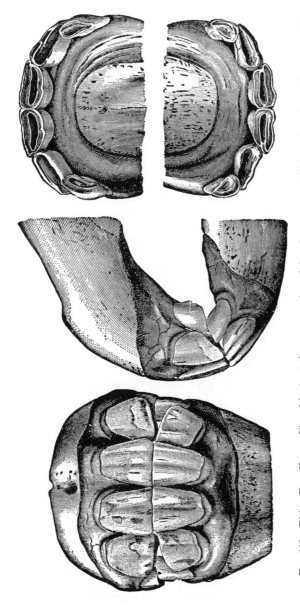

FIG. 102.—Rising Four Years: Viewed in *front*, there are seen, in each jaw, four permanent incisors; two pincers, in contact with each other, the superior with the inferior, and two intermediates which are not yet on a level with the pincers. In *profile*, this fact is shown by an interval between the superior and inferior intermediates. In the corners, the tables appear little worn. This is due to the fact that the animal, during its first dentition, was nourished upon soft aliment. The pincers are very much worn in both jaws; their central enamel is separated from the peripheral, especially in the superior incisors, because it is in this jaw that the eruption of these teeth commences. Finally, the intermediates, still virgin, almost touch, and consequently are at the point of being used. All these characters sufficiently correct the aberrant state of the corners, whose wear is not in harmony with that of the other incisors.

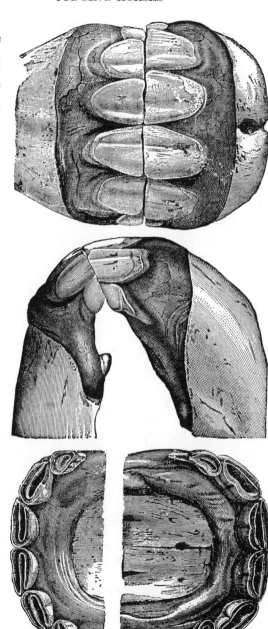

Fig. 103.—Four Years: Viewed in *front*, all the permanent superior teeth are in contact with the inferior; the jaws, in the part which corresponds to the pincers and the intermediates, have acquired so much width, from one side to the other, that the deciduous corners can scarcely be seen. In *profile*, the latter appear very small; the superior commence to be pushed from their sockets; behind the inferior is seen the extremity of the canine tooth. The *tables* of the intermediates are much worn, especially of the superior, which came out first. The central enamel in the pincers forms a distinct oval only in the superior incisors; if this character be absent in the others, it is due to the fact that the external dental cavity is more or less fissured in the vicinity of its external border. The inferior corners are almost levelled; the superior are more so; besides, they are stripped around their base; a portion of their root is seen.

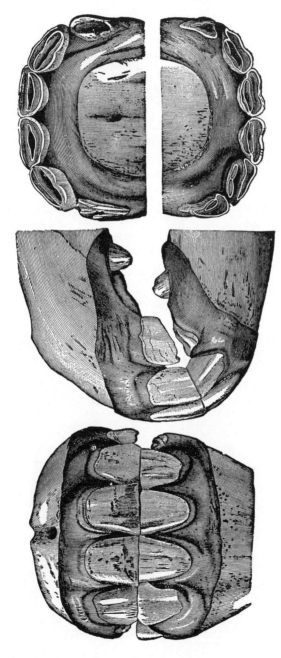

Fig. 104.—Four Years Past: Viewed in *front*, the superior permanent intermediates are in contact with the inferior intermediates, and on the same level as the pincers. The superior and inferior corners are permanent incisors. In *profile*, it is easy to see that the eruption of the latter teeth is not yet completed, especially that of the inferior, which just pierces the gum. Upon the *tables*, the right superior corner is ready to fall out; nothing but its root remains. The inferior corner of the same side is levelled, but is still firm. The superior left corner tooth is permanent and still virgin; its posterior border has just come through the gum. As to the inferior left, it commences to show itself. The superior intermediates, coming out before the inferior, show more marked wear upon their posterior border. The central enamel, in the inferior pincers, is distinct from the peripheral; in the superior pincers this already exists.

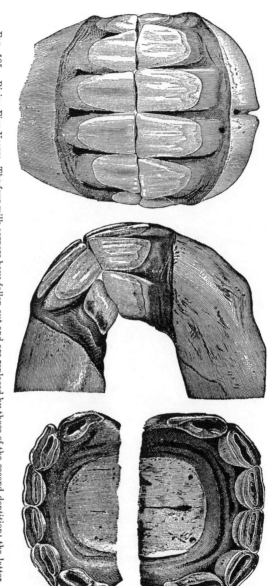

Fig. 105.—Rising Five Years: The four milk corners have fallen out and are replaced by those of the second dentition; the latter, not being on a level yet with the intermediates, are absolutely virgin. The *tables* of the other teeth show more wear than at the preceding age. In the superior incisors, the central enamel is well circumscribed in the pincers and the intermediates. Below, it is at the point of becoming so in the intermediates.

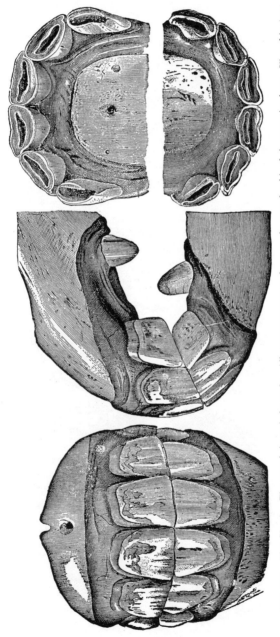

Fig. 106.—Five Years: The mouth is entirely *made*. All the permanent teeth are on the same level in their respective jaws. Viewed in *front*, the jaws appear very convex in both directions. In *profile*, they have a similar disposition; the canines are completely out. Upon the *tables*, it is seen that the corners are already commencing to wear at their anterior border. The pincers are almost levelled, but the infundibulum or cup is still very elongated transversely, and narrow from before to behind; it is closer to their posterior border. This form of the infundibulum indicates that the external dental cavity was not very deep, in consequence of the abundance of the central cement; these teeth are also soon levelled. Almost the same disposition, as regards the external dental cavity, exists in the inferior intermediates. In order, therefore, not to make a misinterpretation of the signification of the levelling, it is necessary to take into consideration the form and dimensions of the central enamel. In this way alone can the degree of wear of the tooth be inferred. The incisive arcades form an almost regular semicircle in each jaw.

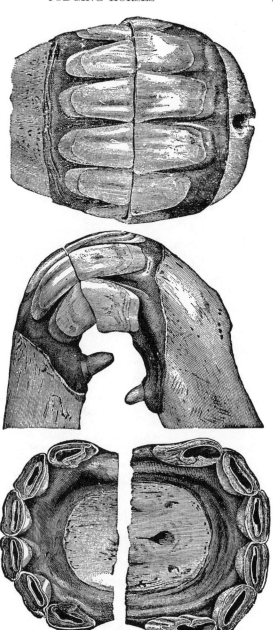

FIG. 107.—Six Years: Viewed in *front*, the jaws present almost the same characters as at five years. In *profile*, we see here a retarded eruption of the canines; these teeth have not yet reached their full length; they are therefore incapable of giving any exact information as to the age. The *tables* furnish by far the best indications. The posterior border of the inferior and superior corners is notably worn. The pincers are ordinarily levelled, and the table tends to take an oval form. In the figure, the levelling of the inferior pincers is not altogether complete. Nevertheless, the central enamel is wider from before to behind, and narrower from one side to the other, than at five years; it is also closer to the posterior border of the table. The same remarks apply to the intermediates. It will be noticed that the external dental cavity is fissured upon its posterior face in the two superior corners. This irregularity of form, somewhat common, amounts to little in the determination of the age.

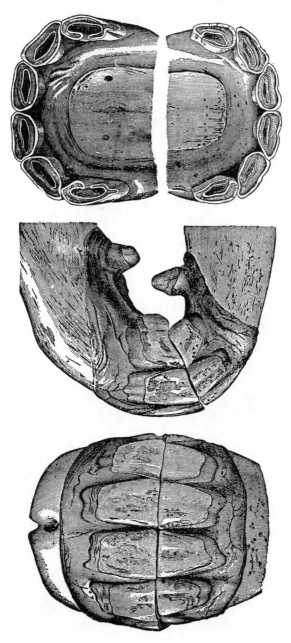

Fig. 108.—Seven Years: Nothing special is shown by the jaws viewed in *front*, excepting that the teeth appear whiter. This is due to the fact that the layer of cement, which at first covered their anterior face, is worn off. In *profile*, it is found that the table of the inferior corners is narrower from side to side than that of the superior; this results in the formation of a notch upon the latter. The incidence of the incisive arcades is always less perpendicular than at six years. As to the *tables*, they are levelled upon the pincers and upon the intermediates; the ring of central enamel is wider anteroposteriorly and shorter from side to side. The surface of friction in the corners is larger; sometimes the central enamel forms a complete ring, and sometimes it is incomplete. These differences often result from an irregular form of these teeth. In some subjects, their posterior border is almost absent. It then requires a longer time for the table to be completed behind. The pincers are oval; the intermediates tend to become so. The superior corners are fissured at their posterior border.

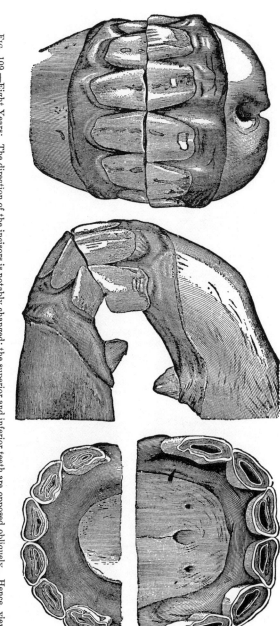

Fig. 109.—Eight Years: The direction of the incisors is notably changed; the superior and inferior teeth are opposed obliquely. Hence, viewed in *front*, the jaws project at the level of their line of meeting. In *profile*, this fact is more apparent, for the anterior face of the incisive arcades has no longer the form of a regular semicircle, as at five years. Their arc appears broken at the place where the tables of the superior and inferior incisors meet, and it acquires more and more the curve of an ogive. The base of the corner is cut squarely by the gum. The incisive arcades are still regular, but narrower than at five years; the surfaces of friction represent, in fact, sections closer to the summit of the cones constituted by the teeth. All the inferior teeth are levelled. The pincers and intermediates are oval; the corners are becoming oval. Finally, the *dental star* appears upon the pincers and intermediates, between the anterior border of the table and the corresponding border of the central enamel.

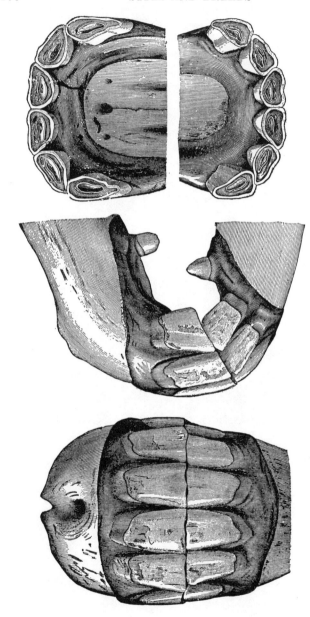

Fig. 110.—Nine Years: Nothing special is to be seen upon the jaws viewed in *front* or in *profile*. The teeth are ordinarily more oblique and less fresh-looking than at eight years of age. The notch on the superior corner has often disappeared. The characters furnished by the *tables* are more positive. The pincers are round; their central enamel has a triangular form; their dental star is narrower but more distinct, and occupies almost the middle of the dental table. The intermediate teeth are becoming round, and the corner teeth are oval. At this age, the superior pincer teeth are levelled in most jaws. The inferior incisive arcade is narrower transversely and depressed in the centre.

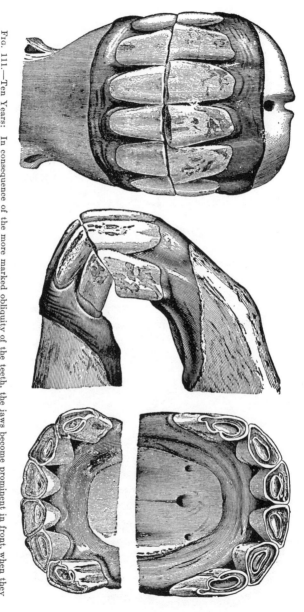

FIG. 111.—Ten Years: In consequence of the more marked obliquity of the teeth, the jaws become prominent in front, when they are examined from this point, and it is necessary to raise the head of the horse higher in order to have a good view of the inferior incisors. In *profile*, this character is still more apparent; the ogive formed by the contact of the two arcades is smaller; the inclination of the corners augments, and the interspace which separates them from the intermediates is larger. Upon the *tables*, the inferior pincers are still more round; their central enamel is smaller, distinctly triangular, and also closer to their posterior border. Finally, their dental star, more visible, encroaches upon the middle of their surface of friction. The intermediates are round, and the corners tend to assume this form. In the plate, the latter have an irregular table, because they as well as the superior corners are fissured on their posterior border; this border has been checked in its development, and hence it is but slightly prominent. The inferior incisive arc is more depressed in its middle.

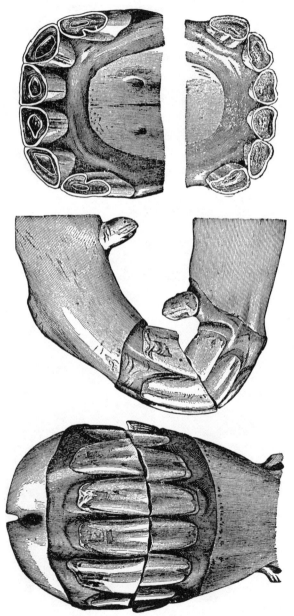

Fig. 112.—Eleven Years: The incidence of the jaws augments in obliquity in such a manner that, in order to see the teeth in *front*, it is necessary to raise the horse's head. In *profile*, the superior corner shows a greater obliquity than the intermediates; the inferior is almost as wide at its free extremity as at its base, which, besides, is cut squarely by the gum. The inferior *tables* are round in the intermediates and in the corners. In all the teeth of the same arcade, the central enamel forms a small ring only, very close to the posterior border of the surface of friction, while the dental star becomes narrower transversely, and also approaches this border. In the superior incisors, the central enamel becomes elliptical in the corners and tends to disappear from their table.

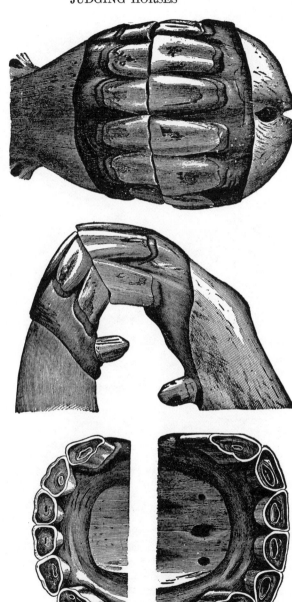

FIG. 113.—Twelve Years: The incidence of the jaws is more oblique than at the preceding age. In *profile*, the obliquity of the superior corner is increased; it carries a notch behind, and the interspace which separates it from the intermediate is more marked. All the inferior *tables* are round, and sometimes the central enamel has disappeared. Some, however, often still present traces of the enamel; those in which it is absent present, in their centre, a small yellowish spot, which is the dental star. In the superior corners the central enamel is about to disappear. Finally, the incisive arcades are much narrower and less convex than at eight years.

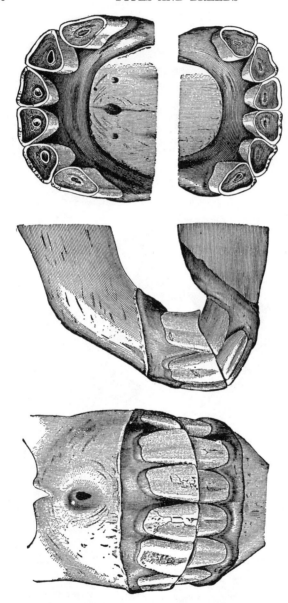

FIG. 114.—Fifteen Years: Viewed in *front*, the inferior teeth appear shorter than the superior; this is due to the fact that the jaws are viewed without being elevated. In *profile*, the incisors are found to be almost of the same length. The notch in the superior corner always exists. The inferior *tables* all present in their centre a rounded and very distinct dental star. The pincers are almost triangular; the intermediates are becoming so. The central enamel, in the superior pincers, is much smaller than at thirteen years. The incisive arcade is greatly depressed in front and narrow transversely.

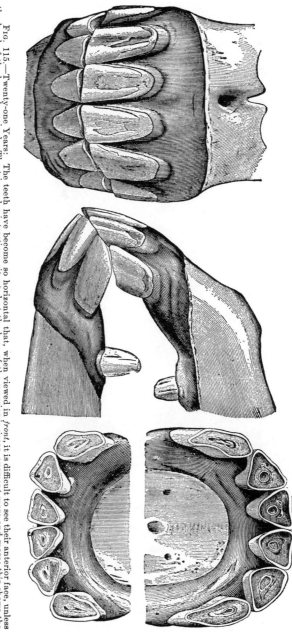

Fig. 115.—Twenty-one Years: The teeth have become so horizontal that, when viewed in *front*, it is difficult to see their anterior face, unless the head of the horse be raised. The triangular interstices, situated at the base of the superior incisors, augment more and more; this shows the convergence of the intermediates and the corners at their free extremity. In *profile*, the jaws are thin. The inferior corner, almost horizontal, has caused the disappearance of the notch on the superior corner. This disposition causes the formation, in these two teeth, of a surface of friction which is elongated from before to behind, or, rather, from the external to the internal side, instead of remaining triangular. The superior *tables*, in the pincers and the intermediates, are wide from their anterior to their posterior border; they are regularly triangular; the central enamel, in most instances, is absent. The inferior tables tend to become flattened from one side to the other and more and more divergent in front.

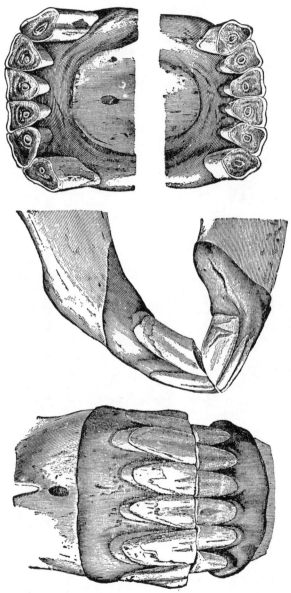

Fig. 116.—Thirty Years: The characters of this period are those of extreme old age. They may be recapitulated as follows: in *front*, the superior arcade overlaps the inferior, which is considerably narrowed; the convergence of the corners and the intermediates becomes more and more distinct. In *profile*, the inferior incisors are very horizontal, especially the corners; the jaws are thin and separated from each other at the level of the bars. The inferior *tables* are flattened from side to side, or biangular; the peripheral enamel tends to disappear from their posterior border. Above, the tables are flattened in the same sense, and their peripheral enamel has a similar disposition. Sometimes in one of the incisive arcades, and at times in both, the teeth have acquired an excessive length, and then the central enamel has not yet disappeared; at other times, on the contrary, they are worn down almost to the gums and surrounded by a thick layer of radical cement, directly applied upon the dentine, which is deprived of its peripheral enamel. Finally, the incisive arcs are very narrow and rectilinear from one side to the other.

This is more in response to demands of buyers than to any real depreciation in the serviceability of the horse. The average horseman reckons the probable period of usefulness as the difference between the present age and the age to which the average horse lives; but there are too many other influences which may impair a horse's usefulness or terminate his existence altogether to make this a sound line of reasoning. A horse that has with-

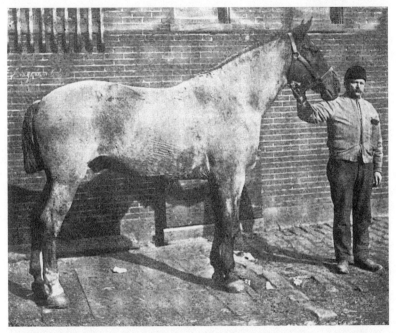

Fig. 117.—This horse has a record of twenty-three years in the delivery service of a large city department store. The reason is evident in the superior breeding and conformation which he manifests.

stood ordinary wear so well that he is comparatively fresh and sound at twelve years of age gives promise of having more years of usefulness ahead of him than the average six-year-old just from the country. Both city stables and the farm afford numerous instances of horses that have been from sixteen to twenty years on the job and still give little evidence of the infirmities that are supposed to come with advancing years (Fig. 117). The

Fig. 118.—This horse has served eighteen years in the city as an ambulance horse and, by
virtue of his superior type, conformation, and intelligence, is still serviceable.

Fig. 119.—This horse, off type and of inferior conformation, with little sense, has been
rendered unserviceable by the same work in one year.

mechanical excellence of conformation is a much more important factor in determining the period of usefulness of a horse than his age (Figs. 118 and 119).

Disposition and intelligence have much to do with a horse's usefulness. Together they determine the character of his performance, within the limits of his possibilities as fixed by type, conformation, and soundness. A good, honest, game horse will oftentimes give more satisfactory service in spite of some physical infirmity than a sound horse that is sour, crabbed, or deficient in horse sense. Whether one rides or drives for profit or pleasure, that end is greatly enhanced by the cheerful responsiveness with which the horses do their work. Horses are being more and more exclusively used for sporting purposes and to realize the greatest delight from a ride or a drive the horse should enter fully into the spirit of the occasion.

Both intelligence and disposition are reflected in the horse's countenance—the expression of the eye, the poise of the ear, and his general behavior. Some horses are much more demonstrative than others.

REVIEW

1. What are the responsibilities of the judge?
2. What does judging involve beside an analysis of the individuals under consideration?
3. Of what assistance is the law of correlation to the practical judge?
4. What is the importance of a system of examination in judging? Outline the most logical system.
5. What features are to be considered in judging?
6. Discuss the proper use of the score card.
7. Upon what will the importance of an unsoundness depend?
8. What is the relation of conformation to the possible occurrence of unsoundness?
9. How do the teeth come to have a definite appearance at different ages?
10. What can be said in defence of the old horse?

PART III
THE PRINCIPLES OF BREEDING

CHAPTER XII

THE BREEDING OF HORSES

THE breeding of horses is done on a limited scale as a side issue to a general farming proposition, more commonly than the breeding of any other class of stock. The majority of farmers raise only a few colts, the bulk of the market supply being produced on a small rather than a large scale.

Ideals Differ Geographically.—The corn belt farmer is most concerned with the weight of a horse, and scorns all that cannot work, no matter how proficient they may be in other lines of service. On the other hand, the Kentuckian is for a "model" horse, possessing quality in the extreme and capable of a sporty performance, either in the show ring or on the race track, be he saddle or harness horse. The Southerner has no more time for a "bull" of a drafter than his contemporary of the Middle West has for the "dude" show or iniquitous race horse. In many parts of Virginia the first thought concerning a horse is "How well can he jump?" and it is regarded as desecration of blood to breed to anything but a Thoroughbred stallion. The average Eastern breeder measures all other types to a road horse standard, and he may be found stinting common farm mares to a little crooked legged pacer that may happen to be the idol of the community since winning the county race at the last fair. It is all a matter of difference in the point of view, and in some communities this point is so indelibly fixed as to make it unwise to advocate a change, but rather to recommend the pursuit of the local ideal in the most intelligent manner. There is a ready market for a good horse of almost any type, and a breeder will usually do best by that which he favors most. It may be impracticable, for instance, to force the breeding of draft horses on the Kentucky farmer whose family traditions, intuitive genius, and available blood all make for a very different stamp of horse.

Investment.—Horse breeding requires a larger initial investment for a longer time than most other live stock enterprises, but if well managed yields a proportionately greater return.

Principles of Breeding.—Breeding is the direction and control of the inherent life forces, heredity and variation, by means of selection and mating. Its practice offers a means of regulating the progeny by control of the parentage. Improvement should be the motive, it being something more than a mere multiplication of numbers in the next generation.

The forces involved are heredity, by means of which characters are transmitted from generation to generation; and variation, through the agency of which new characters are introduced. The natural tendency in reproduction is toward variation, or the production of unlike individuals, with heredity acting as a brake or check, opposed. The more intense the hereditary force, the less marked the variation. The strength of the hereditary force, so far as a specific character is concerned, is determined by the extent to which that character is represented in the ancestry. The greater the number of individual ancestors there are which possess it, and the greater the degree in which it is possessed, the stronger the likelihood of its being transmitted.

Heredity is, therefore, not a matter which involves only the individuals mated, but all those ancestors whose characters and hereditary forces the individuals in question possess. If the prepotency of all individuals in the ancestry were equal, the relative influence of succeeding generations and individual ancestors would be in accordance with Galton's law as shown in the following table : *

Effective Heritage Contributed by Each Generation and by Each Separate Ancestor According to the Law of Ancestral Heredity as Stated by Galton.

Generation backward	Effective contribution of each generation	Number of ancestors involved	Effective contribution of each ancestor
1	½ or 0.5	2	¼ or 25.0%
2	¼ or $(0.5)^2$	4	1/16 or 6.25%
3	1/8 or $(0.5)^3$	8	1/64 or 1.56+%
4	1/16 or $(0.5)^4$	16	1/256 or 0.39+%
5	1/32 or $(0.5)^5$	32	1/1024 or 0.09+%

* Davenport, " The Principles of Breeding."

There are usually a few individual ancestors who, by their great prepotency, dominate the ancestry and have more than their regular fractional influence in determining the nature of the progeny. The more of such impressive ancestors there are, provided their impressiveness is along the same line, the stronger the transmission of their characters will become. Line, or inbreeding, is practiced with this in view, the same individuals being used as many times as possible, thus intensifying the hereditary transmission of their characters.

The germ plasm, representing the union of the two sex cells, is the physical basis of heredity. It represents both the characters of the ancestry which are dominant in this generation, and will therefore be manifested by the individual developed from the germ plasm, and the potential characters of the entire ancestry, which may remain recessive in this generation and not be manifested in this particular individual, but may, in the next succeeding generations, become dominant, some in one individual descendant and some in another. Thus the unlikeness of brothers may be accounted for.

Transmission is, therefore, not from the individual parent but from the ancestry through the parent. The individual manifests but a part of the characters which he inherits, and is consequently capable of transmitting characters which he himself does not possess. All the possibilities of transmission can be learned only by a study of the ancestry. Unknown individuals in the ancestry introduce unknown possibilities into the progeny, hence the advantage of the pure-bred parent, the known excellence of whose ancestry is established. A superior but short-bred individual may happen to manifest all the good qualities of his or her ancestors but transmit none of them. A lack of uniformity in the ancestry is sure to result in a miscellaneous progeny. However, registration and pure breeding are not sufficient, as inferiority possessed in uniform degree by the ancestors will render the progeny of a correspondingly low order of merit; and even some pure-bred and registered horses are inferior in both individuality and ancestry.

Pedigree is but a record of the ancestry, and the value of the pedigree, provided it is complete in recording all ancestors of the first five or six generations, is in proportion to the merit of the individuals recorded.

Prepotency is the breeding power of a stallion or mare, measured by the degree with which their likeness is transmitted to their get. It should be distinguished from fecundity, which is the reproductive power, measured by the regularity with which progeny are begotten by the sire or produced by the dam. Prepotency is determined by the uniformity of the ancestry, which, in turn, is most intensively insured by line and inbreeding. There is, furthermore, a difference in the prepotency of individuals similarly bred.

Fecundity is marked in certain families, showing its hereditary and transmissible nature, and is frequently associated with longevity. The individual element is also a factor in fecundity.

Line breeding is the mating of two individuals having a common ancestor but a few generations removed. It is practiced for the purpose of intensifying the hereditary force derived from certain individuals. It is a compromise on inbreeding.

Inbreeding is the mating of brother and sister, sire and daughter, son and dam, thus eliminating all but the blood from certain individuals. It is rarely practiced by horse breeders.

Cross-breeding is the mating of pure-bred individuals but of different breeds. Indiscriminate cross-breeding is to be condemned, but intelligently conducted it is justifiable for certain purposes, as in the production of hunters in this country. Cross-breeding has the effect of producing variation. The more radical the cross the more extreme and uncertain the variation. It is resorted to for several purposes: (1) Either to restore vigor and fecundity to stock that has been bred too long in one line or under the same environment; (2) to graft on one breed some desirable characters of another; (3) to blend, permanently, the breed characters of two breeds; or simply to combine these characters in the progeny of one generation. To this end it may consist either of making a single infusion of the blood of an alien breed, as the Thoroughbred cross on the Standardbred; of making cross-breds the basis of a new breed, as in the foundation of the French Coach from the *demi sang;* or continuing to cross breed without interbreeding the cross breeds, as in the production of the original *demi sang* (French half-breed) for army service; also in the production of hunters.

Most uniform results are obtained when the hereditary tendencies of the two breeds crossed incline in the same general direction, as in mating a Standardbred and a Saddle horse, or a Thoroughbred with either, and are least satisfactory when radically opposed hereditary forces are united, as in breeding a trotter to a Shire. Such extreme crosses may prohibit any blend of characters and often result in a colt possessed of a draft horse head and body on a trotter's legs and feet, or some similar combination of the extreme characters of each.

Cross-breeding was attended by much greater advantages during the formative periods of our breeds than can be claimed for it at the present time. With a particular breed especially well adapted to almost all requirements, there is little excuse for mixing them up.

Some of the renovating effects of cross-breeding may be secured, yet the identity and integrity of the breed maintained, by resorting to the so-called climatic out-cross, the mating of individuals of the same breed but reared under different conditions of environment, as English and American or Australian Thoroughbreds, or Kentucky and California Standardbreds. The most extreme system of crossing involves species instead of breeds, and is called *hybridization.*

Equine hybrids are the mule and the zebroid. The common ancestor within the genus, in this case, is so extremely remote as to render the hybrids sterile. Bovine hybrids, however, are more or less completely fertile, the supposition being that their common ancestor was more proximate.

The nick, commonly referred to by horse breeders, is a mating resulting especially favorably in a foal superior to either parent. It is supposed to be due to a special affinity of hereditary forces which results in a most harmonious blend or union. A mare may produce good colts to the service of one stallion, but mating with another stallion of equal merit as a sire may result in utter failure, so far as the character of the get is concerned.

Atavism or reversion is the reappearance of the type of a remote ancestor or a harking back to a preëxisting form. It is most likely to follow hybridization, and is exemplified by the line back and leg stripes commonly seen on mules.

A pure bred is, practically, one whose sire and dam are both registered. The " purity " of the breeding depends upon the eligibility rules of the respective registry associations. Literally, a pure bred is one in whom there is no trace of alien blood, but such a degree of purity is approached only by the breeds of greatest antiquity, as the Thoroughbred and the Arab.

Grading up is the mating of common bred mares to pure bred stallions, or the reverse, producing half-breds. By mating the half-breds back to pure breds, of the same breed, the percentage increase of the pure blood will follow the proportions of three-quarters, seven-eighths, and so on, for each successive generation. A horse so bred is called a grade, and the greater the number of generations through which the grading-up process has been carried, the higher the grade.

A mongrel or scrub is one whose fractional breed identity cannot be established.

Top cross refers to the male line of ancestors—the sire's sire, his sire, and thus on back.

Dams.—First, second, third, and fourth dams represent the female line of ancestors—the dam's dam, her dam, etc.

Brothers in blood are the progeny of mating full brothers with full sisters, the same stallion with full sisters or the same mare with full brothers. In each case the mating results in individuals whose pedigrees after the first generation are identical.

Pedigree and Studbook Registration.—In order to keep pedigree records complete and accurate, as well as reliable and authentic, registry associations representing the different breeds have been formed. Entries are made in either alphabetical or numerical order, and show the name, date of foaling, description, breeder, and owner of the horse, with the name and number of sire, and name, number, and usually some of the breeding of the dam. These records are published in book form at more or less regular periods, annually, if the association does sufficient business, and are available to any one at a nominal charge.

Transfers of ownership of registered horses are required to be recorded for the purpose of keeping all records up to date.

A pedigree certificate of registration (Fig. 120) has no negotiable value unless properly issued and executed by the officers of the association whose seal and signature it bears. Its value, even then, is contingent upon the standing of the association. Formerly an accredited list of studbooks was issued and vouched for by the United States Department of Agriculture, but their authorization has since been withdrawn, and the standing of the different associations is based on the personnel of their officers and members.

The eligibility rules for registry are drawn up by the associations themselves and are not uniform in their requirements. The term " pure-bred," as applied to the different breeds, has a significance that is arbitrarily determined by the respective associations. For instance, a horse may be " pure-bred " on the basis of eligibility to registry in the French Draft Studbook yet be ineligible to the Percheron Studbook, and therefore of impure Percheron breeding. In the same way a " pure-bred " Morgan may not be eligible to Standard registration and, as a matter of fact, may possess but a small percentage of Morgan blood, on account of the open nature of the Morgan register.

When a pure-bred, registered horse or mare is bought for breeding purposes, the pedigree certificate often plays a more important part in the transaction than the horse itself. The real value of such a horse lies in the blood lines which he is capable of transmitting, and no just claim to these blood lines can be made unless verified by a pedigree certificate. Title to breeding can be conveyed by no other means. Many pure-bred stallions are deprived of the full credit to which they are entitled through the carelessness or indifference of owners in keeping up records and transfers.

Duplicate pedigree registry certificates can be secured upon application to the secretaries of the associations and by submitting satisfactory evidence that the original has been lost or destroyed.

Eligibility to registration is established by conforming to the rules of entry of the registry associations. These rules are not uniform in the different associations, nor are they fixed, but are subject to change whenever authorized by vote of the association.

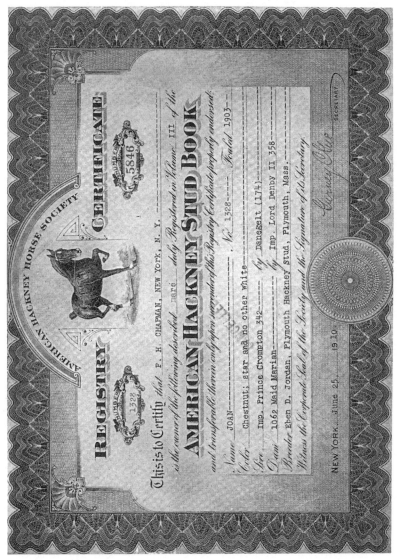

Fig. 120.—A pedigree registry certificate.

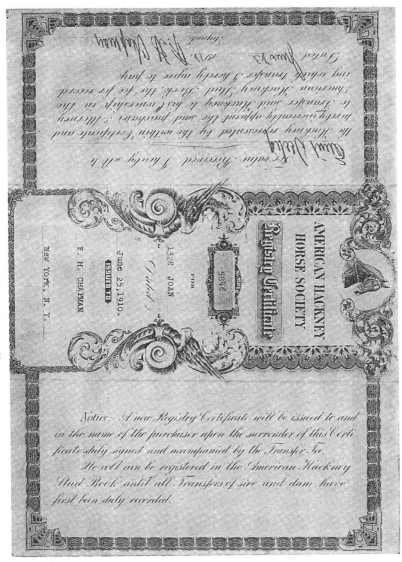

FIG. 120a. Reverse side of registry certificate.

Revision of the rules is generally in the direction of increased requirements and is justified in the case of comparatively new or young breeds which have increased in numbers to a point where the old and more liberal rules are no longer necessary. The American Trotting Registry Association has already dropped rules which during the formative period of the breed were essential. It is reported that they contemplate further tightening up their requirements by elimination of the " standard by performance " clause.

Stallion Legislation.—Stallion license laws have been passed by a number of the States. Because of the much longer time and greater capital involved in the breeding of horses than of other classes of live stock, some legal regulation of the standing of stallions for public service, having in view the protection of the mare owner and the promotion of the interests of the good breeding sires, is important. The idea is not new; all foreign countries in which horse breeding has made any great advancement have either patronized or protected the horse breeding interests by statute. The French system is perhaps the most elaborate.

The French System.—All breeding stallions in France are either owned by the government or have government authority to stand for service. All privately owned stallions which are accepted for service must be free from roaring and moon blindness or periodic ophthalmia, as determined by inspection to which they are required to submit, and this fact is attested by the star branded on their necks. Then they are classified according to merit. Those of the best class are designated as " approved," and many of them are liberally subsidized in order that they may be made available to all owners of high class mares; those which are not quite up to the requirements for approval but are yet desirable sires are classed as " authorized "; while all others which have passed the veterinary inspection covering roaring and moon blindness are simply " certified." The stallions from the government " haras " are systematically distributed throughout the breeding districts during the season.

Ideals in stallion license laws differ, there being a marked lack of uniformity in the provisions of those enacted in the different States. A stallion may be licensed to stand for service in one State while barred from service in another. Local conditions govern, of course, in the case of each State, but there can hardly be sufficient difference in the prevailing conditions to warrant such a variety of laws.

The objects of stallion laws should be (1) to protect the mare owner, by preventing misrepresentation of the breeding or the soundness of the stallion; (2) to protect the owners of superior breeding stallions by eliminating or discouraging the use of inferior competitors; (3) to promote the interests of the mare owners by encouraging the purchase and standing of better stallions; and (4) to promote the interests of the stallion owner by educating the mare owner to be discriminating in his patronage.

The first object is best insured by requiring an examination of the pedigree registry certificates and a uniform inspection, by one board or commission, of every stallion for which application for license is made, all stallions found acceptable to be classified according to breeding, whether pure-bred, grade or scrub, sound or unsound, and said classification to be specified clearly in the license certificate.

Purity of Breeding.—Pure-bred is such an arbitrary term, contingent upon so many conditions, that it is more accurate and just in many cases to certify a stallion to be registered or unregistered rather than of pure breeding or not of pure breeding. In many instances ineligibility to registry may be strictly technical, due to neglect on the part of previous owners, and may not in any way alter the purity of breeding of the stallion or his value as a sire. The fact that the horse is unregistered, however, cannot be disputed.

Hereditary unsoundness is such an elusive condition, so difficult of prognosis, that to specify just what conditions of unsoundness shall, by their presence, disqualify for service, will necessitate the elimination of many individuals of much breeding value, although their get may be in no way predisposed to the unsoundness which they themselves possess. The same unsoundness may be quite regularly transmitted in one case while perhaps never appearing to be hereditary in another. The most careful observation and inquiry warrant the conclusion that spavin and roaring, for instance, can only be regarded as of an hereditary nature when their transmission has actually been demonstrated in the progeny.

The existence of a defective conformation is to be regarded with as much apprehension as the actual unsoundness itself, especially if the latter be unaccompanied by an apparent predisposing cause. In making such a determination, it must be borne in mind that some unsoundnesses, as roaring, may not manifest themselves, even though transmitted, until such age that the horse in question may have been lost track of, although, as a rule, a sire of colts that develop unsoundness with any degree of uniformity can soon be detected.

Suitable Laws.—Any law to be workable and meet the varied conditions, as they exist in most States, should have some flexibility in its application, permitting arbitrary consideration of each case by those in charge of its administration. With a sufficient number of registered, sound stallions available to the breeders of a community, a law might be very strict in its requirements as to breeding and soundness, but there are localities where the interest in horse breeding is such as to need a boost and is not capable of withstanding much of a knock. As long as the State itself is not empowered or equipped to place there a good stallion, but must depend upon private ownership for whatever breeding there is done, stallions that should be barred from service, if in competition with good sires, may be permitted to stand, if not doing more harm than good. Meanwhile, the efforts of the stallion board or commission may be devoted to an educational campaign which will ultimately bring better stallions into that district.

Difficult Points.—It is most difficult to establish the fact that a stallion is unfit for service on account of an existing unsoundness or a short pedigree, while his get are annually selling for more than the colts of other stallions fully accredited on the basis of strict stallion law requirements. Not until the poorest pure-bred is superior as a sire to the best grade and until much more is known of hereditary unsoundness, can we consistently make legal discrimination against *all* grade and *all* unsound stallions, without effecting detriment to the breeding industry. Elimination of the unfit is only one means of protecting and promoting the interests of the fit, and what constitutes fitness itself is more or less arbitrarily determined by local conditions.

The average of merit of stallions standing for service is so low that it will take time to attain to the theoretical or ideal in actual practice. France, with her system of government ownership, can afford to be much more independent and dictatorial than our States, which are dependent on private enterprise and capital for whatever breeding there is done. Too oppressive restrictions may be so discouraging as to destroy the business altogether. An individual or company, for instance, may invest $2,500 in a two-year-old draft stallion, which at the time of purchase passes an examination for soundness and is accompanied by a registry certificate. In the course of a year or two this colt may develop an unsoundness or some fraud may be detected in his pedigree registry certificate. To require his retirement from service on either of these accounts, would entail a most unjust financial loss upon his owners, and would undoubtedly dissuade them from ever making a similar investment.

The Attitude of Mare Owners.—The mare owners, while not directly named in stallion license laws, should receive a share of the consideration of the administrative boards. They really hold the key to the whole situation, in the discrimination they show and the amount of the fees they will allow in their patronage of stallions. Stallions capable of becoming good sires are costly, and their fee must be sufficient to insure some return on the investment. With a liberal policy adopted by the mare owners, there need be no dearth of good sires. The scrub is costly to patronize though the fee is low. As long as the scrub can command his share of the patronage, there is little to induce one to invest in a first-class stallion. It is a fact worthy of note that the average stud fee prevailing in those States from which the bulk of the market supply of horses of this country is drawn is about double that of those districts where the horse business is given up as unprofitable.

No law can compel mare owners to patronize superior stallions, nor is it constitutional to deny them the patronage of the inferior ones, unless they are proven to be an absolute menace to the industry. Education is the only solution, and that **is** within the province of, and should be vigorously prosecuted by, the licensing officials.

The Community System of Breeding.—There are many advantages in the breeders of a community getting together and working to a common end within the same breed. Such a system makes possible the use of a stallion which no individual member of the community could own. It promotes coöperation and mutual helpfulness, which in time revert to the benefit of all concerned in the way of a district reputation for horses of whatever type produced. Buyers are thus attracted where they could not be induced to come to see but a few widely scattered horses or colts, in the hands of jealous owners who were not disposed to reveal the whereabouts of other possibilities in case their own failed to meet the buyers' requirements. Individual advantages are subordinate to the interests of the community, the general policy being to insure the buyers finding the horses sought, each owner helping his neighbor to make a sale, in case he himself has nothing to suit. Once satisfied, the buyers are most likely to return when those who were unable to sell the first time may have their inning.

When different types and breeds are represented in a community, partisan sentiment is almost certain to prevail. Each breeder cannot accomplish alone what might be possible by the combined effort of all, and their offerings in any one line are not sufficient to attract the best buyers.

The Breeding Stud.—A horse breeding establishment is spoken of either as a stud or stud farm, the breeding sire as the stud horse (Fig. 121).

The equipment of a stud farm should consist of comfortable and hygienic quarters, productive pastures, preferably underlaid with limestone and provided with ample shade and running water, safe fences, and competent help.

Quarters.—Breeding stock does not do well in close confinement, but dry, light, roomy, loose boxes or sheds, well bedded, should be provided, to which the horses may have ready access voluntarily, if not regularly stabled. For stallions, box stalls opening into paddocks, the doors fastened back, are best; mares are better cared for in the same way if practicable, although they do fairly well in open sheds and lots, if too many are not turned together and there are no quarrelsome ones in the lot. For draft mares that are worked regularly, the paddock would be superfluous, but they should be allowed loose boxes in which they can lie more comfortably as pregnancy advances.

Maternity stalls may be kept purposely for foaling, but as mares are more finicky than other females at parturition time there is some advantage, so far as their peace of mind is concerned, in keeping them regularly in the quarters that they are to be permitted to foal in, alongside of their accustomed mates.

Pastures.—The greatest horse breeding districts are characterized by luxuriant pastures, a most important feature of any

Fig. 121.—A breeding stud. In the work ring are two Hackney stallions in the foreground, two Hackney pony stallions to the left, two show pony mares, the product of the stud, on the right; show horses, brood mares and foals, weaning colts and fillies in the background. The stallion stable is on the right, the quarters for mares and colts on the left.

breeding farm. Size and early maturity are sought in all but the ponies, and since the body is 6 to 9 per cent bone, and bone is 60 to 70 per cent ash, and 80 per cent of the ash is calcium phosphate, a limestone foundation is a pasture essential. The seeding should include such variety of grasses and legumes as to keep the forage coming all through the season. Pastures should be well drained, not too rough or stony; all dangerous places, such as quarry holes, pits, bogs, and stump lots, should be well guarded. Shade, running water, and possibly a fly flap complete the pasture requisites.

Fences should be at least four and one-half feet high, strong, and of material and construction affording no opportunity for the horses to be snagged or cut. The post and rail, common in the East and South, is perhaps the most satisfactory horse fence. If any barbed wire is used, it should be the top strand kept tight. The ideal fence has been described as " hog tight, bull strong, and horse high "—such is the post and rail, four rails high.

THE STALLION

Selection of the sire is the most important single step pertaining to the establishment of a breeding stud. His is the most potent influence for either good or bad in the operation. Like the bull, he is more than half the herd. On account of his being the parent of so many individual offspring in a given season, his influence is much more extended than that of the mares. It would require the use of as many superior mares as a stallion may beget foals to accomplish the results that might be attained with a single stallion, and then the progeny would be much less uniform. In the case of an individual, his dam may have as much to do with determining his merit as the sire, and it is important that only good mares be bred, but the most practical method of improving the mares of future generations is to grade up by means of a superior sire. But one parent being pure-bred, his or her characters will dominate in the offspring, since purity of breeding is a cause of prepotency. As a rule, the pure-bred parent will be the sire. In selecting a stallion, whether it be to head a select band of pure-bred mares or to patronize with but a single mare, he must be considered from three angles,—as an individual, as representing and transmitting the characters of an ancestry, and as the progenitor of a future generation.

As an individual, he should be just what is desired in his get, *i.e.*, of the right type, good conformation and sound, being strongest in those respects in which the mare or mares with which he is to be mated are most deficient (Fig. 122). Furthermore, he must be masculine in appearance, possessing that development of forehand, hardness of feature, and boldness of demeanor which bespeak the impressive sire.

Testing Stallions.—The ancestry is the antecedent of the progeny and should be carefully studied in order to forecast the character of the progeny. Just as the proof of the pudding is in the eating, so the real value of a sire cannot be determined without an inspection of his get. They alone are sufficient either to

FIGS. 122a and 122b.—A successful sire of the right type, good conformation, sound, and masculine in appearance, whose prepotency is demonstrated by the trueness to type and uniform excellence of his get.

commend or condemn the individual as a breeder. None but a proven sire should be put at the head of a breeding stud. The inferiority of a horse as a breeder may not be manifested until his get are fairly mature; in the meantime, the best mares have been bred to him, perhaps for more than one season, and the damage wrought in the stock as well as the time lost may take generations to efface. The prospective sire should be tried out in a limited way with a few mares before being trusted in premier place. It is only for this purpose that the use of stud colts is justifiable.

Early service cannot improve the development of the colt, and unless carefully managed may be harmful, yet from the owner's point of view it is often desirable to know, early, something of the youngster's ability as a sire. To this end he may be used as a two- or a three-year-old on a few selected mares, all to be served in a short period, so that there may be no interruption in his growth.

The care and management of the stallion through the breeding season may be summarized in a discussion of the feeding, exercise, regulation of service, and grooming. A mutual balance between food and exercise is the key to condition of the stallion in service. A most effective prescription employed by a prominent veterinarian in one of the most extensive horse breeding districts of this country is, " Halve the ration and double the exercise when the stallion is not giving a vigorous, sure service."

Feeding.—Vigor and tone are secured for the sire by a ration rich in tissue-building, protein and ash, but with little of the fat forming starches, the whole to be counterbalanced by exercise of some form in the open air. No better grain ration can be offered than oats, but for the sake of variety and relish there may be substituted a little barley or corn, and bran is always a valuable supplement to any grain ration, since it relaxes the system generally, corrects or prevents digestive disorders, and furnishes an abundance of bone and tissue-building material.

The draft stallion is most likely to be the victim of a stimulating ration that is not counterbalanced by sufficient exercise. The demand for ton horses is responsible for a system of fitting which is not intended to insure foals. Many draft stallions offered for show or sale are in anything but breeding condition. On the other hand, it should not be considered necessary to reduce a draft stallion to anything like race horse condition in order to insure virility. It is natural for a draft horse to be fat in a degree which would be abnormal in a road horse, and he is not at his best in any other condition. There is what might be termed an optimum or best normal weight for any horse, *i.e.,* his weight when in normal condition as to flesh, muscular tone, and vigor. If that can be determined and then maintained by establishing a balance between feed consumed and exercise taken, the greatest virility may be expected.

Exercise.—If a horse is gaining over his normal weight, increase his exercise first, and if he continues to gain, reduce his ration. If he falls below normal weight and is receiving only a reasonable amount of exercise, increase his ration first, then, if necessary, reduce the exercise. But it is generally the former rather than the latter condition which the stud groom has to meet. The old country practice of travelling the horse is one of the most practical means of solving the exercise problem, and is for that reason commendable, although there seems to be a prejudice against it in some parts of this country. It is often found practicable to give the draft stallion work about the farm. If there is no such opportunity, he should be led or driven several miles per day, but at a walk. This is the draft horse's gait, and if a more ingenious than industrious groom imagines that he can concentrate the benefits of a long walk into a short trot, he will find the results much in favor of the walk.

Exercise is just as essential to the best breeding condition of the light stallion, but the trotter is more certain of his daily jog and the Thoroughbred of his morning gallop than is the drafter of his walk. In the lighter classes of stallions there is not the premium placed on weight which induces the feeder to fatten the horse beyond all reason.

Regulation of the services of the stallion is of vital importance. Opinions differ as to just what such regulation should be, but nearly all agree that many horses are misused in service. It is well to remember that a horse's success is not measured by the number of mares he serves, but by the number and character of the colts he gets in a given season. No definite number of mares can be assigned as best to allow the horse, since the number that can be properly bred will depend upon their distribution through the season, the age of the horse, and his preparation and fitness for the work. The most conservative estimate is an average of one service per day the season through for a mature horse. However, the mares do not always come in regular order, distributed throughout the entire season. Hence, it often becomes necessary to make two or even three covers in a single day, and this may be done, occasionally, with no injury to the horse. It should not be repeated, however.

Grooming is necessary, not only to make the horse more attractive in appearance, but to assist exercise in maintaining the best of health and condition. The functions of the skin must be kept active. A lack of exercise and neglect in grooming are together responsible for many serious conditions about the legs and feet of the big, lymphatic draft stallions, especially those with much coarse feather. The grooming must not be so rough nor severe as to cause irritation either of the skin or temper, but it should be thorough, with special care taken to keep all parts clean and free from any foulness.

THE BROOD MARE

We have as yet no definite information to show that the parent of either sex has any special influence in determining the character of the offspring apart from what is governed by prepotency. The relative influence of sire and dam is *apparently* in favor of the sire because the female line is so often lost or untraced. Many noted families, however, have been founded by females, and the evidence of Arab pedigrees, which have been traced through the dams for centuries, demonstrates the importance of the mare.

The dam is not only a source of hereditary transmission, like the sire, but she serves as a host to the developing fœtus. Selection of the brood mare involves the same general consideration as selection of the stallion. Her manifestation of sex character is found in a comparatively light forehand, a sweet, refined head and neck, and a matronly appearance throughout (Fig. 123). In order to sustain the growth of the fœtus well, she should be deep-ribbed and roomy, and somewhat more openly made, with more length, than is desirable in the stallion. She should possess every indication of capacity and vigor (Fig. 124).

Care and Management of the Brood Mare.—The feed, work, and care, at and after foaling, are of greatest importance in con-

FIG. 123.—A producer—sweet, refined, and feminine.

nection with the mare. Food and exercise, together, so regulate the condition of the mare as to determine success or failure in the production of a foal. It is a matter of give and take between them. A balance is manifested by the condition which is indicative of the greatest activity of the vital functions, *i.e.*, vigor, expressed in the clear eye, the sleek coat, and the keen appetite which the feeder describes as " hearty," together with a general evidence of nerve and muscle tone. The mare in this condition

will carry no superfluous flesh, but is herself sufficiently well
nourished to insure ample nutriment for the perfect development
of the foal.

The *ideal conditions* for the brood mare, namely those in
which the balance between feed and exercise is most easily maintained and the feed of the best sort secured, are those surrounding mares at pasture. Fresh air and sunshine, without exposure,

Fig. 124.—A brood mare of proven worth, deep-ribbed and roomy, with every indication
of capacity and vigor.

freedom to move about at will, with little danger of slips or
fatigue, and an abundance of nutritious, succulent forage, furnishing the elements essential to the growth of the foal and the
production of milk by the dam, are the things nature has provided at the season of the year when most females naturally bring
forth their young. These can hardly be improved upon, and if
they must be modified or substituted on account of economy, they
should still be the standard by which other systems are measured.

However, the average farmer must either breed his working mares or work his brood mares. The question which confronts him is how to secure natural conditions for his mares while performing artificial service.

It must be borne in mind that feed furnishes energy and tissue-forming material, and that the performance of work requires energy and uses up tissue. Thus the balance between them is maintained. The mare at work is just as well off, in the matter of exercise, fresh air, and sunshine, as the one at pasture, but she has imposed upon her labor which demands more energy and uses more tissue-building material. She is also subject to fatigue, mechanical injuries, and nervous disturbances that never come to the mare at pasture.

Exercise and Work.—In general, the management of the brood mare should have for its object the feeding of such a ration as will supply the demand for energy and tissue and still allow ample nourishment for the development of the foal, either before or after birth, together with such a regulation of the work as will protect the mare from becoming tired, overheated, or injured in any way. She must not be fretted either by another horse or by a rough hand, while heavy, jerky pulls, extreme speed, rough saddle work, or jumping are to be strictly prohibited as pregnancy advances. But to work a mare up to within a month of foaling and then confine her in a stall with no exercise whatever is almost as injurious as to begin working her hard after ten months' rest, following breeding. It is not unusual for mares to foal, successfully, while in the field at work, but it is safer to gradually diminish the work, so that during the last few weeks of pregnancy only the lightest work is done or exercise in the yard is taken.

Avoid Extremes.—It is a peculiar fact that, while the two extremes in condition are both unfavorable to breeding, statistics indicate that the birth rate among nations has shown a marked increase following devastation by war and famine, conditions of life in which the females become reduced to the extreme of low condition. This would seem to be in response to a natural law for the preservation of the race, and should not be taken to indicate that starvation and extremely low condition are favorable to reproduction. It is true that a thin mare is more apt to breed than a pampered one, but a mare in low condition has no reserve on which to draw for the nourishment and growth of her colt. Her whole system is in an impoverished condition, which must be corrected before the nutrients will be available for the growth of the foal.

Feeding.—The quality of the ration is of as much importance as the quantity. Fat production is to be avoided, and the formation of blood, muscle, and bone sought instead. Hence, a comparatively narrow ration should be fed.

The tendency of females to fatten as pregnancy advances must be guarded, as mares may become so fat as to interfere with the development of the foal, and cause abortion or trouble at birth. Just before and after foaling, the ration of the dam should be lightened and made more laxative by the addition of bran, either dry or in a mash, to be continued until both dam and foal have fully recovered from the ordeal through which they have just passed.

After Foaling.—Exercise should be permitted after the system of the mare has readjusted itself, but regular work should not be begun inside of three weeks. It is better not to work the mare until the foal is weaned.

THE FOAL

Navel Infection and Impaction of the Bowels in Young Foals.—There are two active causes of death in young foals, a better understanding of which might materially reduce the fatalities ordinarily reported during the foaling season. One, perhaps the most common, is due to an impaction in the bowels of the excrement accumulated during the development prior to birth. This material is called meconium, and its prompt removal is essential to the well-being of the new born animal. Nature has provided for the accomplishment of this by giving to the fore-milk or colostrum, as it is called, purgative properties. Thus, if Nature's plans are not interfered with and the first milk is taken, there is usually no trouble in clearing the bowels after birth. However, the dam may have some trouble with her milk at first, or the young, through weakness, may not get a good draft of fore-milk; in some cases even, care is taken to draw off the colostrum before the young thing suckles, in the belief that it is unfit to be taken; and the colt suffers accordingly. In order to avoid the difficulties arising from this cause, the first care should be to insure a good portion of the fore-milk for the young creature. Then if, from any cause, the digestive tract has not been cleared of its contents within twenty-four hours, the bowels must be stimulated to action by a tablespoonful of castor oil and a warm water injection.

The other cause of many deaths in young animals is infection with pus and disease germs through the navel. At the moment the umbilical cord is ruptured there is a direct communication from without to some of the vital internal organs and blood of the foal. This opening is later closed naturally by the swelling and final drying and sloughing off of the end of the cord. There is thus a brief opportunity for the entrance of bacteria which may later affect the system generally or locally and produce serious results. It has been satisfactorily demonstrated that the so-called navel or joint ill, in foals, is due to organisms entering through this channel.

If this affection has prevailed in a stable it would be well to remove pregnant mares to clean, uninfected quarters and allow them to foal there. The new-born foal should be dropped only on fresh litter, and it would be safer to wash the stump of the cord with a saturated solution of boracic acid and then dust with boric acid powder. These precautions have been the means of eradicating the difficulty from many stables where deaths had occurred year after year.

It is not advisable to cut or ligate the cord, but allow it to break naturally, as it will do if left alone. A torn or broken blood-vessel will not bleed, whereas, one that is cut directly across will, and it takes a skilled hand and sterilized materials to make a ligature that will not do more harm than good. If it were more generally known that the newly broken umbilical cord offers a channel of infection which may admit the most dangerous bacteria, more care would be taken to prevent such infection.

During the existence of the colt as a suckling some especial precautions must be taken in addition to those already mentioned. The milk flow must be maintained by succulent forage, the colt must be fed often, and the dam must at no time be in such a condition as to render the milk injurious to the foal.

Most breeders advise leaving the colt in the stable while the dam is at work, but others allow the colt to follow the dam to the field. The objection to the former method is that unless the mare is returned at least once during each half day the colt becomes very hungry, and when the mare comes to him sweating he gorges himself on the milk with which the udder is distended. This milk is often rendered injurious by the heated condition of the mare, and it thus becomes a cause of serious digestive disorder, especially when so much is taken. It is a good thing to encourage the colt, as it grows older, to take a few oats, preferably crushed, from its mother's allowance, or a creep may be especially constructed for the foal to feed in. If two mares and foals are allowed together, the youngsters will form an attachment for each other which will prove of great service in reconciling them to the weaning process.

The Next Breeding.—Observations have shown that a mare may be bred with greater certainty of success on the ninth day after foaling than at any subsequent date. It is also known that mares which have their sexual ardor somewhat suppressed by a moderate degree of fatigue are more apt to conceive than mares in an extremely nervous condition at the time of service. It is for this purpose that the Arab gives his mare a sharp run just prior to service.

Breeding Two-Year-Old Fillies.—The advisability of breeding fillies at two years of age is an economic question which is frequently considered, and concerning which there is a great deal of difference of opinion. It may be said, in the first place, that it all depends upon the filly. Horses of draft breeding mature much earlier than the hot-blooded sort, so that a draft filly at two years of age is often as forward as one of trotting breeding almost or fully a year older. Again, there is a great difference in individuals and their development. Usually a smoothly turned, neat, well-finished youngster makes its growth much sooner than an apparently rougher but more growthy individual, although as a rule the latter attains, eventually, to much greater scale. Furthermore, the same individual may develop in much less time in the hands of the feeder who keeps her continually " doing " than when required to make all her growth on pasture, with a material setback due to improper feeding each winter season.

It does not seem feasible to include in this discussion any but the well-matured draft filly, she being the only one which should, under any circumstances, be bred as a two-year-old. It is not reasonable to suppose that, from the point of view of the filly herself, early breeding is beneficial, but as a business proposition it has been demonstrated that, whatever slight injurious effect the filly may suffer, it is not sufficient to offset the advantage of having her make some return, as a three-year-old, to the man who has his money invested and is paying for her keep. It is more satisfactory to have a two-year-old filly pay her way by raising a foal than by going to work in the field, as she is very much more apt to suffer permanent injury from this than from being bred. Even though a great many two-year-olds are capable of doing a considerable amount of selected work, they cannot take the full part of a horse's work without danger of its becoming detrimental to their ultimate worth.

The breeding of fillies is believed to insure their becoming better mothers and more certain and regular breeders, eventually, than though they be permitted to fully develop and become somewhat " staggy," as they do occasionally, before being bred.

Practice Elsewhere.—The best means of solving this problem is to accept the findings of the other great horse-producing countries where it has been thoroughly worked out. In Scotland, for instance, the practice is to breed the Clyde fillies the spring they are two years old, allowing them no work whatever that season. Then, after weaning their foals, they are taken up as three-year-olds and put to work, but not bred again until they are four years old. This seems to be a very practical system and worthy of our adoption.

Spring or Fall Foaling.—The natural time for foals to arrive is the spring, and under ordinary conditions, especially in breeding studs, this is customary. However, nature is perverted in many ways by modern methods of domestication, so there are circumstances which make it more desirable to raise fall colts. With good stables, abundance of feed, and the necessary help, there is no reason why mares should not be made to foal in the fall, if it is more convenient to have them do so. This may be the case with farm mares which are expected to do the season's work in addition to raising a colt. In fact, if one is forced to choose between a spring foal, with no chance to properly favor the mare, and a fall colt which arrives and is suckled while the mare is laid by, the latter would be more desirable. During the winter, however, both mares and foals will require.more attention and should not be "roughed through." By late foaling the youngsters can be given a good start before they are set back by the inevitable short pastures and flies of midsummer.

Of course, breeders of race and show horses take every advantage of the age limit and therefore favor early foaling. There are also the unquestioned benefits to be derived from the life in the open and the new grass to commend the spring time for foaling, but prejudice against the fall date is not altogether warranted and circumstances may be such as to make it most advantageous.

Weaning the Foal.—The foal is usually weaned at from four and one-half to six months of age, depending upon the circumstances. If pasture is short, or if for any reason either mare or foal is not doing well, it is advisable to wean the foal comparatively early. If, on the other hand, the mare has a full flow of milk and her services are not needed, there is no reason for making a change under six months. Weaning is. more a matter of preparation than of the absolute removal of the foal from the dam, and the simplicity of the weaning process itself depends upon the thoroughness of the preparation.

If the proper provision is made for the foal to take more and more grain as he grows older, he will gradually reduce the amount of milk taken from his dam, so that when the time for weaning arrives very little if any setback or disturbance is caused either foal or dam. If, however, the foal must learn to eat after being deprived of his ordinary source of sustenance, he will require some time to accommodate himself to the new régime, while the mare will demand especial care on account of the removal of the colt before her milk supply has been to any extent diminished. Furthermore, a little foal acquires a spirit of independence as he becomes self-sustaining, and for that reason the absence of the dam becomes a less disturbing factor to him, especially if he has the company of another foal, than to the young thing which has been entirely dependent upon its dam until she is suddenly taken away. When once the dam and foal are separated it is better for both if the separation is complete; if, after both have become reconciled to the parting, they are permitted to see, hear, or smell each other again, all that has been gained up to this time is lost, and it will be necessary to begin over. Especial care should be taken to see that the new quarters, where the weanlings are confined, are so constructed and arranged as to make it impossible for them to injure themselves, in case they make a demonstration of their resentment at being so treated.

Care of the Colt's Feet.—The relation between the direction of the colt's legs and the form of his feet is so close as to make the care of the latter a most important means of enhancing his usefulness in later years. In the first place, the natural attitude of the leg determines, in large part, the form of the foot. But, on the other hand, the natural attitude of the leg may become altered to conform to an unnatural condition of the foot resulting from neglect. Therefore, if the natural attitude of the leg is correct, the natural form of the foot should be guarded in order to preserve the correct position of the leg. It is even possible, within certain limits, to so shape a colt's foot as to induce correction of some defect in the position of the legs which existed at birth. For example, the horse which stands toe wide, nigger heeled, or splay footed as it is commonly called, will have the inner wall of his foot much shorter and more upright than the outer wall. The condition is probably due primarily to the position of the legs, the foot at birth appearing normal. If, however, the animal had been born with the legs straight, but for some reason during the first few months of his life the outer wall of his foot had been allowed to become longer than the inner wall, this unnatural form of the foot would tend to bring about a toe wide position of the legs which were originally straight. Or, if the feet of a toe wide colt had been kept in proper form, they would have influenced the toe wide legs to assume a proper direction.

Horses become unsound of limb when the wear and tear is not equally distributed, certain parts bearing an undue amount. Equal distribution of weight bearing and other functional activities are possible only when the form of the foot and the direction of the leg are correct. Any deviation from the proper standing position of whatever degree will, in all probability, cause a proportionate overtaxing of certain parts with its resulting unsoundness.

Handling the Foal.—It is much easier to train the young plant or to mold the clay before they are set in some definite form. In the same way the young animal, and notably the horse, has fewer ideas of his own, and is more ready to accept the directions of a superior intelligence the younger this work is taken up.

The too common notion that education and work are inseparable is largely responsible for the fact that so many colts are allowed to assert their independence until such time as they are fit to go to work, their general usefulness being in most cases impaired on this account. The horse should be reasonably mature before he is called upon to do any service, but any time spent on his education prior to the date at which he first goes into commission, as it were, will be repaid many-fold in the more satisfactory manner in which he performs his service.

The profit and pleasure to be derived from the use of a horse of any class are so dependent upon his being readily subservient to his master's will that the earlier this spirit is created the better horse he will be. A common custom in the Middle West is to take the unbroken two- or three-year-old, put him between two or three other horses to the gang plow, and thus " break " him. He pulls when the others pull, makes the turns when they do, and finally becomes of about as much service at that work as the other horses in the team, but he is not broken. Take him by himself and he will not stand, back, lead, rein, or allow a foot to be picked up without as much or more resistance than was offered before the breaking process began.

Subordination.—Little foals should be taught subordination at the very start, and not allowed to become wilful or head-strong. An early effort in this direction will not only simplify that culmination of their education, too often most properly termed " breaking," but it will insure that end being more completely accomplished. On the other hand, the idea of fear must be kept as remote as possible, as the timid horse is usually the one which has some terrifying experience to remember. Even before the time for haltering arrives, the youngsters may be taught to stand over, have their feet raised, and in a general way to respond to the master mind.

Halter Breaking.—When halters are to be placed on the colts in order that they may become accustomed to them, one of the light web variety is preferable to the heavier strap halter commonly used, and care should be taken not to pull heavily on the nose band at any time. Many deformed face lines have been caused by this means. It is not necessary to drag a colt by the halter in order to suggest to him that his business is to follow. As a matter of fact, the reverse effect is usual, and the harder a colt is pulled, the harder he pulls back. If, on the contrary, he is coaxed along some accustomed route, as to the water trough and back, he will soon catch on and follow promptly whenever the halter is taken in hand.

The first time the colt is tied up by the head, see to it that the halter will hold him in case he pulls. If it does and he fails in the first few attempts, a string will probably serve as well as a chain to keep him in his place thereafter, while if he succeeds in freeing himself at the first few attempts he will never cease trying to repeat what he has once accomplished.

Bridle and Harness.—The first step toward getting a colt going successfully in harness is to properly bit and mouth him. In the old countries a common practice is to back the colt into a slip stall and hold him there by cross-ties snapped in the bit rings. He thus works against the iron, first bearing, then yielding, until he becomes accustomed to its presence and the pressure exerted by it. The dumb jockey or more simple bitting ring, commonly used here, serves much the same purpose, but no mechanical device is as effective as the pressure of the hand on the rein; better mouths are made in this way. One of the most effective ways of developing a good mouth in a colt and of teaching him to flex his neck is by riding him as soon as he is old enough to be " backed." Many of the best harness horses received much of their preliminary schooling from the saddle. Inasmuch as the conveyance of the master's thought to the horse's mind, for execution, is *via* hands, reins, bit, and mouth, no progress can be made and none should be attempted until this fundamental means of communication has been established. Simple physical power is a poor means of control when applied to the horse. On the contrary, control is a matter which involves to a greater extent the mental faculties of both horse and master. If he has been inspired from colthood with the idea of man's dominance, obedience will receive a great deal more consideration from him than will rebellion.

While teaching the horse subordination by leading him to underestimate certain of his powers, it is also essential that he be made to believe that there is no limit to certain others. In the breaking process the kick strap should not be left off until the habit has been acquired, nor should any pains be spared to prevent an initial performance at either rearing, backing, wheeling, or running. On the other hand, it is just as important not to overload a pair of draft colts, with a view of creating in them the notion that they can pull anything with two ends loose. For the same reason a prospective race horse should be given no occasion to believe that he is anything but invincible. Thus by exaggerating our equine servant's notion of those of his powers which are most useful to us, and at the same time deceiving him as to those attributes which, if realized, might impair his usefulness, we promote his serviceability.

It is not necessary here to discuss the various systems of breaking, nor the art of driving. The idea is simply to impress upon the breeder the importance of properly handling the colts and fillies which he has bred. At all events, give them a liberal education and begin early. Then, when the buyer comes along, the colt so handled is more likely to sell well for three reasons: (1) He is worth more; (2) the owner has a better opportunity to show the colt off to his own advantage, presenting him with the best foot forward, as it were; and (3) the buyer has a much better chance to observe the real merit that he possesses.

STERILITY

Sterility is the cause of considerable loss to horse breeders annually. Since actual test in the stud is the only means of determining its existence, large prices may be paid for breeding animals which prove utterly useless for that purpose. Some knowledge of the causes of sterility may enable the breeder to guard against the purchase of barren animals, to prevent it in his breeding stock, or to regain the breeding power of animals in which it is temporarily impaired.

Sterility may be either permanent or temporary, and involves both sexes. Permanent sterility is usually congenital, the result of an incomplete or abnormal development of the generative organs. Temporary sterility is caused by injuries or disease affecting the genital system, or such general constitutional conditions as may result from a change of environment, either extreme obesity or general debility, and excessive use in the stud.

Sterility in the stallion may consist either of an inability or an indisposition to serve a mare; or that operation may be accomplished but with no resulting impregnation on account of the absence of live, vigorous spermatozoa. Sterility of the latter class may be complete or only partial, as when the breeding powers are impaired but not lost. Double cryptorchids, in which both testicles are retained undeveloped in the abdomen, are usually sterile, while single cryptorchids (ridglings), in which one testicle only is involved, may be sure breeders. The latter are objectionable as sires, however, since the condition is frequently transmitted, thereby seriously complicating the operation of castration.

Many instances are reported of imported stallions which have had successful stud seasons abroad proving impotent the first year or two in this country, after which their potency is regained.

Stallions remain potent to an old age as a rule. Many valuable sires are sacrificed just as their true worth is beginning to be appreciated, because they are growing old. Experienced breeders who retain their proven sires find them potent to an advanced age and much more valuable than many untried young stallions prove to be. Most stallions are sold with a guarantee to get 60 per cent of breedable mares in foal, but a much higher percentage is maintained by some.

Sterility or barrenness of the mare consists of an inability to produce a living colt. She may either be unable to conceive, to carry the foal the full period of fœtal development, or to deliver the foal alive at the conclusion of gestation.

Some mares are so irritable or excitable in the presence of the stallion as to make it necessary to resort to artificial impregnation in order to get them bred.

If a twelve- or fourteen-year-old mare has never had a foal, her generative organs have probably undergone more or less atrophy from disuse, and the possibility of getting her with foal is much lessened. There are numerous instances, however, of quite old mares having become pregnant for the first time. Mares frequently suffer from cysts or tumors of the ovaries, the irritation of which keeps them almost continually in heat and renders them practically useless, yet they fail to get in foal, when bred. Such mares should be spayed and considered as work geldings rather than brood mares.

Extensive breeders of imported mares have experienced considerable difficulty in getting some of them in foal the first season or two after their arrival unless they were in foal when brought over; others breed as readily as native mares.

Occasionally a mare is encountered which breeds only every other year. Others will not come in season, or at least conceive, while suckling a foal. It is usually more difficult to get mares in foal in the fall than in the spring. The age to which mares will continue to breed is variable, but many have remained productive after passing the quarter century mark. Their breeding power declines gradually, being marked by occasional misses, occurring with increased frequency.

A mare which produces a good foal regularly is of priceless value in the breeding stud. When an apparently valuable breeder, although not in foal at the time, is offered for sale, it is safe to assume that she has proven herself barren or at least a shy breeder, unless, of course, there are other obviously good reasons to account for her being sold.

Hermaphrodites, individuals in which the sexual organs of both sexes are more or less completely represented, are, of course, sterile.

Reproduction is a natural function which requires simply a normal state of health and vigor for its accomplishment. The stallion does not need the artificial stimulation of drugs to insure his potency, neither can there be any virtue in " breeding remedies " for mares, other than that they may, like any antiseptic preparation, overcome acidity or correct a catarrhal condition in the genital tract.

When intelligent management of breeding animals, insuring, especially, a balance between feed and exercise, fails, it is probable that breeding is either structurally or functionally impossible.

Artificial impregnation is quite generally resorted to now by breeders of all classes of horses, both as a means of extending the services of the stallion and to insure the mares' getting in foal. The method of conveying the spermatic fluid from the vagina of the mare served, into the uterus of the same or other mares, by means of either the gelatine capsule or the impregnator—a specially designed syringe—is familiar to most horse breeders. When first advocated, artificial impregnation was opposed by mare owners, but when it is demonstrated that colts so conceived can not be distinguished from colts sired in the natural way, this prejudice gradually disappears. Peter the Great, the leading sire of trotters, got from seventy to eighty foals a year as a result of artificial impregnation being used in his case.

It is fundamental to the successful practice of artificial impregnation to know that the vitality of the male germ cell is so susceptible to the influence of light and temperature that it must be carefully handled and quickly transferred. " Colts by mail " is hardly feasible.

COST OF RAISING HORSES

Reports have been received from about ten thousand correspondents of the Bureau of Statistics of the Department of Agriculture upon the cost of raising colts on farms to the age of three years. The average for the United States is found to be $104.06; or, if we deduct the value of work done by the horse before he has passed his third year, namely, $7.52, the net cost is $96.54; this is 70.9 per cent of the selling value ($136.17) of such horses.

The cost varies widely by States, from an average of $69.50 for New Mexico, $71.59 for Wyoming, and $82.47 for Texas, to $156.60 for Rhode Island, $149.98 for Connecticut, and $141.80 for Massachusetts.

Itemized, the cost is made up as follows: Service fee, $12.95; value of time lost by mare in foaling, $10.06; breaking to halter, $2.22; veterinary service, $2.04; care and shelter, first year, $4.98; second year, $5.36; third year, $6.35; cost of grain fed, first year, $4.98; second year, $7.14; third year, $9.56; hay, first year, $4.14; second year, $6.61; third year, $8.48; pasture, first year, $2.56; second year, $5.41; third year, $6.21; other costs, $5.01; total, $104.06.

The total cost for all feed is $56.30, being $21.68 for grain,

$19.23 for hay, $14.18 for pasture, and $1.21 for other feeds. The total cost of care and shelter is $16.69. Of the total cost, 54 per cent is charged to feeds, 16 per cent to care and shelter, and 30 per cent to other items, as enumerated above.

As more than half the cost of raising a three-year-old horse on the farm is chargeable to feeds, it is readily observed how important is the influence of variation in prices of feedstuffs upon such cost.

REVIEW

1. Describe the forces involved in breeding.
2. What is the relation of the parent to the ancestry on the one hand and the progeny on the other?
3. Explain the greater breeding value of the pure-bred parent. What is the pedigree?
4. What is meant by prepotency and upon what may it depend?
5. What are the objections to cross-breeding and when is it justifiable?
6. What is the importance of studbook registration?
7. What are the objects of stallion legislation?
8. Why is " pure bred " an arbitrary term?
9. When may an unsoundness be considered hereditary?
10. Name the advantages of the community system of breeding.
11. Of what does the proper equipment of a breeding stud consist?
12. Describe the ideal sire and direct his care and management.
13. Describe the ideal brood mare and direct her care and management.
14. What can be said of breeding two-year-old fillies; of fall foaling?
15. What should the proper care of the foal from birth to marketable age include and how much should it cost?

PART IV
THE HORSE IN SERVICE

CHAPTER XIII

RELATION BETWEEN HORSE AND MASTER

History.—The first reference to the domesticated horse is in the Book of Genesis, Chapter xii, verse 43, and records him in use by the Egyptians in Joseph's time, 1715 B.C. Modern research, however, leads us to believe that the Egyptians derived their horses and ideas of horsemanship from the Libyans, the people of the other division of the Hamitic branch of the white race inhabiting Northern Africa and with whom the Egyptians were frequently brought in contact. From this centre the general distribution of horses throughout Arabia, Asia Minor, Asia, and Europe was accomplished with greater rapidity than has marked the advance in the domestication of any other animal. Contrary to a popular belief, there were no horses in Arabia at the beginning of the Christian Era. The horse has been and is yet, in primitive countries, preceded as a beast of burden by the dog, camel, ox, and ass.

Recently archæologists have unearthed evidence that the horse not only existed but was subjugated to the service of man in the Old Stone Age, when men lived in caves, worked and fought with implements and weapons of stone of most crude design, and were supposed to have domesticated only the dog and the reindeer.

The first use made of the horse was in warfare. The war chariot has been regarded as a creation of the Egyptians, but it is believed now that the design was borrowed from the Libyans. Later, the war horses were ridden, and hand-to-hand combat with spear or lance and shield was waged by their riders, although at first the horses served only for the transportation of the combatants to the field of battle, where they dismounted and fought on foot. With the adoption of armor, the size of the horse was materially increased, in order that he might be capable of carrying the gross weight of rider and armor both for man and horse.

219

With the invention of gunpowder the type of war horse was modified in accordance with the change in methods of warfare. Our modern cavalry charger is quite a different horse from the ancient " Great Horse " of the armored knight, which eventually became the prototype of our present drafter.

In ancient times it was customary for the victors in a conflict to drive their chariots through the towns in celebration of their victory, a practice now emulated by college students. This led to the adoption of the chariot as a feature not allied to war but representing the Church and State. White horses were preferred for this service, and a race of white horses was perpetuated in Lombardy and the purity of their lineage was guarded with great zeal solely for this purpose. The horse has been an important factor in civil and religious ceremonies ever since.

At an early period the horse was engaged in the sports and pastimes of the people. During the latter half of the twelfth century primitive horse sports, the most remote antecedents of modern polo and the gymkhana, were popular in England. In 1377 the first race was run between Richard Second and the Earl of Arundel. Racing and hunting have been followed in England for five centuries.

The general use of horses in the industries came later, although there is evidence of their having worked at draft in England during the eleventh century. Their importance in this line of service has increased in proportion to the development of agriculture and commerce.

Man's Obligation to the Horse in Service.—The horse is an involuntary, dependent party of the second part to all contracts; a silent and submissive partner in his alliance with his master. Theirs is a business relation in which the credits are all on one side, the debits on the other, and the horse is never accorded an accounting. Yet if the master would be fair and equitable, he must either concede a moral if not a civil obligation to pay for services rendered, or exact only such service as his care and management of his horses has placed to his credit.

In the feral state the horse is self-sustaining, expending his energy by utilizing his power or speed in securing feed, water, and protection from the elements and predatory foes; under natural conditions such expenditure may be considerable.

In Domestication.—The husbandman, with his system of domestication, substitutes an artificial for a natural environment, relieving the horse of all responsibility in the matter of feed, water, and protection, conserving to himself the energy that would otherwise be expended for that purpose. There is thus made available to the husbandman energy for work of whatever character the horse is capable, and to just the extent that energy has been saved. To balance the account, horses working up to their full capacity must be furnished all that is required for their subsistence and comfort; to underfeed or overwork is to overdraw the account, and against one who has not the usual privilege of protest.

Economic efficiency of the horse in service is more essential now than ever before, on account of the high cost of feedstuffs and the continued improvement in the motor vehicles with which the horse is in competition.

Two men may ride or drive the same horse or team over the same route with the same load and in the same time, yet there will be a marked difference in the condition of their horses after having accomplished the same task. This difference is due to a more intelligent use of the available motive power in the one case than in the other. If the various ways in which energy may be expended in the performance of work were more carefully taken into account, both the period of usefulness and the daily capacity of the average horse would be much increased.

A Horse's Capacity for Work.—The unit of measurement by which work is expressed is the foot pound or the foot ton, *i.e.,* the power required to lift a weight of one pound or one ton to a height of one foot against the force of gravity. The energy required to do work equivalent to 33,000 foot pounds per minute constitutes a horse-power. This estimate of a horse's power is not literally correct, however, but exceeds the capacity for work of the average horse by about one-third.

Horses have been forced, experimentally, to do the equivalent of 7800 foot tons in a day, but that is far in excess of their normal capacity, as shown by the marked loss in weight which attended such efforts. Three thousand foot tons has been fixed by Col. Fred Smith, Veterinary Department, English Army,* as a reasonable daily requirement of the horse, in work. This amounts, in actual performance, to:

Distance travelled.

Walking   at   3 miles an hour for 8.7 hours...... 26 miles
Walking   at   4 miles an hour for 5.3 hours...... 21 miles
Walking   at   5 miles an hour for 3.7 hours...... 18 miles
Trotting   at   8 miles an hour for 1.5 hours...... 12 miles
Cantering at 11 miles an hour for 1 ....11 miles

The same authority has determined a horse's maximum muscular exertion to be 68 to 78 per cent of his body weight, as registered by his pull on the dynamometer, not on the load. Such a pull, however, could be exerted but a few seconds, as in the starting of a very heavy load. The walking draft of a horse is given by King† as about 50 per cent of his body weight, while for a steady, continuous pull a draft of from one-eighth to one-tenth of his own weight is all that can be expected.

The weight-carrying capacity of a horse as reported by Smith is from one-fifth to one-sixth his weight, at severe exertion. If the pace is more moderate the weight carried may be increased. The weight carried is expressed in England by stone—one stone being fourteen pounds.

The factors determining the severity of a horse's work are the draft of the load, the pace at which the load is hauled or carried, and the duration of the period of work.

Draft of the Load.—The traction required to move a load is dependent upon the following conditions, acording to King:

1. The extent to which the pull is opposed by the force of gravity. The increase in the draft required to move a load up hill is proportionate to the increase in the grade. A 10 per cent grade increases the draft 10 per cent of the load.

2. The resistance offered by the road-bed to the wheel. This is least when the road is smooth and hard; greatest when rough or yielding. Rough roads impose a series of obstacles over which

---

* Veterinary Hygiene.
† Agricultural Physics.

the wheel must travel, while the depression of a soft road surface by the wheel creates a grade up which the wheel is continually being drawn, in effect, the degree of the grade being proportionate to the depth to which the wheel cuts. Experiments have shown that the traction of a given load over a common road is from three to five times as great as in the case of a well-paved surface.

3. Friction of the box on the axle. The degree of friction depends, primarily, upon the weight of the load, but may be modified by the style and condition of the axle and bearings.

4. Width of the tire. On the ordinary road the wide tire reduces the necessary draft by distributing the weight borne by the wheel over a greater area of road surface, thereby reducing the tendency of the wheel to cut into the roadway and giving the effect of a hard road, with its advantages. In an unusually soft or muddy road the wide tire may be a disadvantage. The saving in draft of as much as 120 per cent has been effected by the use of a six-inch tire instead of a one and one-half inch tire on ordinary going.

5. Size of wheel. It has already been shown that the depression of the road by the wheel results in that wheel being continually pulled up a grade, the steepness of which is in inverse proportion to the diameter of the wheel. Furthermore, the liability of the wheel to cut is in direct proportion to its diameter. The larger the wheel the greater the base of support for the load and the less the tendency to depress. Therefore, the smaller the wheel the greater the draft. Also, the greater the diameter of the wheel the more easily it is lifted over the obstacles which the rough surfaces of some roads present (Fig. 125).

6. The distribution of the load on the wagon. When only part of a load is carried it is customary with teamsters to place it well forward on the wagon for obvious reasons, but when a full load is put on it should be so distributed as to balance and divide the weight equally on all four corners, if the wheels are of equal size, or if the hind wheels are somewhat larger, as is usually the case, more weight should be allowed on the rear axle. Lightening the load forward has the advantage of permitting a certain amount of play in the front axle over rough

going. If the load is not evenly distributed, whichever wheel or wheels are overloaded cut more deeply into the road-bed, thus increasing the draft as described above. Furthermore, by the cutting in of one or more wheels the weight of the load is shifted in that direction, which increases the degree of the cutting still deeper.

7. The line of draft. As a general principle the line of draft should be parallel to the direction in which the wheels travel. On an absolutely unyielding surface this plane is parallel to the general surface of the roadway, hence the draw bars on railway cars and locomotives line up parallel with the rails. The ordinary wagon, however, is hauled over surfaces more or less yielding, consequently, allowing for the depression of the wheels,

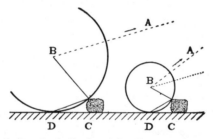

Fig. 125.—The draft acting in the line *A B* pulls on a bent lever, *B C D*, raising the weight which may be considered as concentrated at *D*. The longer the arm *B C* and the shorter the arm *C D*, the more easily will the draft raise the weight of the wheel and for the same sized obstacle the larger wheel will evidently have the advantage. In the figure the lines of draft make the same angle with the radius-arm of the lever. If the lines of draft are parallel, the advantage of the larger wheel is still greater.

they are really travelling more or less up hill at an angle with the apparent surface of the road. There should, therefore, be a corresponding slant in the line of draft, to avoid pulling down upon or against the incline of the depressed surface. The adjustment of the line of draft is governed by the length of the traces, on the one hand, and the height of their attachment at both hame and single-tree, on the other. In making such adjustment it should be borne in mind that, other things being equal, the traction is less the nearer the team is to its load.

8. Attachment of traces to hames. Whatever adjustment of traces is made for the purpose of giving the proper line of draft, it should not interefere with the angle which this line

forms with the hames. With a properly fitted collar, the pull should be as near as possible at right angles to the line of resistance, the hames, in order that the collar may bear directly against the shoulder, and not be borne down upon the withers nor up against the trachea. Furthermore, the height on the hames at which the attachment of the traces is made should be such as to distribute the bearing proportionately over the collar-bed, and allow the greatest freedom of shoulder motion. If attached too high the greatest weight is borne on that part of the collar-bed which is least capable of sustaining it, while if attached too low, as is more commonly the case, the point of the shoulder is overworked as well as being seriously hampered in its movement (Fig. 126).

9. The fit of the collar. While not directly influencing the degree of traction required to move a load, it has much to do with the application of the power by which the load is pulled. A horse's draft capacity is very often seriously impaired by his inability to exert himself to the limit against an ill-fitting collar. It is far easier to keep shoulders right than to restore them to that condition once they have gone wrong. The collar should be so well made as to retain its shape in use; it should be perfectly smooth and quite hard on its bearing surface, sweat pads more often inducing than correcting shoulder ills; it should conform to the general shape of the forehand of the horse, draft horses, with their comparatively low but muscular withers, requiring ample width at this point; and it should fit in such a way as to insure the best relation between the collar itself and those structures constituting the collar-bed with which it comes in contact (Fig. 127). A properly fitted collar should admit the thickness of the fingers between it and the shoulder all around, with sufficient room for the hand or even the wrist, over the trachea and the withers. Made-to-measure collars are a good investment, and, needless to say, the fitting should be made with the horse in working condition.

Dutch or breast collars should be so adjusted as to just miss the point of the shoulder below, yet not compress the windpipe above (Fig. 128).

The Rate at which the Load is Moved.—The pace at which

a horse is capable of exerting his draft power to the best advantage is from two to two and a half miles per hour, the ordinary walking rate. Power and pace are not correlated; the speed horse to accomplish his utmost must have the lightest impost of weight, while the draft horse requires full time allowance for the best performance of which he is capable; therefore, as more pace is required, less load can be hauled.

The Duration of the Period of Work, or the Distance Travelled.—The traction which a horse is capable of maintaining continuously, for a day's work, as plowing, is much less

  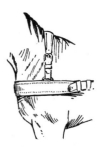

Fig. 126. — The angle formed by the traces with the hames should be as near a right angle as possible in order to insure the proper distribution of collar bearing on the collar bed.

Fig. 127.—The scapulo-humeral and elbow-joints, showing the position of the bones of the shoulder and arm and their relation to collar bearing.

Fig. 128. — The breast or Dutch collar in proper position.

than that which can be accomplished in one short, supreme effort, as in the starting of a load or even for a short haul.

There is an intimate give-and-take relationship existing among these factors by which the severity of a horse's work is determined. They represent the means by which energy is expended.

The Application of the Power.—What might be considered as the application of the power, on the part of the rider or driver, is a most important factor in limiting what a horse can do. Two drivers will show very different results in what they take out of their horses in accomplishing the same work. One husbands his horse's strength, speed, and stamina in such a way as to secure the maximum return for every unit of energy expended, with always a reserve upon which to draw, if need be. His horses are working or going well within themselves. Another, either by his ignorance or inconsideration, is always expending more of his horse's resources than is necessary to accomplish a given task, with the result that he is continually overdrawing the amount of energy available, and his horses are soon spent.

Warming Up Slowly.—To suddenly open wide the throttle of an engine or to throw to the last position, in one stroke, the control lever of a trolley car is productive of great mechanical injury, yet such abrupt application of horse power is common. A new engine runs " stiff " till warmed up; so does a horse, and especially an unsound one. A horse starting on a day's work or a road trip should have the collar warmed and shaped to his shoulders, his muscles actively contracting and extending, his joints thoroughly lubricated, breathing and heart action gradually accelerated, and bowels evacuated before he is called upon for his best effort. In the reverse order he should be gradually cooled and blown out before being put away at the conclusion of the day's work or road trip.

Notice to Drivers.—The following advice to drivers copied from a large city stable is typical of what is sought in most well-managed establishments:

1. Walk your horses for five squares going to and from the stable.

2. Water horses as often as possible.

3. In case of a sick horse notify the stable immediately.

4. Have your horses' manes and tails brushed, buckles straight, and straps in keepers before starting.

5. Reliable information of the ill treatment of any of our stock by drivers will result in suspension and, in serious cases, in prosecution.

Trotting down hill is much more injurious to legs and feet, though less fatiguing, than trotting up hill. A horse holds his breath during extreme effort, as in pulling; one with a tube in his throat will have his pulling power much impaired because he cannot hold his breath by closing the glottis. Therefore, an opportunity to fill the lungs by a couple of full, deep breaths at frequent intervals during a hard pull will not only slow down the hurried, shallow breathing, but will actually increase the power of the horse to pull. Every advantage of grade and going should be availed of, and the horse spared most when great effort would be most futile.

The Natural Gait.—The majority of horses acquire a natural pace which they maintain with little effort. If continually urged to a slightly faster rate of speed they are soon distressed, even though the actual saving of time in the distance travelled is immaterial.

Condition.—The fundamental factor determining efficiency for work, other things being equal, is condition or fitness. Fitting renders a horse more efficient, because by it there is established a state of health, vigor, and muscular tone in which there is a concordant action between lungs, heart, muscles, digestion, and nerve control. Condition is indicated by a spirit of keenness for work, brightness of the eye, bloom of the coat, and an absence of fat, exposing the outline of the individual muscles, with a characteristic hardness of the muscles themselves. Condition is a matter of degree, the most extreme of which is found in the race horse and hunter, less in the road and work horse, and still less in the park or show horse, a surplus of fat being desirable in the latter case.

Fat is an element of condition in the draft horse in which it has the real advantage of adding to his weight in the most natural way, as well as affording him a reserve store of energy upon which to draw in his long hours of arduous daily service. It must be put on, however, under the same conditions as obtain in the regular life of the draft horse, namely, while at work; otherwise it will prove an impediment and will not be retained long.

Balance Between Feed and Exercise.—Condition is the result of the mutual balance between feed and exercise, and requires the keenest powers of observation for its detection. Overfeeding and insufficient exercise on the one hand, and under-

feeding with overwork on the other, are the two causes which
destroy the balance necessary for condition. It can only be
obtained by degrees and cannot be forced without disastrous
results. Exercise and feeding should be gradually begun and
results carefully noted day by day, with a uniform increase up
to the maximum and a correspondingly gradual decrease when
the horse is to be thrown out of training.

Hardening the Skin.—Draft and saddle horses should have
their skins hardened to the friction of the collar and saddle in
addition to being rendered physically fit.

A marked difference between individuals is found in the
manner in which they round into form, in the fitting process.
Frequently those which attain fitness most readily are the first
to go stale.

Degree and Time.—The more extreme the degree to which a
horse is conditioned the shorter the period during which that
degree of fitness can be maintained. The modern practice of
keeping race horses in training and fit to start at any time during
prolonged campaign seasons presents many more difficulties than
fitting for a single race, when the horses can be trained to the
minute.

An Intuitive Art.—The fitting of horses for racing, showing,
or work is an art which requires the keenest horse sense, judgment, and discernment. There is no school for trainers; the
art is natural, not acquired, and it is doubtful if the master
trainers themselves could coach another to do what is intuitive
with them.

Condition has an economic importance, for a horse is capable
of his maximum efficiency, in his respective fields of service,
only when fit. The work horse, on account of the regularity of
his occupation, offers the least difficulty to the conditioner;
while the saddle and harness horse, whose work is more severe
when it does come, and it comes with the greatest degree of
irregularity, in accordance with the whim of their owner, require special care. There is no correlation between fitness for
work and resistance to unsoundness, but a leg-weary horse is
especially liable to interfere, forge, stumble or slip, thus predisposing to permanent injury.

REVIEW

1. When, where, by whom and for what purpose were horses first used?
2. What is the master's obligation to his horse?
3. What is a horse's average capacity in foot tons per day, draft, and weight carrying?
4. What factors determine the severity of a horse's labor?
5. Upon what does the draft of a load depend?
6. Describe the proper fit of collar and adjustment of traces and hames.
7. How should horse power be used for greatest efficiency?
8. When is a horse in condition and how is it indicated?
9. Of what does conditioning a horse consist? and what personal qualifications are involved?
10. What may be the consequences of working horses when not in condition?

CHAPTER XIV

THE FEEDING OF HORSES

ONE of our leading texts on feeding has this most appropriate quotation on its fly leaf: " The *eye* of the master fattens his cattle."

The feeding of stock is both an art and a science. The artist does not employ a **T**-square and compass, nor does he resort to mathematical equations to express his conceptions on canvas. The accuracy of his results is in proportion to his skill. The scientist, on the other hand, is exact to the fifth decimal and is held to the most absolute accuracy in his methods of determination.

Scientific research has provided us with most valuable data bearing on the subject of nutrition, but the possession of such data alone does not constitute all of the qualifications of a successful feeder. In an effort to make feeding an exact science there is danger of losing the art. Provide two feeders of similar classes of stock with the same scientific data and allow them both access to the same mows and bins, yet there may be a wide variation in the results obtained by each. One lacks the *art* of applying the *science;* it is as essential to know how as what to feed.

Art in Feeding Horses.—This is especially true of the feeding of horses. The block animal has simply to *be* a superior carcass, and to this end he is provided with every advantage, and requires from but a few weeks to three years, at the most, for its attainment. A horse's obligation is to *do* rather than to *be;* he is required to perform more complex functions, and for a period of such duration as will justify the greater initial investment which he represents. The nature of a horse's work is so exacting and yet so variable, his opportunity for mental and physical disturbances so great, and his misuse so common, that in his case no standard or rule can be applied unalterably.

Successful horse feeders are " artists " with eyes for the " fattening " of their stock. They balance their rations, not so

231

much from a knowledge of either German or American feeding standards, as from the actual requirements of the horses themselves. These requirements are indicated by their spirit or " feel "; the expression of their countenance; the condition of their coats and legs; and the color, odor and consistency of the fæces. If feeders read these signs aright it will usually be found that the rations fed will check up very closely to what would be a balanced ration if calculated on the basis of generally accepted feeding standards.

Two Systems Compared.—In the feeding of cattle and hogs the lot is the usual unit, but in the case of horses, even more than with dairy cows, the individual is the unit, and even his individual requirements may be subject to considerable variation. One system of supposedly economic feeding is to calculate, in the office, from the requirements set forth in the Wolff-Lehmann or modified standards, the rations to be fed, compare them with the stock of feed on hand and the number of horses to be fed, then notify the stable boss that his feed should last till a certain date, and hold him responsible for any shortage. This system ignores, completely, the individual requirements of the different horses, which only the artist feeder can appreciate and meet. Another way is to employ a thoroughly competent feeder, provide anything and everything that he may desire in the feed line, allow him every latitude in the use of it, and then hold him responsible for results only, as measured by the fitness and capacity of his horses for their work. The former method may be more economic of feed consumed, but the latter will be much more productive per unit of feed consumed, which is the real economic consideration.

How the Feed is Used.—The horse utilizes the constituents of his ration,—the water, ash, protein, carbohydrates and fat chemical compounds,—in the growth and maintenance of his body structure, in supporting the vital processes by which he lives, and in performing those functions which we designate as work. The extent to which the ration contributes to either or all of these depends upon the relative proportions of each of the compounds it contains.

Water is present in considerable amount in all tissues, being contained in the protoplasm of the cell, the unit of structure of the animal body.

The inorganic material of bone, to which its strength and texture are due, is largely calcium phosphate, although other mineral or ash constituents are present in other tissues of the body.

Protein is the chief source of the cell protoplasm and is the most important tissue builder.

The carbohydrates are fat formers and, in addition, furnish the energy necessary to do work, after the operation of the vital functions and the maintenance of the body temperature have been taken care of.

Fat serves the same purposes, but with a caloric or heat value 2.25 times as great.

Rations Not All Alike.—It is obvious that mature animals at work, at rest, pregnant mares, or growing colts require rations made up of these compounds in different proportions. When the proportions of the protein on the one hand and the carbohydrates plus the fats on the other are such as to just meet the requirements of the horse in question, with no excess of either, the ration is said to be *balanced*. The relation of the protein to the carbohydrates plus fats is expressed as the *nutritive ratio*. This is determined by adding to the digestible carbohydrates contained in the ration, the fats multiplied by 2.25, then dividing the sum by the amount of the protein. The protein is to the carbohydrate as one is to the quotient.

The ration is considered *wide* if the ratio of carbohydrates plus fats is large when compared with the protein. If the ratio is small the ration is called *narrow*.

There is no relation between the balance and the sufficiency of the ration. A horse may starve on a perfectly balanced ration of insufficient quantity, or he may be surfeited with feed and yet suffer from malnutrition if the relative amounts of protein and carbohydrates plus fats are not properly balanced.

In view of the fact that maintenance requirements, which amount to about 50 per cent of a full ration, will be satisfied before anything is available to be turned to work, the full ration, so far as quantity is concerned, is most productive.

Nutritive Requirements of the Horse.—The horse's daily nutritive requirements, according to the Wolff-Lehmann feeding standards, are as follows. The amounts are for one thousand pounds of live weight:

	Dry matter	Protein	Carbo-hydrates	Fats	Nutritive ratio
Light work	20 lb.	1.5 lb.	9.5 lb.	.4 lb.	1 : 7
Medium work	24 lb.	2 lb.	11 lb.	.6 lb.	1 : 6.2
Heavy work	26 lb.	2.5 lb.	13.3 lb.	.8 lb.	1 : 6

Smith * concludes, however, from the investigations of Langworth, of the United States Department of Agriculture, and others, that the protein standard is too high; that the majority of American work horses are doing their work acceptably, without loss in condition, on a ration of 1 to 8 instead of 1 to 6.

Three Types of Feed.—A ration may be composed of three types of feedstuffs,—concentrates, roughage, and succulence. The relative amounts of each, which the ration should contain, will be determined by the class of horses fed. The horse is an automobile in that he moves by his own power, and is not a stationary engine, as are cattle, sheep, and hogs, so far as their productiveness is concerned. It is important, therefore, that he expend as little as possible of energy available, in simply transporting the mass of his own body. Hence, the horse at work must carry his ration in more or less concentrated form, according to the nature of the work. But some bulk in the digestive tract is necessary, for physiological reasons. A horse would practically starve to death on concentrates alone. Roughage should be allowed but its amount regulated according to the nature of the work, and it should be fed mostly at night, when it will cause least interference. An idle horse can take a greater proportion of his ration in roughage than one at work, and the drafter moving at a walk, with weight an advantage, can be allowed more roughage than the race horse, in whose case weight is a handicap and bulk an impediment.

Succulence is useful in the ration, not only for the nutrients it contains but for the palatability which it lends and its physio-

---

* Profitable Stock Feeding.

logical effect on the digestive tract and condition of the animal in general. The use of succulence for horses at work must be guarded or it will induce such a lax condition of the bowels as to seriously interfere with their serviceability. Succulence is admissible according to the nature of the work a horse does, as in the case of roughage.

CONCENTRATES FOR HORSES

Oats.—The concentrate best adapted to the feeding of horses is oats; on account of both chemical and physical composition, they stand first in this class. They not only meet the protein and carbohydrate requirements best, but the hull is an advantage, in so extending the kernel as to insure most complete digestion. Besides, there seems ample reason for believing that oats improve the fettle, especially of harness and saddle horses. The cost price of oats is high, however, and in the interests of economy they may be displaced by the other feeds, either wholly or in part, without any serious detriment to the ration.

Corn is the logical substitute for oats in most sections of this country. In fact, economy demands the use of corn in the ration of the work horse to a much greater extent than it is used at present.

When its general use in the corn belt States is considered, much of the prejudice of the Eastern feeders loses weight. The average Iowa horse, for instance, is produced by a dam which was raised on corn, and had no other grain during the period of carrying and suckling her foal. The foal receives a little cracked corn or even cob corn for his first bite, with the amount gradually increased until he is allowed from 20 to 40 ears per day at maturity. In spite of this fact, when these very horses come East, top our markets, and pass under the management of the city stable boss, corn is absolutely prohibited as dangerous to feed; yet it requires a long time to induce and teach some of these horses to eat anything else.

Corn Supplements.—An exclusive corn ration is not to be recommended, but corn in combination with either oats and bran, bran or cottonseed meal alone is all right. Recent investigations at the Iowa station have shown that corn with cottonseed meal, in the proportions of 9 to 1, constitutes a perfectly satisfactory ration for the work horse, and is effective of a very material saving in cost.

Ear corn is most desirable for horse feeding, as the kernels keep best in the original package, as it were. There is a certain freshness about it that horses prefer, and, besides, they are compelled to eat it slowly. Corn in this form, however, is bulky to handle in the trade and few city stables are equipped to store it in any quantity. The most reasonable objection to the more general feeding of corn, off the farm, is the difficulty in securing ear corn in good condition.

Shelled or cracked corn is more convenient for all but the farmer feeder. It is not so safe nor satisfactory as ear corn, however.

Cornmeal coarsely ground, and in combination with oats, bran, or cottonseed meal is excellent, providing the corn can be ground as required. But the commercial meal is more liable to cause trouble by its oil becoming rancid and the mass spoiling than is corn in any other form.

It is probable that the opposition to corn for horses, so common among both city feeders and their veterinary advisers, is due more to the quality and condition of the corn which usually reaches city horses than to the composition of the corn itself. The satisfactory results which attend its judicious use in the country, generally, would seem to vindicate the contents of the corn crib from responsibility for the alleged evils of corn feeding. By properly balancing the ration of which corn forms a part, the much dreaded " heating " effect may be largely overcome.

Bran ranks third as a horse feed, although it can hardly be considered as an exclusive feed, except for occasional or exceptional use. In work stables it is customary to feed a bran mash, preferably wet, at least once a week, and that Saturday night. The practice is commendable, as it tends to offset the effect of continued high feeding of horses at hard work, as well as being acceptable to the horses for the sake of variety. Much depends upon the preparation of the mash. The coarse, flaky, winter wheat bran is preferable; add sufficient water to moisten it thoroughly, so that it breaks nicely, but without any semblance to a slop, then season with salt and a little ginger or gentian.

Shorts and middlings are too concentrated to be fed to horses except in small quantities, and then they should be in combination with some of the other more bulky grains. Some horses show an especial susceptibility to digestive disturbances when middlings are fed.

Dried brewers' grains, now quite generally fed to dairy cattle, have not been utilized by horse feeders to the extent that trials of their feeding value would seem to justify. The increasing demand for them among dairymen will no doubt advance the price, but they are comparatively much cheaper than either oats or bran. In combination with either of these or with corn they have given satisfaction so far as they have been tried. They are reckoned about equivalent to oats, pound for pound.

Barley is the most common cereal feed for horses in some parts of the country where it is extensively grown. It is well adapted for that purpose provided it is crushed before feeding. The presence of the awns may prove irritating to the horse's mouth.

Canada field peas deserve more general consideration than they receive from horse feeders. When available they may be profitably employed in combination with other concentrates in making up the work horse ration.

Linseed oil meal is more commonly fed as a conditioner than for its nutritive properties, although the Iowa station has shown favorable results from oil meal combined with corn and oats for the purpose of reducing the cost of the ration, the oil meal displacing the oats otherwise required to balance the corn. It has a most valuable physiological effect on the bowels, coat, and the nutritive functions in general. It helps restore condition in horses which have either been overdone by feeding or are in a state of malnutrition. It is usually fed to secure finish and bloom, in fitting horses for show or sale, in quantities up to but not exceeding a pound per day.

Cottonseed meal has been tested in feeding trials at both the Pennsylvania and Iowa stations, with such satisfactory results that it is now generally recommended as a complete or partial substitute for oats, in combination with corn, to cheapen the ration. No bad results are reported from feeding two pounds per day. It is not palatable and its taste should be obscured in the mixture with other feeds.

Molasses.—Little was said of molasses as a horse feed, although it had been fed to a limited extent as a conditioner, until about 1900, when a United States Army veterinarian, Doctor Griffin, reported its exclusive use with hay by the native Cubans, their hardy ponies doing remarkably well. This report was published in the *American Veterinary Review* and engaged the attention of Doctor Geo. L. Berns, of Brooklyn, New York, who gave it a thorough trial in some of the large stables of draft horses under his supervision. The results were such as to thoroughly convince him that molasses deserved a place in the dietary of all work horses, not alone for the sake of economy but because it has a most beneficial effect upon the digestive system. Dr. Berns still holds to this opinion, which has been quite generally confirmed by others who have made observations along this line. Remarkable results have been secured by a liberal feeding of molasses in bringing back to condition horses either convalescent from sickness or those in very poor flesh. It is a valuable " coaxer " to shy feeders. Its laxative effect must be guarded against to a certain extent. Molasses is usually fed in quantities of from one pint to one quart, per feed, diluted with at least an equal quantity of water and preferably mixed with other feeds. Reports are made of feeding as much as ten pounds per day to mules in Louisiana. There are about twelve pounds to the gallon. It is especially well adapted to the coarse, mixed ration in which cut hay or straw forms the base.

Whatever the ration, its palatability as well as its nutritive value is increased by the addition of molasses. It is a constituent of many proprietary feeds, serving to disguise and render more edible the fraudulent ones. The black strap cane molasses, not the beet-sugar product, is the kind fed. Undiluted molasses is unsatisfactory, as it smears the muzzle, and from it the sides of the horse, and is especially objectionable in fly time.

Wheat and rye both make acceptable horse feeds provided

they are crushed to prevent the formation of paste in the mouth. The market price of wheat, especially, allows of its being fed only under unusual conditions.

Other materials, the availability of which is more or less restricted, may prove worthy of a place in the horse's ration when and where they can be secured at low cost. For example, one enterprising Philadelphia city teamster met the high cost of oats and corn, of recent years, by introducing a ration of molasses and stale bread, on which his horses did well.

ROUGHAGE FOR HORSES

Timothy is in a class by itself as a roughage for horses, the leafless nature of the plant insuring nearly perfect curing and freedom from dust in the hay. In addition there is a constringent property in timothy by virtue of which horses filled up with it keep hard and do not become washy on the road, as horses will if fed on the hay from a legume or on fresh grass. The market value of timothy hay is not in accordance with its chemical composition. The very feature which horsemen favor in it is correlated with a low coefficient of digestibility. As a means of affording, in the ration, the bulk and volume necessary for a physiological distention of the digestive tract, to maintain it normally functional, timothy is ideal. Horses like it, if not too ripe, but as a source of nutriment it is inferior to the hay of clover, alfalfa, and other legumes.

Legumes, with their extensive leaf surfaces, are much richer in digestible nutrients but more difficult to properly cure. When improperly cured they are unfit to be fed to horses. The causal relation between clover hay and heaves has been fairly well established. It is alleged not to be due to the dust, in general, with which clover hay is likely to be filled, but to a specific fungus, the growth of which is peculiar to legumes. It is true that the history of most cases of heaves reveals clover hay in the ration, although there is nothing remarkable about this, as the majority of horses are so fed. On the whole, we cannot afford to count clover-mixed hay out of the ration of the average horse. But in view of the possibility that may result from feeding it, we should consider carefully the quality, and guard the quantity, of that allowed. It is best mixed with timothy in about such proportions as come in the second season's cutting from a timothy-clover seeding.

Alfalfa is in the experimental stage as a constituent of the horse's ration. There is no reason why its judicious use, in combination with timothy, should not be recommended. Good alfalfa hay is about the most tempting thing that can be put before a horse in the winter time, as he himself will attest if allowed the opportunity. In addition to its palatability and high content of easily available protein, alfalfa has a beneficial action on the digestive tract. The amount fed, with timothy, can be so regulated as to control the bowels to a fine degree. On account of its 10 to 15 per cent of protein, alfalfa should be balanced by the other constituents of the ration, lest an excess of protein be fed. An excess of nitrogen would require elimination by the kidneys, which may prove injurious.

Alfalfa hay has not been fed in the East extensively enough to determine whether or not it may induce heaves. Those parts of the country where it is most extensively grown and fed furnish only exceptional cases of heaves from any cause. It would be difficult to obtain a cured forage plant in a more perfect state of preservation than some of the alfalfa hay that is produced in the semi-arid Rocky Mountain States. So long as hay produced under the ideal conditions for growth and curing which prevail there can be placed on Eastern markets, to compete with the home-grown product, favor is likely to be shown the former. The Eastern farmer should be encouraged in the production of alfalfa. The addition of alfalfa hay to a ration will both reduce the cost of maintenance and improve the condition of any class of horses.

Ground alfalfa may be used in place of bran, in combination with other concentrates, but unless combined with molasses or moistened it is so light and fine as to be readily blown away, and has the objection of being dusty. Many prepared alfalfa feeds, of this class, are offered to the trade. The hay has the same nutritive value and, if of good quality, will be as completely and enthusiastically consumed as when artificially prepared. These facts argue for the more general use of the hay.

Cow pea and soy bean hay are both reported upon favorably by those who have fed them as a part of the roughage. Like corn stover they are available to feed only on the farms where grown.

Corn Stover.—In the early winter, before the leeching and blowing away of its most nutritive and palatable parts has been accomplished, corn stover is one of the best kinds of roughage for horses, either at rest or at work. It has a nutritive value about equal to timothy hay, from which it affords a change. Horses do not fill to excess on it as they do on hay, and it is positively beneficial to horses which have mild cases of heaves aggravated by the feeding of hay of even good quality. Horses eat the leaves and pick at the stalks readily without shredding. In fact, they seem to prefer stripping the leaves from the stalks rather than seeking out the finer parts from among the sections of stalk, in the cut or shredded stover. Idle horses will strip and eat quite a large portion of the stalk itself, if not over-supplied with the finer parts. More corn stover will be eaten if hay is not furnished at the same time.

In many parts of the South the tops and leaves are pulled from the corn plants, cured, and done up in bundles for horse feed. Pulled corn and sheaf oats are highly esteemed for the purpose of bringing back a stale show or race horse or to start one already in poor condition.

Oat straw, if bright, well cleaned, and not too ripe, does well for horses not at hard work. Its feeding condition is improved by chaffing and moistening with diluted molasses.

Sheaf Oats.—When available, sheaf oats are excellent for horses with ample time in which to feed.

Cereal Hay.—The cereals, especially barley and oats, either or both in combination with field peas, make excellent hay for horses if cut in the dough stage. Their use, like that of sheaf oats and pulled corn, would be resorted to in order to meet special requirements or secure unusual results, rather than in the economic maintenance of horse power.

SUCCULENCE

Succulence is most essential to horses which do not have the stimulating effect of their ration offset by an abundance of exercise, although its use is not objected to either with work horses or even race horses in training.

Pasture.—Grass is the most natural and satisfactory form in which to furnish succulence, as it also necessitates healthful exercise in the open air in order to secure it. Unfortunately, it is not available at all seasons of the year nor under all circumstances. It must, therefore, be substituted or supplemented.

Carrots are the best root crop for horse feeding. Like other roots, their physiological benefits outweigh their nutritive value. For the winter feeding of colts and brood mares they are especially desirable, while they form a staple article of diet in most stallion-importing establishments, where it is necessary to carry the horses along in high condition all the time and yet keep them right. Carrots are fed either whole or sliced, but to slice them to a size too large to swallow but too small to chew is more liable to induce choking than if fed uncut.

Soiling crops are sometimes fed to breeding or show horses. In France it is common to feed green cut alfalfa (Lucerne). Such green material must be fed to horses as soon as wilted and before heating or decomposition of any degree begins.

Silage has been condemned by most horse feeders and justifiably so, for much of the data concerning its use have been unfavorable, fatal results being commonly reported. Recent feeding experiments, however, have demonstrated that silage may be safely fed to work horses and growing colts, if of best quality and limited to from ten to twenty pounds per day. Silage the least bit moldy or spoiled is dangerous for horses.

WATER

Water of good quality and ample quantity is essential to the good health, comfort, and efficiency of horses at work. A thirsty horse does not make the most of his ration; his digestive functions are impaired by the sense of thirst. Horses should be watered regularly, so they may be able to anticipate their opportunities. Regular watering at frequent intervals will probably insure the horse drinking more of fresher water in the course of the day than though allowed free access to water in the stall at ali times. The idea, more prevalent than one would believe, that a horse should be stinted in his water supply is incomprehensible. If the horse has much liberty in this matter he will rarely drink to his own detriment.

Watering when Warm.—It is dangerous to allow a fill of water when the horse is very warm, but better then than never, as is liable to be the case in many poorly managed stables. A moderate drink will refresh and benefit any horse at any time.

Public Watering Troughs.—Indiscriminate patronage of public watering troughs in cities is fraught with the danger of glanders infection. A bucket, which could be filled direct from the inflow, and the horses watered from it, might well be made a part of the equipment of each work horse outfit.

Time to Water.—Theoretically, watering should precede feeding, in order not to flush on into the intestines the incompletely digested feed contained in the stomach, at the time the drink is taken. In practice, however, it is found that many horses will refuse to drink before eating, especially in the morning, and will seek a drink soon after feeding, if allowed any freedom in the matter. It is best not to follow feeding immediately by a drink.

A horse's drinking periods should be so arranged that he will not go to work immediately after a full drink. The common practice of allowing horses to drink their fill upon coming into the stable from work and again when going out is most convenient, but is not safe, although often followed with impunity.

The one time at which a horse requires and appreciates a drink most, yet is offered it least frequently, is the last thing at night, after having consumed his full allowance of roughage and being ready to lie down to sleep. Every horse, having worked through the day, should be allowed an opportunity to drink at this time.

SALT

Salt is required in small quantities, frequently, and regularly. The irregular allowance of too much salt with its consequent drinking of an excess of water does not meet the requirements in this respect. If given frequently or provided for the horse to help himself, only limited amounts will be taken. A satisfactory method of furnishing salt is to season the grain feed. A lump of rock salt in the feed box does fairly well, although the quality of the salt is not good. One of the best patented devices is a container for a cylindrical cake of high-grade salt, so arranged that the cake rotates as the horse licks the bottom of it. This insures the salt being used off evenly, the cylinder lasting until it is but a thin disc. The container screws into the wall of the stall at a convenient height. Loose salt should not be made too easy of access.

METHODS OF FEEDING

Regularity of Feeding.—Horses are creatures of habit and should be so managed that their daily routine is regular in order that each event may be anticipated in turn. This rule applies to feeding with especial force, it being the most important event of the day. Regularity of feeding promotes digestion, assimilation, and peace of mind. All horses in a stable should be fed at once, with as little delay as possible in getting to each, in turn, after the operation has begun. In most large stables the drivers have nothing to do with the feeding, that matter being better attended to by one man, who feeds each horse impartially and in accordance with his individual requirements.

Time of Feeding.—The daily ration is divided into three feeds given, when circumstances will permit, about six hours apart. City delivery service often necessitates much longer intervals between meals. Just a bit of roughage should be allowed in the morning, the bulk of it going with the evening feed. The division of grain is about equal for the three feeds, less being allowed at noon if the dinner hour is short.

Omission of the noon feed is practiced by some employers of horses and with apparent good judgment. The horse's digestive system, unlike that of the ruminating cattle and sheep, is so arranged that he requires feed in small amounts, at comparatively frequent intervals. There can be no argument of the fact that, under ideal or natural conditions, he should receive at least three feeds a day. But it is economically impossible to insure, to all work horses, ideal conditions. Short noon hours, horses hot when noontime arrives, and compelled to stand in the sun and fight flies while eating, wasting much of their ration, and then to go directly to hard work after feeding—this is the experience of many work horses. The nose-bag or other feeding device which will prevent the waste of a large part of its contents, especially in fly time, has not yet been perfected. It is as injurious to feed a hot, tired horse as it is to water him when hot. Feed consumed under such conditions is not well digested and assimilated, even if it does no harm, and its nutritive value to the horse is, therefore, small.

The danger of colic from putting a horse to work immediately after eating is unquestionable, as most cases of indigestion in working horses occur between one and four o'clock in the afternoon. In view of all these facts, there is good reason to conclude that the noontime spent in rest after a moderate drink, and the amount of the noon feed added to the night allowance, would be more beneficial to the horse if it is impossible to allow him proper time and place in which to feed.

The character and amount of the ration should be modified to meet each change in the work of the horses. Those well fed and working regularly are very susceptible to the so-called "Monday morning" disease, if laid off for a day or two. A short period of idleness calls for a material reduction of the concentrates of the ration and an increase in the lighter constituents, as bran or succulence. Horses temporarily put out of business by storms or holidays should be exercised, in addition to having their ration cut down. Once a horse has shown, by previous attacks, that he is especially predisposed to trouble of this character, he demands the closest attention, yet if this be accorded him he may work as satisfactorily as any horse in the stable.

Special preparation of the feed is of little advantage to the normal horse, under usual conditions. The crushing of oats at the ordinary mill is not considered worth while; although the installation of small mills, in stables which are already supplied with the electric current, may bring the cost of crushing down to a point where the end justifies the means. For old or overworked horses, the artificial mastication insures the more complete utilization of the feed. Crushed or rolled oats have a corrective effect on the bowels of horses prone to be washy, which would warrant their use in such cases.

Cutting or chaffing hay or straw makes it possible to combine it with the concentrates of the ration to the mutual improvement of both. The roughage extends the concentrates, so that they will be more slowly eaten and more perfectly digested. The addition of the concentrates induces the horse to eat more of the roughage, especially if the latter is straw.

Moistening hay or straw, especially if chaffed or dusty, improves its condition.

Variety in the ration is most acceptable to the horse and is to be sought, but its introduction should not involve any sudden or radical change, especially if either corn or middlings be used.

REVIEW

1. Why should horse feeders, especially, be " artists "?
2. How is the feed used by the horse?
3. What are the daily nutritive requirements of a horse?
4. Of what three types of feed may the ration be composed, and what are the special requirements of the horse in regard to each?
5. Why are oats considered the most desirable concentrate for horse feeding?
6. What are the advantages and disadvantages of corn as a horse feed?
7. To what extent may molasses be fed to advantage?
8. Why is timothy hay especially in demand by horse feeders?
9. Of what value is alfalfa to the horse feeder and how should it be fed?
10. What is the importance of succulence for horses and what may be its source?
11. At what times, in what quantities, under what conditions and where should horses be permitted to drink?
12. Why should horses be fed at regular periods?
13. Under what circumstances may it be advisable to eliminate the noon feed?
14. What precautions should be observed in the feeding of work horses, temporarily idle?
15. When should the grain be ground, the roughage cut, or the ration varied?

CHAPTER XV

STABLES

The character of the habitations in which horses are required to live varies from the simplest kind of an enclosure, affording no protection whatever, to the most luxuriantly appointed quarters, as those in which some gentlemen's show horses are stabled. As a rule, the more artificial the conditions under which horses are used, the more complete the system of stabling required.

There are two general classes of stables, town and country, the principal features of location, design, construction, and management of which are, necessarily, quite different.

Location.—There can usually be very little option exercised in the selection of the site of the town stable, but in the country the situation of the horse's quarters should be given careful consideration. The horse stable may be distinct from or included within the farm barn; but in either case it should be built on high, well-drained ground, with a southern exposure, if practicable. The benefits of the light and heat of the sun's rays are insured for a longer period in the day, and the temperature of the stable is maintained more uniform, if admitted through southern windows. If a double row of stalls, back to back, are to be provided for, an east and west exposure will be fairest to the occupants of both sides.

The design and arrangement of stables should be made with a view to providing sufficient room to accommodate the requisite number of horses and vehicles to be housed, proper light, ventilation and drainage, comfort and security of the horses, and convenience of attendants and patrons. These being insured, the simpler the design the better.

Construction.—Frame stables predominate in the country, and if well built are entirely satisfactory, so far as the essentials outlined above are concerned, with the exception of greater danger from fire. Town stables are more frequently built of

247

brick, stone, concrete, terra-cotta block, or plaster. In the use of these materials for construction it should be borne in mind that a solid wall of masonry is cold and damp, and therefore sweats when the moist, warm air of the stable comes in contact with it. When horses are to stand next to outside walls they should be built with a hollow centre for a dead air space. Either concrete blocks, the hollow tile, terra cotta, or plaster have this advantage over the solid wall of stone or brick or the poured concrete construction. The plaster or stucco, either rough cast or smooth finished, on expanded metal lath, is a form of construction which has proved very satisfactory in a limited way and is comparatively inexpensive.

Dimensions of a stable are determined by the individual allowance for stalls, alleys, floor space, and other requirements.

Stalls are of two sorts, (1) the loose box stall and (2) the straight, standing, or slip stall. Box stalls allow a horse more liberty, either standing or lying down, and freedom to roll, an opportunity very much appreciated by most horses. Every stable should have at least one, but on account of the additional room and extra care required they are not practicable for all horses in large stables. The idea of turning a horse " loose " to " run " in a box stall is unreasonable. There is no advantage in having them larger than twelve feet square except in the case of a maternity or hospital stall, where it is necessary to get about the horse readily and to accommodate a foal. The straight stall is the one in which the majority of horses are confined, and should be of sufficient length to protect the horse from being kicked back of the heel post, and wide enough to enable him to lie down in comfort, yet not to induce him to attempt to roll. At least eight feet from manger to heel post and five feet in width is necessary for that purpose, the size of the horse to govern. Horses show better in shorter stalls, and in sale and show stables safety is often sacrificed on this account.

Stall partitions should be about eight feet high in front and five to six feet in the rear, heel posts carried to the ceiling, and should not be built up solid, but be open to allow a free circulation of air through the stalls. In a stall with solid walls the horse lying down is deprived of fresh air to such an extent as to almost smother him in some stables. Planks or panels should be horizontal, not upright, in order not to be split or shattered if kicked. This arrangement brings the impression of the shoe across the grain of the wood. Floors can be kept drier and be more thoroughly cleaned if the partition does not come quite to the floor (Fig. 130).

Bales.—One of our most experienced American authorities * is an ardent advocate of the bale in place of the fixed partition to separate horses, claiming for it economy of space and more latitude and comfort for the horses, with equal safety. The bale consists of two planks or boards, ironed together, to make a width of three feet, suspended 18 inches from the floor by a hook and ring in the wall at the head of the stall and by a rope or chain at the rear. Four feet is a sufficient allowance for an ordinary sized horse between bales, and they will do well in even less.

Stall Floors.—Stall floors may be of clay, plank, or pavement. In the selection of flooring material there are many ends to be considered. Well tamped clay is noiseless, affords a firm footing unless wet, and without question places the horse on the most natural tread. It does very well in country stables where the clay is available, straw is cheap, and manure is of value, with the horse out of the stable much of the time. It is especially well adapted for use in box stalls. However, it is not easily cleaned and requires frequent repairing to keep the surface even and free from holes and depressions. Plank floors do not tire a standing horse, are warm to lie upon, and are not slippery, but they are neither durable nor sanitary, being more or less pervious and absorbent. Paved floors have the advantage of durability and are most sanitary, being impervious and easily drained, but they are hard to stand upon, slippery, noisy, cold to lie upon, and generally undesirable from the horse's point of view. Notwithstanding, they are well-nigh indispensable in large city stables, and a satisfactory compromise, in consideration of the horse's personal preference in the matter, is made by supplying a well-fitted rack. This is made of slats running lengthwise of the

---

* Ware, "First Hand Bits of Stable Lore."

stall, fixed at such distance apart as to admit but not catch the narrow calks or to prevent the entrance of broad calks, depending upon the type of horse to be stalled, the entire rack to be readily taken out, permitting thorough cleaning of the floor beneath. These racks, of course, wear out, but are more easily replaced than a floor, and while the horse stands on wood the sanitary features of the paved floor are procured. Concrete, rough cast or corrugated, vitrified or cork brick, are the common paving materials.

Concrete floors may be made comparatively dry and warm by insulating the top coat from the rough bottom with a layer of tar paper or two coats of tar paint. Cork brick has proven satisfactory in dairy stables but has not yet been much used under horses.

Drainage.—The drainage of stalls may be by open or covered drains. Common experience is in favor of the open drain, the covered drain becoming stopped up frequently in spite of gratings and traps to prevent such occurrences. Drains consist of either a central or two lateral troughs, running either from about half way to the front of the stall, or the centre of the box, to a main drain passing in the rear of the stalls. Two lateral drains at the sides of the stall interfere less with the horse standing or getting up and down than does the central drain. The stall floors should incline slightly toward the drain but not enough to unbalance the standing position of the horse. Undrained stalls, in which absorbent litter is depended upon for the removal of the liquid manure, are most practicable for the average country stable and can be kept sanitary provided an abundance of litter is used. The high cost of bedding materials and the objectionable features of accumulated manure, together with the available sewer connections and possibility of frequent flushing, render the drained stable much more desirable in the city.

Litter for Bedding.—Bedding is used for several purposes: (1) To insure comfort to the horse, thereby inducing him to lie down and save his feet and legs as much as possible; (2) to keep the horse clean and free from stable stain; (3) to absorb and thus facilitate the removal of liquid manure; (4) to dilute and thus improve the physical condition of the manure for fertilizing purposes.

Bedding materials consist of straws, sawdust, shavings, peat moss, and, in the country, corn stover and leaves. The durability of the straws is in the order of rye, wheat and oat, while their absorbing capacity is reversed. Their relative values, therefore, will depend upon whether or not they are to be used in drained stalls. If that is the case they will be valued in the order named, but with an abundance of straw, and value attached to the manure, they would have an inverted valuation in the undrained stable, where the absorption by the bedding is depended upon for the removal of the liquid manure. The chaffy nature of oat straw would make it objectionable to use in drained stables. The market price is greatest for untangled rye straw, which is especially demanded in high-class stables, where the appearance is much enhanced by " setting fair " the bedding; then tangled rye, wheat, and oat in the order named.

Shavings and sawdust have the advantages of economy in most locations, a cleanly appearance in the stable, and to a certain extent they counteract odors, but they are difficult to handle, rather cold to lie upon, and undesirable in the manure on account of their dearth of plant food. Sawdust holds better on the stall floor but it is not so easily removed from the horses' coats as are shavings.

Peat moss is much more commonly used in England and Scotland than in America. It is imported by the shipload in large bales, chiefly from Holland and Germany, and is therefore cheapest in the Eastern cities. It has the advantage of durability, will absorb about ten times its volume of water, while straw absorbs but three, prevents stable odor, affords a comfortable bed either to lie or to stand upon, and does not stain gray horses, a property which alone is responsible for its use in many large stables. Like shavings and sawdust, stalls thus bedded are somewhat difficult to muck out. Peat moss has some fertilizing value and is therefore not objectionable in the manure, as are shavings and sawdust. If available at a price of about $12 per ton it will be found a most economical and satisfactory litter.

Corn stover must be either cut or shredded in order to be conveniently used for bedding. It is customary to feed a generous allowance and permit what is not consumed to go under the horses for bedding.

Feed boxes should be easily taken out in order that they may be frequently cleansed and kept sweet. Various schemes have been devised for the purpose of preventing too rapid bolting of feed and throwing it out. Aside from the patent slow feeding contrivances, a broad, flat-bottomed box which insures the feed being spread in a thin layer, or a few good-sized cobblestones placed in the ordinary box will serve to prevent hogging, while a flange about the rim of the feed box will help retain the grain, although increasing the difficulty of removing what feed is left, in case it may be necessary to do so.

Mangers for the roughage should not be placed higher than the level of the feed box and should be provided with either cross slats or some other means to prevent the hay being thrown out. They should be open at the bottom in order that they may be kept clean from dirt, chaff, and all trash. It is recommended by some that feeding be done from the floor, inasmuch as that is the natural position of the grazing horse. It has the advantage of cheapening construction and economizing stall space, as well as enhancing the security of the horse in the stable. It requires a careful allotment of hay, however, as what is not readily consumed will be wasted, and with those horses which have acquired the habit of pawing whatever is in front of them back under their hind feet it will prove a wasteful practice.

Ties.—A horse should be tied securely in his stall for the protection of both himself and others in the stable, but the method of tying should be such as to enable him to rest comfortably, yet without danger of becoming either cast or entangled in the halter shank. Comfort requires that a horse be permitted to lay his head flat on the floor, yet much more length than this will enable him to get a foot over the halter. Both comfort and safety are met by attaching a weight to the end of the halter shank equivalent to the weight of the shank itself, allowing the shank to slip through either a ring or a hole in the manger without being tied. The weight keeps the halter shank taut to the extent of not being slack in whatever position the horse's head may be without exerting any drag on the head. Another method is to tie a short halter shank to a ring which travels a perpendicular rod, in much the same manner as some cow ties are made. The length and adjustment of both rod and halter shank should be such as to allow the horse ample freedom, either standing or lying down, yet never permitting any slack in the strap. Halter shanks, whether rope, strap, or chain, should be attached to the head stall by a snap to insure certain and prompt release of the horse in case of emergency.

Passageways both behind and between stalls should be of ample width, and if paved should be roughed in some manner to prevent slipping. A smoothly finished concrete or asphalt pavement may be made safe by a thin coating of sharp sand replenished daily, or, better yet, the concrete may be corrugated or rough surfaced, even to the extent of a layer of fine crushed stone to give a foothold. This last, however, is more difficult to sweep and clean. If bricks are used they should be laid on an angle and be so bevelled and pointed as to afford a catch for the shoe.

Doors should be so located as to be most convenient yet least productive of drafts in the stable. Single doors should not be less than four feet in width and double doors eight feet. The usual height is eight feet. Rolling doors are preferable to hinged doors, especially in the interior of the stable as on box stalls, for the reason that they are always out of the way, while a partially open hinged door may project into a passage in such a way as to seriously injure a horse.

Windows should be ample in size and number to provide requisite light and ventilation. They should be placed high enough over the horses' heads to protect their eyes from the direct light of the sun. In the simpler systems of ventilation, the windows serve for inlets, and should for that purpose be so constructed as to drop inward from the top, thus directing the air toward the ceiling where it becomes diffused and gradually settles to the floor of the stable. The sides of the windows should be protected by fenders, which prevent side and downward drafts. The opening should be regulated in accordance with the velocity of the wind. Outlets are usually provided at the ridge pole, by direct flues from below or by an open ceiling.

The King system of ventilation is to be recommended whenever its installation is practicable. It is made up of two kinds of flues: (1) Those for intake of fresh air, and (2) those for the outtake of foul air. The intake flues start at a point two feet or more above the ground outside and extend to the inside near the ceiling. The outtake flues start near the floor of the barn and extend above the highest point of the roof.

Fresh Air Requirements.—The fresh air and cubic space requirements per horse should be considered in the construction of stables and the provision of windows. It has been estimated that a horse of average size requires approximately 15,000 cubic feet of fresh air per hour, and this is the ideal aimed at in the English Army. Col. Fred Smith in his book on Veterinary Hygiene describes a simple method of arriving at the horse's fresh air requirements and of determining whether or not these requirements are being met. He bases his conclusions on the fact that the horse inspires about 100 cubic feet of air per hour while in the stable, and his expirations completely vitiate air, to the extent that it would not sustain the life of a mouse, at the rate of twenty-five cubic feet per hour. This air requires a dilution of 150 times in order not to be injurious when rebreathed as it would be in the ordinary stable. De Chaumont's test makes it very simple to detect an injurious amount of respiratory impurity in the air. By actual analysis it has been determined that the sense of smell upon first entering the stable from the outside may be relied upon, not only to detect but to gauge the amount of respiratory impurities present. An amount up to .2 per thousand may be present without being perceptible; .4 per thousand gives to the air a smell suggested by the term " rather close "; .67 per thousand " close "; .9 per thousand " very close—offensive." Therefore, it is concluded that sufficient vitiation to be detected by smell renders the air unfit to be breathed and .2 per thousand has been taken as a standard of requirement. By the equation

$$\frac{\text{Amount of carbonic acid exhaled per hour}}{\text{The permissible organic impurities}} = \left\{ \begin{array}{l} \text{Fresh air required, 15,000} \\ \text{cubic feet per hour is de-} \\ \text{termined to be necessary.} \end{array} \right.$$

The cubic air space of the stable should be ample to insure to each horse the requisite 15,000 cubic feet per hour without such frequent changes of the volume of air as to cause drafts or a continuous fluctuation of temperature. Sixteen hundred cubic feet per head, requiring a complete change in the volume of air nine and one-half times per hour in order to furnish 15,000 cubic feet per head per hour, is the ideal aimed at in the designing of the English Army stable. Changing the air so frequently keeps the stable decidedly fresh and renders a horse more fit for service than for show. About one cubic foot per pound of weight is the usual rule in figuring the air space of the stable. It should be remembered, however, that the nearer the temperature and the atmosphere of the stable approaches that outside, the more capable the horse is of hard and fast work.

The size of the inlet or window necessary to admit the required amount of air is computed from the following table:

Data for Calculating Size of Inlet.

Description of wind	Mean velocity in miles per hour	Size of inlet to admit 15,000 cubic feet of air per hour
		Sq. ft.
Calm.................	3	1
Light air..............	8	0.4
Light breeze...........	13	0.2
Moderate breeze........	23	0.12
Fresh breeze...........	28	0.12

Rule for Computing.—Multiply the number of animals to be supplied with air by the size of the inlet corresponding to the estimated velocity of the wind. This divided by the number of ventilators on the inlet side of the building gives the size in square feet which each ventilator or window should be opened. Outlets should have the same opening in order to facilitate the movement of the air.

Fresh Air for Horses.—On account of the fact that most horses work regularly in the open air, the principles of ventilation are violated with greater impunity in their case than in the case of dairy cows. Existence in some city subway stables would be impossible were it not that the horses spend most of their time outside. The care of the stable and stable drainage are both factors concerned with fresh air, and properly done they remove an important source of contamination of the atmosphere.

The interior of the stable should be made as free from projections and possible sources of injury to the horses as may be. All hardware should be countersunk; harness hooks put

Fig. 129.—A model work horse stable, showing the main alley-way and general interior arrangement.

above the level of the horses' heads; dung forks, shovels, and all other implements put safely away; manure pits and trap doors thoroughly protected.

Wagon and harness rooms should be completely shut off from the stable and so situated as to be convenient for the harnessing and putting-to of the horses. In fact, the whole stable arrangement should be such that the turning out of the equipage, whether for business or pleasure, may be accomplished by progressive steps, with no retracing, from the grooming floor to the outside door.

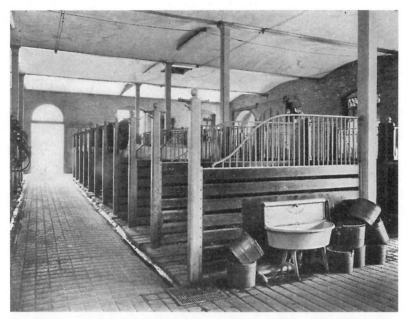

FIG. 130.—A model work horse stable, showing width of stalls, corrugated concrete floors, wooden racks in stall floors, width of alleys, drains and ventilating flues.

FIG. 131.—A model work horse stable, showing length of stalls, open partitions and front doors, the latter being a convenience for caretakers and obviating the danger of backing heavy horses on slippery floors.

The assignment of stalls should be made with a view of promoting congenial relationships between neighboring horses and avoiding the consequences of incompatibility.   Furthermore,

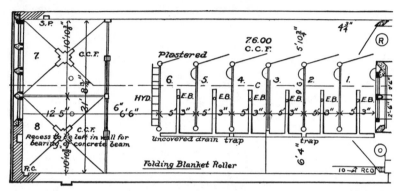

Fig. 132.—Plan and specifications for a small work horse stable with open front stalls.

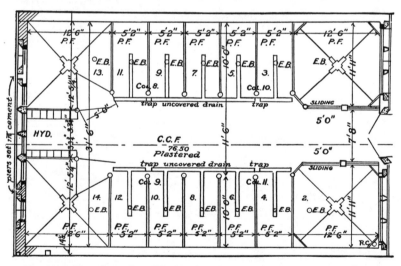

Fig. 133.—Floor plan and specifications for a convenient, comfortable, and sanitary city stable.

in large work stables, it is well to stable together those horses which work during the same hours.   This enables them to rest better, with less disturbance while in the stable (Figs. 129, 130, 131, 132, and 133).

Grooming is essential to the health and general appearance of the horse. Systems of grooming vary from the simple use of the bare hand and arm, as practiced by the Indians, to the most thorough and vigorous employment of a variety of utensils. The more highly bred, finer coated horses require more delicate treatment than the heavier coated and phlegmatic work horses. Utensils in common use are the metal curry-comb, bristle body-brush, corn brush, rub rag, sponge, wisp, and hoof pick. All grooming should be thorough but gentle, with due consideration for the sensibilities of the horse. Dandruff consists of shed particles of skin, waste products of metabolism, fat, and some salt. It complete removal is the primary object of grooming.

The first step usually is the use of the curry-comb the reverse way of the hair for the removal of dandruff and dry stable dirt, if there be any. The curry-comb should never be used about the head nor below the knees and hocks, should be dull (new ones preferably filed dull), and used with the greatest care. It is not permitted in many well-regulated stables, the wisp of straw and the corn brush accomplishing the same purpose. The bristle or body brush is used the right way of the hair to remove what the curry-comb or wisp has brought to the surface, also to brush the head and legs. The corn brush is used chiefly on mane and tail, although the latter may require additional picking by hand. The use of a comb, except on docked tails and pulled manes, is not desirable. The rub rag, used the right way of the hair unless in cooling out hot horses, puts the final finish on the coat.

In show and race horses the rubbing may amount to a most vigorous massage. The eyes, muzzle, and region under the tail should be sponged off; also the feet, after having been picked out. White points may be washed if necessary. Motor brushes and vacuum cleaners have not as yet been very generally adopted, even in large stables (Fig. 134).

Washing.—The frequent application of soap and water destroys the lustre of a horse's coat, beside rendering him especially liable to chill if not thoroughly dried out. Except in the case of pure white horses or in hot weather, washing is not to be commended, but is too frequently resorted to by indolent caretakers. There is really nothing gained in either time or labor, as it is as difficult to properly wash and dry a horse as to groom him completely.

Fig. 134.—A vacuum grooming machine in operation. A vacuum is maintained in the pipes which draws the dirt out of the hair and conveys it to a receptacle where it collects and can be removed.

Care of the Legs.—Horses of a lymphatic temperament, as most business horses are, working continuously in all kinds of going, require especial attention to keep them right in their legs. A proper balance between feed and exercise is the first consideration in keeping legs right. Then they must be thoroughly groomed, and dry grooming keeps the skin much less predisposed to disorder. So does the presence of hair, the arrangement of which, about the fetlock, naturally turns the water off the leg instead of running it down into the heel where the skin is most delicate. The most intelligent and experienced managers of city work horse stables, where the clipping of legs in the winter has been tried out, are opposed to it on this basis. Once the skin becomes affected, it may be necessary to remove the hair in order to reach the seat of the trouble. The old country plan of rubbing out legs with considerable feather is the best means of dry grooming them. Too much rough brushing may be irritating.

Horses' legs should not be washed unless thoroughly dried. If necessary to put away wet, the legs may be loosely bandaged to prevent chilling, until they have dried out. The fetlocks, pasterns, and heels may be protected against the snow brine common on city streets, and other irritating influences, by smearing them thoroughly with a coating of linseed oil before leaving the stable.

Care of the Feet.—The importance of having a horse " good on the ground," as the saying goes, is generally appreciated; but the structure of the foot itself, as a most important feature of conformation, is not always well understood. Furthermore, the necessity for keeping horses shod, which, in itself, is an injurious practice at best, renders consideration of the principles involved especially essential.

Shoeing.—The foot is not an immobile block to which a shoe can be nailed, but is capable of motion, interference with which will defeat the purpose which the foot is most ingeniously designed to serve, namely, the relief of concussion. Compare the unshod foot of the colt with the foot of the horse that has been shod in the ordinary way, for a number of years, and the detrimental influence of shoeing will be apparent. Notice the smooth, worn foot surface of the shoe that has been properly applied and the extent to which the foot expands and contracts, laterally, will be indicated.

Physiological Movements of the Foot.—This is what happens when the foot comes to the ground at the conclusion of the stride: As the weight drops on the foot the fetlock and pastern settle downward and backward, the internal structures of the foot are borne down upon, and in the normal unshod foot further depression is opposed by the contact of the frog with the ground. The structures compressed between the pedal or coffin bone above and the unyielding ground or roadway beneath are elastic, and yield in the line of least resistance, which is laterally. This sidewise expansion of the internal structures of the foot presses the bars and lateral cartilages outward, and with them the wall at the quarter, thus increasing the transverse diameter of the foot from one-fiftieth to one-twelfth of an inch. As this expansion is most marked in the back half of the foot, there is a corresponding narrowing of the hoof head in front.

Interference, by shoeing or otherwise, with this lateral expansion of the quarters, not only causes the full force of the concussion incident to the contact of the foot with the ground to be felt, but induces a cramped, stilty stride, as a result of the horse's effort to come down easily and thus spare himself the pain of concussion. It is a condition analogous to that of a man with a tight, unyielding shoe which pinches at every step as the weight is borne on it.

The destruction of the elasticity of the lateral cartilages by ossification, in the formation of side bones, has the same effect, marked both in the stride and in the altered form of the foot, the quarters becoming more narrow and straight.

Proper shoeing consists, first, in so dressing the foot that the removal of surplus horn does not destroy the balance of the foot, but leaves it with its axis unbroken either up or down, in or out, thus insuring an even distribution of weight and wear on the joints above (Figs. 135, 136 and 137). Only such horn should be removed from the sole or frog as is loose; the bars, natural braces to prevent contraction, should not be cut through, the heels " opened up," nor the sole concaved. The shoe must be made to fit the foot, not the converse, its upper surface being perfectly level and smooth to favor the sliding of the wall in the outward expansion of the quarters, not bevelled to turn the heels out; the nails should be placed far enough forward to leave the back of the foot free to expand on the branches of the shoe. Hot fitting, properly done, insures a better fit than is possible when the shoe is fitted cold, and is not injurious to the horn; in fact, there is some advantage in searing over the ends of the horn tubules.

Common styles of shoes are the plain open shoe, the bar shoe, designed for the purpose of giving frog pressure or protecting weak heels, tips, and pads.

Hoof Dressings.—The boot blacking idea applied to the feet of horses is inexcusable. No dressing is so attractive as the natural horn, perfectly clean. If it is desired to prevent the drying out of the horn after the removal of the natural varnish in the operation of shoeing, neatsfoot oil without the customary lampblack does not disguise but rather improves the natural appearance of the foot.

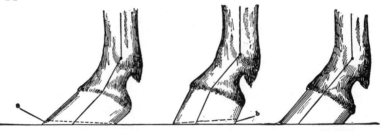

FIG. 135.—An untrimmed hoof with an excess of horn (a) at the toe which breaks the foot axis backward.

FIG. 136.—An untrimmed hoof with an excess of horn (b) at the heel, which breaks the foot axis forward.

FIG. 137.—Hoof dressed and foot axis straightened by removing excess of horn below dotted lines in the two preceding illustrations.

Clipping.—The removal of the hair consists of trimming and incomplete or complete clipping.

Trimming is the removal of the hair from certain parts only, as the foretop, fetlocks, or ears. Trimming is largely a matter of fashion.

Fashion in Horses.—The rule of fashion is not confined to the boxes about the arena of the horse show; it prevails also in the loose boxes adjoining the paddock. In compliance with the dictates of fashion heavy harness and walk-trot-canter saddle horses are docked, their manes pulled, but foretops left. By the same authority, light harness and gaited saddle horses carry full manes and tails; as a rule, while the former have foretops removed, the latter have their tails artificially set and have been known to wear " wigs." Hunters and polo ponies must submit to a hogging of manes and foretops, while the tails nowadays are suffered to remain full length, except for a square blocking of the end, perhaps, while the bulk of the tail is reduced by plucking the hair from the sides of the dock.

Drafters are docked but the hair is not trimmed. In the show ring their manes are rolled and plaited. The docked tail of the harness and saddle horse may be trimmed short like a brush, or have the hair parted, breaking straight down when the tail is set, with the ends evenly trimmed off, or the hair may be left untrimmed, as in the case of the so-called French tails; the second method is most popular in this country.

All " light-legged " horses have the feather and fetlocks removed to give a trim appearance, while some feather at least is desirable on the draft horse, to augment the appearance of bone, and even mild blisters may be resorted to for the purpose of stimulating its growth.

Business horses may have foretops trimmed and tails blocked as a matter of convenience. In stables of 100 horses, for instance, the additional time required in doing up and brushing out a long tail in bad weather is a considerable item in labor.

Partial clipping consists in removing the hair from the legs but not from the body, as is frequently done with business and road horses ; or the reverse, as is customary with hunters, the hair being left on the legs for the protection it affords in the hunting field.

Complete clipping is justifiable and even necessary under certain conditions. The horse naturally grows a heavy protective coat of hair in the fall which would be of the greatest service to him under his original natural conditions. However, the artificial conditions under which the average horse lives and works render an excessively heavy coat objectionable. The horse thus protected sweats unduly at either ordinary or fast work, is generally enervated and his system is relaxed, thereby rendering him especially liable to contract colds. Furthermore, it is difficult and sometimes impossible to completely dry him after a day's work. The removal of such a coat early enough in the fall so that a light, protective coat may yet be grown before severe weather is encountered, with care that artificial protection is always afforded, will render the horse more fit for work. Unless a horse is afflicted with an exceptionally heavy coat, and certainly not unless he will be provided with ample clothing at all times when not at work, he should not be clipped.

Clipping is also resorted to in the spring after the shedding process has begun, but before the new coat has started to grow out, to obviate the disagreeable features of the shedding coat, especially in the case of gray horses. Here, too, the substitution of blankets for the natural coat is required.

Clothing consists of blankets of various weights, hoods, and bandages. It serves to protect from cold, flies, and dirt. Show horses are heavily blanketed and covered for the purpose of keeping down their coats, although some fitters of draft horses secure the highest bloom without blankets. All blankets should fit comfortably, have their girths adjusted, and be put on in such a way as to leave the hair smooth beneath them.

The blanket is usually folded once each way, the cross fold being made first, then caught up so as to double lengthwise. The blanket should be taken up in such manner as to unfold in the reverse order from that in which it was folded up. If this is done the longitudinal fold will open as it is thrown over the horse, and if carried well over his withers, with the open edges of the transverse fold forward, the last step in the unfolding will bring the blanket over the horse's loins and croup, drawing it in the direction of the hair. To remove, it should be folded transversely backward, then caught up where the lengthwise fold is to come and drawn off backwards in such· a manner as to leave the hair smooth.

Hoods are used in conjunction with blankets on race and show horses to cover all but the eyes, ears, and muzzle. It is important that they should fit well about the eyes and ears.

Bandages are used either to protect the extremities from chill, in which case they are rolled loosely, or to exert gentle pressure in order to prevent filling of the subcutaneous tissue, commonly termed stocking. They are applied by starting at the middle of the canon, rolling down to or including the fetlock joint, then up to the knee, and back to the starting point. By rolling downward first better support for the bandage is secured.

Stable Vices.—*Wind sucking,* as indicated by the name, is a practice in which the horse assumes a position with the upper teeth bearing on the manger or other projecting object and proceeds to suck wind into his stomach, accompanied by a long grunting sound. Wind suckers are difficult to keep in condition.

Crib-biting is a vice in which the edge of the manger or any other projection is grasped between the teeth and gradually bitten away. The habit results in a characteristic bevelling of the front margins of the teeth, although the wear of a rounded iron feed box may produce much the same appearance of the teeth. Wind sucking and crib-biting are usually associated, although a horse may be subject to one and not the other. The habit is not confined to the stable, but may be practiced whenever the opportunity offers. Either a smoothly finished stall in which there is nothing to offer a toothhold or the use of a strap fitted closely enough about the throat to compress the larynx when pressure is borne on the teeth but causing the horse no discomfort when not indulging in the vice, are the usual means of preventing, although not curing, the habit.

Weaving is a rhythmical shifting of the weight of the forehand from one forefoot to the other in much the same manner that is displayed by a bear in captivity. As a rule, enforced idleness is an active cause. It has been suggested that horses tied with chain halter shanks have acquired this habit in order to rattle the chains.

Kicking.—Horses kick from various motives, such as maliciousness, good feeling, or wilful attempts to injure either companions or attendants. A great many horses which never manifest an inclination to kick elsewhere acquire the habit of kicking in the stable. Mares are more frequently kickers than geldings. Some horses kick only at feeding time, thus giving vent to their impatience. A true stable kicker appears to have no other excuse than the satisfaction of kicking; for such horses a swinging bale partition is recommended. It offers little resistance to the kick and for that reason seems to destroy the desire. Either hobbling the two hind feet or even shackling one to a weight is sometimes resorted to, but such practices are attended with more serious danger than the original offence.

Some horses kick only in the dark, and the presence of a light in the stable will stop them. Some are provoked to kick by an especially uncongenial companion in the next stall. Finally, horses perfectly well behaved in the stable under ordinary circumstances kick from sheer spirit and energy when confined for an unusually long period.

Tail Rubbing.—The presence of animal parasites or neglect of the region under the tail, which may become foul, are usually the causes of the first offence at tail rubbing. Once acquired, however, the practice will be persisted in, even after the correction of the conditions which originally induced it. If thorough grooming will not stop it, the horse may have to be put into a specially constructed loose box, provided either with a fender arranged at such a level that the horse can neither rub his tail against it nor touch any other part of the stall, or, better yet, a bevelled wall to about the height of the horse, giving it an upward and outward slope from the floor so that the horse, with his heel against the wall, cannot reach it to rub, at the height of his tail. Shields and bandages may be employed, but they are liable to injure the hair of the tail.

Halter Pulling.—Confirmed halter pullers are best secured by ropes or chains snapped across behind them. The habit may be broken in the earlier stages by a slip noose about the flank, the rope being carried forward between the front legs, through the halter ring, and then fastened securely. After pulling back and tightening the noose about the flank the horse will usually take great care to keep the rope slack.

Bad Habits.—Horses are most likely to fall into bad habits from want of something else to do. A regular daily routine, therefore, of either moderate exercise or work, and a ration not too stimulating, are the best safeguards against their acquisition. Furthermore, much can be done to make the stable life of a horse congenial by so arranging the occupants as to promote good fellowship and avoid incompatibility among them.

REVIEW

1. What should well-arranged stables provide?
2. What determines the dimensions of a stable?
3. Give specifications for a straight stall.
4. How large should a box stall be and why?
5. What are the advantages and disadvantages of paved stall floors? and how may the disadvantages be partially overcome?
6. What purposes does bedding serve? Name the bedding materials in common use and the relative merits of each.
7. What should govern the number, size, and placing of the windows?
8. What are the fresh air requirements of the average horse and what cubic space in the stable is necessary to meet them?
9. What consideration should be given to the assignment of stalls in the stabling of horses?
10. What special care do the legs of horses require?
11. Of what does proper shoeing consist?
12. Discuss the advisability of clipping horses.
13. How does fashion govern the trimming of horses?
14. To what extent do horses require clothing?
15. To what are most bad habits, which horses acquire in the stable, due?

CHAPTER XVI

EQUITATION

HORSEMANSHIP involves the mastery of mind over matter in a way, but the control of the matter is accomplished, indirectly, by the mastery of a superior over an inferior intellect. A horse's usefulness is in proportion to the completeness of his subjugation, and the more we know of his mental capacity the more completely may we accomplish his subjugation.

Control of the Horse.—There is a sentimental opposition to a recital of the horse's mental limitations which must be overcome, and these limitations appreciated, if the most satisfactory service is to be had from him. For instance, it has been alleged that the horse is both a fool and a coward, and while these uncomplimentary terms may arouse the ire of horse lovers, and apparently justly so, it is the actual possession of these two traits, perhaps more moderately called credulity and dependence, which makes it possible to use horses, at all, with safety and satisfaction. Our whole system of breaking, schooling, and driving is fundamentally deceptive. We aim to give the horse an exalted notion of those of his powers which are useful to us and at the same time create the idea that certain others, which might prove detrimental to our purpose, are hardly worthy of the horse's consideration.

The all too common notion that the primary essential in riding or driving is to be able to " hold him " leads one wide of the mark in the rudiments of real horsemanship. Such misconception of facts is responsible for many of the disasters in which runaway horses are conspicuous. Most convincing proof of the absurdity of such an idea is the faultless performance which a pair of horses may put up in a class for ladies to drive, while the same pair, under identical conditions, had proved unmanageable for some heavy-handed, strong-armed man driver in a preceding class. Control, or at least the only system which renders horses serviceably safe, is of the mental, not muscular activities of the

269

horse; therefore, the proper method is by suggestion rather than by force. The execution of whatever act has its origin, so far as the horse is concerned, in his brain, not his brawn; so that is the logical headquarters through which to transmit instructions. If the orders, emanating from this centre, for execution on the horse's own initiative, should happen to conflict with the physical efforts of the rider or driver, there is liable to be a rebellion in favor of the horse, who regards his own motive as taking precedence. On the other hand, by suggesting to the extent of bringing the horse to be of the same mind as the driver, there can be no conflict of orders, and most harmonious response on the part of the horse results.

Compare the horse which has been educated and driven by the strong arm method, which requires a flogging to make him go, a man's weight to stop him, and two hands to pull him round a corner, with the possibility that he may conceive and carry out, at any time, some fool notion which it is beyond the physical power of man to check, with the thoroughly schooled horse responding to the light yet firm and strongly suggestive hand of the master reinsman, who is able to stop, back, start, and drive any place, without a word or even a perceptible twist of the wrist.

Transmitting the Impulse to Act.—Now that the principle has been exposed, the system may be outlined. It may be summarized in a consideration of hands and mouths. These are the two essential factors in the system of control, serving alternately as transmitters and receivers. By means of the former, either the instructions or demands in the mind of the driver are conveyed, by the medium of the reins, to the sensitive structures constituting the mouth of the horse; to be forwarded after being received through the sensory nerve-trunks to the brain of the horse; thence the motor nerves convey the authorized instructions, as it were, to the proper parts for execution. What is here described at length and in detail is accomplished in a flash, but it is well to follow the actual transmission of an impulse in order to appreciate good horsemanship.

If we are to realize the most prompt and delicate response, the horse must be taken and kept well in hand, so that, telegraphically speaking, the line of transmission from hand to mouth may be instantly called into requisition without waiting to get the wires up and connections made. Driving with a careless rein or continually jabbing not only lets the driver but the horse off his guard, and both must be called to attention by taking in hand, before communication can be established. Delays of even this long may be disastrous.

Hands of the right sort are capable of such delicate manipulation as to constantly feel and be felt by the mouth, without maintaining a drag, which destroys all sensibility in both. Such hands convey to the mouth graduated pressure, from the lightest touch to the most compelling pull if occasion demands, and all with a firmness that is convincing.

Relation of Hands and Mouth.—Mouths are the product of hands, therefore reciprocal in every respect. The heavy, rough hand is productive of a hard, unresponsive mouth and destruction of any other kind; while the light, impressionable hand can be relied upon to create or preserve a most sensitive mouth. There are features of this relationship between hands and mouths which can neither be described nor prescribed. They are best learned by contact, the one with the other; only one who has experienced the intimacy of such a fine system of communication has any conception of all that it means. With many the possession of good hands is intuitive; they can neither tell why or how they do as they do; others are heavy handed in spite of themselves, and are fully conscious of their offence and its attendant bad result. Of course, practice has much to do with this; one accustomed to driving trotters will find himself in trouble with the lighter mouth and different bitting arrangement of the actor; while he who has had his schooling with the latter class of horses may be incapable of taking a strong enough hold to steady and support the horse at speed.

The bit is the instrument by means of which communication between the hands of the driver and the mouth of the horse is carried on. An impulse arising in the mind of the driver is represented in a manipulation of the reins, so as to bring the pressure of the bit on the structures of the mouth with which it is in contact in such a manner as to suggest a corresponding notion in the mind of the horse, which, if he be well schooled, he imme-

diately executes. In the reverse order the horse may conceive
the idea of taking some steps on his own initiative, the premedi-
tation of which will be felt by the driver, and if not in order
he flashes back counter instructions. This is the advantage of
keeping the horse always in hand.

Intelligent use of the bit requires some knowledge of the

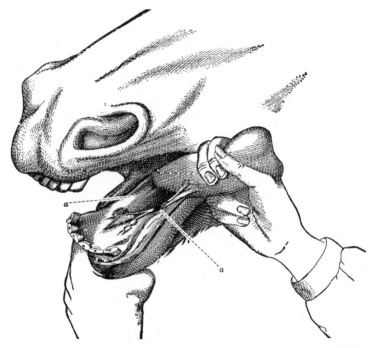

Fig. 138.—Tongue held back to show the bars (*a*) of the mouth upon which the bit bears.

structures of the mouth involved and the methods by which the
bit operates.

Following are the structures with which the bit is more or
less in contact, the extent and nature of their importance depending upon the style of the bit:

1. The bars of the mouth, that region of the lower jaw between the incisor and molar teeth (Fig. 138).

2. The tongue.

3. Angles of the lips.

4. The skin of the groove on the under surface of the lower jaw just in front of the union of its branches.

5. The lower premolar teeth, in some instances.

Classification of Bits.—Bits may be classified as snaffle, curb, and special. Snaffle bits consist of a straight or jointed bar, in which the principle involved is a direct pull on the mouth. The jointed snaffle (Fig. 139) is more severe, as it puts the pressure chiefly on the bars of the mouth, while the plain snaffle bears equally on the tongue, which has a cushioning effect.

The four-ring snaffle (Fig. 140) is doubly severe on account of the rings at the ends of the cheek pieces being drawn into the mouth.

Curb bits consist of a plain or port bar furnished with a cheek lever or shank at each end, in place of snaffle rings, at the

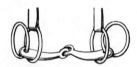

FIG. 139.—The jointed snaffle bit.

FIG. 140.—The four-ring snaffle bit.

upper ends of which are attached the chain or strap which bears in the groove under the lower jaw, while near the lower extremity of the shank the reins are attached. The length of the shank is usually one-third above the mouth-piece and two-thirds below. The principle involved with the curb is one of leverage, the restraint of the upper arm of the shank by the curb chain or strap constituting the fulcrum, the power being applied on the lower arm of the shank, the position of the attachment of the reins determining the leverage, while the weight is the mouth-piece of the bit borne by the bars and tongue. The lower the loop into which the reins are buckled, the stronger the leverage. The possible attachments of reins are the plain cheek, the half cheek, the first or second loop. The bearing of the curb chain is intended to be sufficient only to establish the leverage of the shank by holding its upper extremities stationary and establishing a fulcrum. The severity of the bit may be increased, however, by shortening the chain or strap or roughing the chain by twisting its links. The action of the curb bit is also made more severe by the U-shaped mouth-piece (Fig. 141) which provides a port, into which the tongue passes when the bit is in operation, thus throwing all the pressure upon the bars of the mouth. Without the port in the bit, the pressure is cushioned on the tongue before being borne by the bars.

The plain bit is usually corrugated on one side, if of the reversible Liverpool pattern, which makes it a little more severe than if the smooth side is used.

There are four standard styles of curb bits: The Liverpool, the elbow, the Buxton, and the Pelham. The Liverpool (Fig. 142) has a straight shank. The elbow (Fig. 143) has an angle

Fig. 141.—Port of curb bit.   Fig. 142.—The
                                Liverpool bit.

in the shank to prevent the horse from catching it in his lips and preventing the operation of the bit. The Buxton (Fig. 144) has a long S-shaped shank serving the same purpose as the elbow, the lower extremities being united by a cross-bar to prevent their becoming caught in parts of the harness. The Pelham (Fig. 145) is the style of bit commonly used in riding bridles.

The special class of bits includes all those designed to meet extraordinary requirements, and they are too numerous to mention. The majority of them are a modification or corruption of the snaffle type, causing such distortion of the horse's mouth as to make any hold of the bit impossible. Many are ruinous to a good mouth and aggravating to a bad one.

The Bitless Bridle.—There has recently been put on the market a bitless bridle, in which a metal nose band is equipped with rings through which pass the ends of a flexible chin strap into which the reins are buckled. The idea is an old one, similar bridles having long been in common use in Southern Europe. For some horses with spoiled mouths this bridle might give good service, but with it the nicer responsiveness of a good mouth to light hands is impossible.

The proper fit and adjustment of a bit are as essential to the preservation of a good mouth as is the type of the bit itself. It should just hang easily in the mouth, wide enough not to pinch the cheeks and low enough neither to stretch the angles of the mouth nor to draw the cheeks in against the teeth. Curb bits should be lower in the mouth, as a rule, than the snaffle, some

FIG. 143. — The elbow bit.

FIG. 144.—The Buxton bit.

FIG. 145.—The Pelham bit.

being constructed so that the bar has play up and down on the shank in order that the position of the bit may be, to a certain extent, automatically adjusted. The curb chain should be loose enough to admit from two to three fingers when the bit hangs naturally with no pressure upon it. Then the bit should be so adjusted as to bring the chain into its proper groove. If too high, its pressure comes on the sharp margins of the lower jaw with injurious effect.

Accessories.—*Check or Bearing Rein.*—The overdraw check, attached either to a small check bit, a chin strap, or some modification of either or both, takes the bearing directly over the pole and therefore has the effect of extending the nose and at least favoring, if not suggesting, an extension of stride. It also prevents the compression of the larynx and the interference with breathing, which come from sharp flexion of the neck under a pull. The overdraw check rein accompanies the snaffle bit, never the curb. The rein should not be attached to the snaffle bit itself, as its bearing will displace the bit in the horse's mouth, thereby destroying its relation with the structures on which it is supposed to bear.

This rein is used on speed and road horses which are not reined up long periods at a time and are driven at a pace, at which they go against the bit in such a way as to put the head

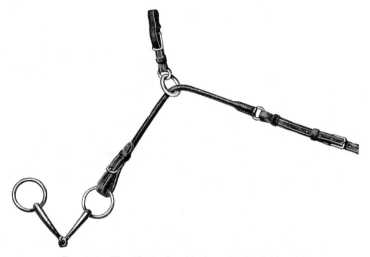

Fig. 146.—The side check or bearing rein with bridoon bit.

and neck in a position in which the bearing of the check rein is very much relieved. The check bit may even be dropped completely out of the mouth, although the rein seemed tight when the horse was standing.

They are out of place on the horse which is required either to do continuous road work, to pull any load, especially up hill, or to stand hitched for any length of time. Ignorant or thoughtless use of the overdraw check is one of the most common and severe abuses which horses have to endure.

The side or bearing rein is attached either directly to the

bridoon bit (Fig. 146) or to a pulley bridoon (Fig. 147). It places the bearing at the side of the head, having the effect of drawing the chin in and arching the neck without necessarily elevating the head very much. This rein is an adjunct to the curb bit, co-operating with it in suggesting a shorter but higher stride and a more collected way of going.

Its use is especially indicated in the case of horses which yield to the curb with the entire neck instead of with the head only, which brings the chin to a position almost against the breast. Severe reining of this character, especially in short, thick-necked horses, may seriously compress the larynx, in addition to causing extreme discomfort and muscular cramp.

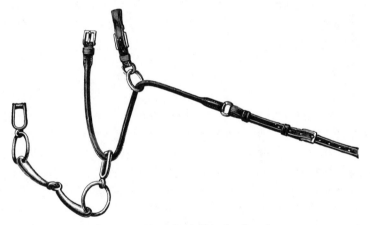

Fig. 147.—The pulley bridoon bearing rein.

The Coupling Rein.—In pair harness the reins consist of the draught or outside reins and the inside or coupling reins, one of which is attached to each draught rein and passes to the inside of the bit of the opposite horse. A pull to right, for instance, is thus communicated to the off side of each horse's mouth and in equal degree, provided the adjustment of the coupling reins has been properly made.

Coupling is the finishing touch in putting a pair of horses together, and determines whether they are to drive " like one horse " or whether the driver is to be ever conscious of the presence of two horses in his team. In order to exert equal pressure on both sides of each mouth, the relative carriage of heads, promptness in driving, disposition, etc., of both horses must be taken into consideration. With a pair of horses closely matched in every way, the coupling reins should be from four to six inches longer than the draught reins, since they are the hypotheni of triangles. If one horse carries his head higher than the other, his coupling rein should be on top in order not to be borne down upon by that of the lower headed horse. If one horse sets his head and neck in a flexed position, his rein should be shortened to take up the slack so produced. Or if one drives more freely than the other, his rein must be shorter to keep him under restraint without pulling the other horse. In order, however, to keep the horses' heads an equal distance apart and their bodies

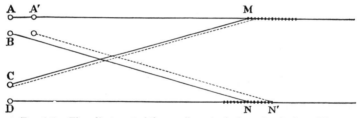

Fig. 148.—The adjustment of the coupling reins is shown by the dotted lines.

parallel with the pole, whatever is taken up in one rein must be let out in the other. Having the coupling reins too short draws the heads together and throws the horses out from the pole, sometimes causing them to fall, on pavements and down grades. Too long coupling reins turn the heads out and the bodies in against the pole.

Figure 148 illustrates by solid lines the position of the reins when the horses carry their heads and necks alike, AB and CD representing the bits of the two horses, AM and DN the draught reins, BN and CM the coupling reins. If, however, the off horse carries his chin in, or for other reasons requires his rein to be shortened, the altered position of the coupling reins is shown by the dotted lines. Coupling rein BN is taken up on the draught rein to N^1, the take back on the draught rein to A^1 being made by the hand of the driver. This, however, would shorten coupling rein CM unless it be let out on its draught rein to the same extent that BN has been shortened.

The more nervous horse is often put on the off side so as to bring the other horse between him and objects to be passed in the road, it being the American rule of the road to keep to the right. It also brings him closer to the hands of the driver, who sits on the right side. The largest horse is customarily put on the off side for the reason that in turning to the right on roads the surfaces of which are crowned, as is usually the case, the off horse is called upon to pull more in returning the load to the centre of the road.

Blinds or Winkers.—Many horses are rendered much more serviceable by having their field of vision restricted to the direction in which they are supposed to go. Both nervous horses, which will jump at any sudden movement of those behind them, and lazy horses, which are disposed to loaf, usually drive much more steadily and promptly with winkers. Careful adjustment of the winker, both as to height and as to length of the winker stay, should be made so as to prevent the horse's looking over it, but allowing full vision forward. A sudden change from a blind to an open bridle or the reverse may be most disconcerting to the horse. Appointments require winkers on heavy harness; with light harness they are optional.

Martingale.—There are two varieties, standing and ring. A standing martingale is a strap passing from the belly band, between the forelegs, to either the bit or nose band, and has the effect of preventing the elevation of the head beyond a certain level. It is most generally employed on trotters that are difficult to catch in breaks, saddle horses that rear, and polo ponies that endanger their riders by throwing their heads up in response to the severe curb, when pulled up sharply.

The ring martingale is not attached to the horse's head, but terminates in two rings through which the reins pass. Its action is generally the same as the standing martingale but in less degree. Its adjustment should always permit of the reins being almost at the level of the bit and turret rings, thus holding but not pulling the horse's head down. It is used on both light harness and saddle horses; the snaffle rein only, in the case of the latter, passing through it.

Nose Band.—The object of the nose band is to keep the mouth shut and the bit in position, thus preventing yawing and lugging. It also serves as an attachment for the standing martingale. Heavy harness and most riding bridles are regularly equipped with nose bands.

Chin Strap.—This is a strap that passes under the chin either in front of or through the bit especially designed for it, and serves to place the bearing of the check rein under the chin instead of on the upper jaw, to keep the mouth shut, and to prevent the lateral pulling of the bit through the horse's mouth.

The bristle burr is a round leather disc fitted around the bit inside the ring or shank, against the cheek, and is often applied to one side only. It is used on horses which either side rein or bolt to one side, in order to keep them off that side of the bit.

The Word.—Well-schooled horses, in competent hands, may either be started, pulled up, stopped, backed, or changed in their gait without a word being spoken. Only a few words, such as " whoa," " back," and possibly " steady," are justifiable under any circumstances, and they should be spoken distinctly and always for the same purpose. It is more the tone and modulation of the voice, in speaking, than the word itself, which the horse interprets. The objection to a careless and indiscriminate use of words in either driving or riding is that they are not only confusing oftentimes to the horse for which they are intended, but may disturb all other horses within hearing. Every horse should know and heed the command " whoa," which should always mean a full stop.

The whip should be used more for punishment than persuasion. The continued tapping of the whip, like the jabbing of the reins, will make a loafer of any horse. Discretion in its application will insure both uniform and prompt response.

FORM

There are two ends sought by good horsemanship: First, the safety and comfort of the individuals who are riding or driving, which depends upon one's ability to keep his horse both between fences and on his feet; and second, the ease with which this is accomplished.

Form may be simply defined as the manner in which a thing is done. So much importance is attached to form in some instances that results are all form and nothing else. Form usually marks the made equestrian, whose real horsemanship still lacks something. On the other hand, it is probable that the naturally good rider or driver will number form with his other accomplishments.

Following the thought of the definition, it may be inferred that good form consists in doing a thing in the correct way.

Fig. 149.—Reins held in left hand, right hand free for take-back or whip.

Right, in this sense, does not mean according to the dictates of fashion but in that manner which insures its being done with greatest efficiency and readiness. We should accept what has been established as the correct manner of riding and driving as that which contributes most to the safety, comfort, and appearance of those directly concerned. If beginners in horsemanship could be induced to take advice from some one who really knows, ultimate results would be much more satisfactory to both themselves and their horses. One frequently sees accidents narrowly averted or the most flagrant cruelties practiced purely through the ignorance of the perpetrators, who would be as much distressed as any one if they fully realized the seriousness of their mistakes.

The Rudiments of Driving.—The rudiments of the proper way to drive are as follows: Under ordinary conditions drive with the left hand, with the right hand free for either take-up or whip; hold the near rein over the forefinger, the off rein between the middle and ring fingers, thus leaving the reins separated by two fingers, which allows sufficient space to introduce the fingers of the right hand quickly, to take back (Fig. 149). This is done by dropping the thumb and forefinger of the right hand over

Fig. 150.—The take-back.

the near rein, slipping the remaining three fingers between the two reins at such distance in advance of the left hand as may be required (Fig. 150). The reins should be gripped by their edges rather than by their flat sides. Either rein may be taken up by the right hand as in the case of a turn, and the off rein may be released by the left hand, passing through the right hand and over the thumb in case a two-hand grip is desired (Fig. 151).

The position of the left hand should be with the knuckles turned forward and perpendicular, the forearm horizontal and at very nearly right angles with the reins. This position insures the greatest freedom of wrist and fingers, is conducive to a light hand, and renders almost impossible a continuous, dragging pull.

Gloves permit of both a better grip and more easy manipulation of the reins, but they should be a size too large and unbuttoned to allow the greatest freedom of the fingers and wrist.

Riding,—Holding the Reins.—The usual method of holding the reins of a curb and snaffle riding bridle is to take the near snaffle rein over the little finger of the left hand, the near curb rein between the little and ring fingers, then pass the off curb rein between the ring and middle fingers and the off snaffle rein

FIG. 151.—The two-hand grip.

between the middle and index fingers, the ends of all four reins coming out of the hand over the index finger and clasped by the thumb (Fig. 152). Either curb or snaffle reins can be taken up independently by the right hand back of the left, or the right hand may be dropped in front of the left, the little finger between the off curb and snaffle reins in case a two-hand grip is desired (Fig. 153). The hands may be separated and their position on the reins changed by running the reins through the fingers as the hands are drawn apart.

The single rein from the plain snaffle bridle is usually simply crossed through the hands.

The trooper holds his single curb reins in the left hand, the two separated by the little finger, then passed through the hand and over the index finger, where they are clasped by the thumb.

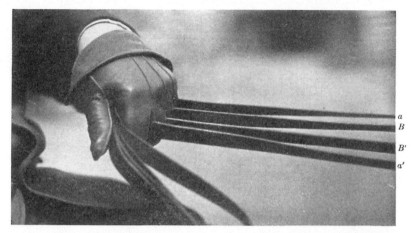

Fig. 152.—Riding, reins in one-hand grip.   a, a', snaffle reins; B, B', curb reins.

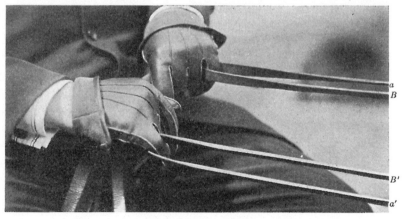

Fig. 153.—Riding, two-hand grip.   a, a', snaffle reins; B, B', curb reins.

The cow puncher uses an open, unbuckled rein which falls to the ground the moment it is released from the hand, serving to hold his pony as though anchored securely.   He usually holds the reins loosely, separated by the forefinger, or with both reins gripped between the thumb and forefinger.

The trooper, mounted officer, or cowboy rides with one hand in order to have a free hand for sabre, gun, stick, or rope, but for riding in the park and cross country it is not only permissible but advisable to use both hands. Continued one-hand riding with the other hand hanging disengaged has a tendency toward an unsymmetrical development and carriage of shoulders. Since the trooper and cow puncher guide their horses by the rein on the neck exclusively, using the bit only for restraint, the fingering of the reins in their cases is quite different from that which is employed in riding a gaited or high school horse, for instance.

The use of the reins implies pressure on the bit, with one notable exception—the saddle horse. All saddle horses, but especially those ridden with a single rein, are schooled to respond to pressure of the rein on the neck (rein wise), turning away from the side against which the rein is carried. If the reins are crossed in front of the horse's neck, pressure on one side of the neck puts pressure also on the opposite side of the mouth, with the usual result so far as the horse is concerned. Gradually he can be taught to respond to the rein on the neck without waiting for the pressure on the bit; clever horses even learn to follow the movement of the hand as though bringing the rein against the neck on one side or the other. Of course, the reins are not crossed after the habit has been acquired.

REVIEW

1. Of what importance are the horse's mental limitations?
2. What is the principle which underlies our system of control?
3. What is the line of transmission, from driver or rider to horse, of instructions for execution?
4. What are good hands; a good mouth; and what is their relation?
5. Describe the snaffle and the curb bits, naming the structures of the mouth involved by each.
6. When is a bit of the right size and properly adjusted?
7. For what purpose was the over-draw check designed and to what extent is it abused?
8. When are the coupling reins of a pair of horses properly adjusted?
9. To what extent should the word be used in riding or driving? Why?
10. What is the proper manner of holding the reins in driving? Why?

CHAPTER XVII

VEHICLE, HARNESS, AND SADDLE

It is quite natural to assume that horses were ridden long before they were driven, although the war chariot is mentioned in some of the earliest references to the horse in the service of man. The use of the vehicle is so generally dependent upon the construction of roads, and the nature of the roads in early times was so poor, that the comfort of passengers and safety of goods were much greater on the backs of horses and mules. It is so even to-day in the newer parts of our own country. Even after roads were built, the primitive vehicles were so crude and lumbering that they were used chiefly for agricultural hauling.

After the pillion method of conveying people came the horse litter (fifteenth century), a carriage swung between two poles which were supported at both ends by horses which were either led or ridden.

The evolution of the wheeled vehicle may be traced in steps: First, the most crude sort of a sledge, often consisting of the forked branches of a tree, dragged in the manner of a stone boat; second, the addition of fixed rollers; third, the turning of large rollers into the form of wheels or rollers on the ends of a revolving axle, this being the first semblance of wheels (Fig. 154); fourth, a fixed wooden axle on which the wheels revolved, being held in place by pins; fifth, the construction of the metal axle with boxed hub wheel, designed to meet if not to minimize friction; sixth, the highest development of this idea, represented in the modern lubricated or even roller and ball-bearing axles, with wheels of the strongest yet lightest construction.

The Wheel.—The roller is the means by which rubbing friction is transformed into rolling friction, which requires very much less draught to overcome, and the wheel is the highest type of roller. The two parts of the wheel concerned with friction are the tire, which rolls on the road, and the box of the hub,

286

which rubs on the axle. The tire rolls not only on the ground but also over any obstacle which the surface of the road may present. The width of the tire has already been discussed under " Draft of the Load," Chapter XIII.

The resilience of the tire is a matter the importance of which has been made more apparent by the development of bicycling and motoring. The resilience is the springing back of the tread behind the point of contact of the wheel with the ground. It may be present either in the tire of the wheel or the surface over which the wheel rolls. The force of the resilience is equivalent to the additional force required to compress the tread ahead of the point of contact, as the wheel rolls.

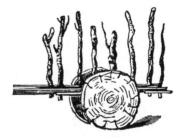

Rubber tires have the general effect of the wheel travelling over a yielding surface, which increases the draft, but if the rubber is sufficiently resilient to restore the force thus expended, the actual draft required may be reduced, since the rubber cushion acts like a spring in absorbing shock and thus preventing waste of power in lifting the load over every little obstacle, then letting it fall, with a pound, on the road again. This saving is greater the higher the speed at which the vehicle is pulled.

Fig. 154.—The evolution of the wheel.

The pneumatic tire, acting on the same principle, very materially reduces the draft of vehicles so equipped, as shown by the experiments of Morin:

Iron tires—Walk three miles per hour .require traction of 48 lb. per ton
Iron tires—Trot 6½ miles per hour. . . .require traction of 59 lb. per ton
Iron tires—Fast trot 9.4 miles per hour .require traction of 77 lb. per ton
Pneumatic tires—Walk . . . . .require traction of 48 lb. per ton
Pneumatic tires—At other paces . . . . .require traction of 50 lb. per ton

Bearings.—Rubbing friction between the axle and the box of the hub with which it is in contact is controlled by *lubrication* and special bearings of rollers, cones or balls, in place of the simple friction bearing.

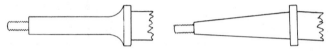

FIG. 155.—The cylindrical axle arm.   FIG. 156.—The tapered axle arm.

Axles are either cylindrical or tapered. The cylindrical axle arm (Fig. 155) insures a truer bearing and easier running, in case the road is level from side to side, the tire at right angles to the face of the wheel and the arm itself horizontal. There are many reasons for modifying these conditions prerequisite to the best results from the cylindrical axle, however, which render the tapered axle better adapted to common use. The tapered arm

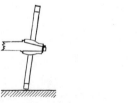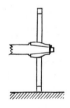

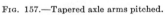

FIG. 157.—Tapered axle arms pitched.   FIG. 158.—An unpitched tapered axle.

(Fig. 156) is stronger for a given weight, since it is heaviest at the point of greatest strain, the shoulder. With the tapered axle it is a much simpler matter to maintain a good fit between axle and box by the use of leather washers placed between the wheel and the shoulder of the axle than in the case of the cylindrical axle, in which no subsequent adjustment is possible. For this reason the tapered axle is much more easily constructed. Axle arms are so pitched (Fig. 157) as to keep the wheel running snug to the shoulder instead of running off as it would tend to do with an unpitched tapered axle (Fig. 158). Incidentally, this pitch places the tops of the wheels farther apart and, therefore, throws the mud or dust away from instead of against the body of the wagon.

Wheels are dished, that is the spokes are set in the hub at an angle, instead of perpendicularly, for several reasons (Fig. 159). In the case of a pitched axle, dishing brings the spokes of the lower half of the wheel into an upright position, in which they are capable of sustaining the greatest weight. Dishing also braces the wheel against being sprung by a lateral thrust from the inside, as occurs when the vehicle bounds back and forth from side to side over the road. Dishing also affords an automatic means of keeping wheels tight. The effect of wear and continued battering over stones, rails, and all kinds of rough roads is to expand metal tires, thus allowing the spokes to loosen in both hub and felloe. In the dished wheel, however, the spokes are not only set at an angle, but the tire, after being expanded by fire, is fitted so close that when suddenly contracted by cold water it draws the ends of the spokes into a still greater dished position than they were originally set in. Therefore, any expansion that occurs in the tires is immediately taken up by the spokes springing toward the perpendicular. The centrifugal force of the revolving wheel also operates to throw the spokes into a perpendicular position, which assists in keeping them taut against the felloe and tire, by which they are bound.

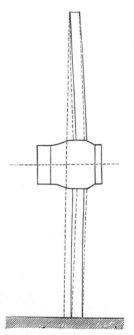

Fig. 159.—The dished arrangement of the spokes in the hub.

In pitching the axle arms or dishing the wheels, care must be taken to keep the tire parallel with the road surface so as not to drag or scuff, as motorists say, but roll evenly over its entire width.

Very light wheels may have the spokes set in the hub in staggered fashion (Fig. 160) in order to brace the wheel against being sprung by a side thrust from either direction. Instead of

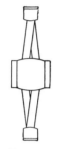

being lined up in the hub every other spoke is set outside the centre of the hub, which is directly in line with the felloe, the other spokes being set inside. Thus each alternate half of the spokes braces the wheel in opposite directions.

Wheeled passenger vehicles were first introduced into England in 1555, according to Sir Walter Gilbey, and were in limited use in France a little before that time. Queen Elizabeth was the first sovereign to use a coach, it having been brought from the Netherlands and presented to her by a Dutchman, William Boonen, who later became her coachman. This was one

FIG. 160.—The staggered arrangement of the spokes in the hub.

of the first carriages seen in England and was of most cumbersome but pretentious design (Fig. 161).

Progress in carriage building was as rapid as the gradual im-

FIG. 161.—One of the cumbersome and pretentious early coaches.

provement of the roads would permit, and they remained in very bad condition until late in the eighteenth century.

Steel springs were first used in 1670, although our buckboard idea had been represented at a much earlier time, in the way of strap supports in which the body of the vehicle was slung (Fig. 162), or two long, supple poles, supported at the ends by the axles, and upon which the body was suspended. Iron tires were reported in the first half of the nineteenth century, although wooden rims, braced with iron at the joints, had been previously used.

Use of Rubber.—Early attempts were made at shock absorption, it being no doubt more imperative then than now, on account of the rough condition of the roads. The pneumatic tire was patented in France in 1846, but proved impracticable at that time. Before this, inflated cushions over the springs,

FIG. 162.—Strap supports in which the body of the vehicle was slung.

rubber cushions inside the hubs, and spring spokes had all been attempted. In 1883 rubber cushions under the iron tires were tried.

The first brakes were used 1860 to 1865.

Superior Woods.—A distinct advantage is claimed for American carriage builders over those of any other country on account of the superior woods which are available to them. Hickory is fast replacing oak in carriage construction, and American woods are extensively exported for the use of foreign manufacturers. The American idea in carriage design is light, rigid strength of the " split hickory " sort, while foreign carriages are much heavier. It is interesting to note the exchange of ideas between England and the United States; while carriages of English type have come to dominate our show rings, the Englishmen are showing their high steppers to a bike wheeled vehicle not unlike our American road wagon (Fig. 163).

FIG. 163.—A class of English harness horses.

Vehicles Classified.—Vehicles may be classified as follows:

I. For the transportation of merchandise:

1. Van
2. Dray
3. Truck
4. Cart

5. Wagon
6. Express Delivery
7. Light Delivery

II. Four-wheelers for the transportation of passengers:

1. Omnibus
2. Opera Bus
3. Wagonette
4. Station Wagon
5. Berlin
6. Landau
7. Brougham
8. Coupé

9. Rockaway
10. Mail Phaeton
11. Demi Mail Phaeton
12. Stanhope Phaeton
13. Spider Phaeton
14. George IV (Lady's) Phaeton
15. Sayler Wagon
16. Victoria

17. Cabriolet
18. Surrey
19. Runabout
20. Road Wagon
21. Speed Wagon

22. Trap
23. Park Drag
24. Road Coach
25. Brake

Two-wheelers for the transportation of passengers:

1. Gig
2. Hansom
3. Jaunting Car

4. Brake Cart
5. Jogging Cart
6. Sulky

THE HARNESS

There are three general classes of harness,—work, heavy, and light. The chief distinctions between the latter have already been referred to. Heavy harnesses are differentiated as coach, gig, and runabout. The typical light harness is also designated as a single strap or track harness.

THE SADDLE

Horses were ridden long before saddles were thought of, but saddles of various sorts were described at an early period. The horse cloth was used first (800 B.C.), but real saddles, with trees, were reported in the fourth century A.D. The side-saddle was introduced by Anne of Bohemia in the last half of the fourteenth century.

Types.—There are in general three types of saddles and, correspondingly, three ways of sitting them or "seats":

The English or flat, pig skin saddle is used for park riding, hunting, polo, and racing, with some modifications especially adapting it to each purpose. Its chief characteristics are a low tree, also low pommel and cantle, padding, skirts usually with knee pads, buckled girths usually double, and open steel stirrups. *Seat.*—Natural sitting posture, stirrups medium length, knee grip, posting the trot. See illustrations of gaited and walk-trot-canter saddle horses, Chapter V.

The McClellan saddle is the regulation United States Army saddle. Its features are a medium high, open tree, open seat,

Fɪɢ. 164.—Philadelphia mounted police equipped with McClellan saddles and single-rein curb bridles.

Fɪɢ. 165.—The style of riding to which the stock saddle is best adapted.

high pommel and cantle, blanket pad, cinch, and hooded stirrups. *Seat.*—Close, pommel and cantle support, long stirrup and thigh grip (Fig. 164).

The stock or Texas saddle is used exclusively for range work and for rough riding in general throughout the West. Its features are a heavy steel tree, a very high pommel surmounted with a horn for roping, deep seat, very high cantle, heavy square skirts, double cinch, no buckles, and heavy wooden or steel, hooded or open stirrups. *Seat.*—Comparatively loose but balanced, straight leg and long stirrup (Fig. 165).

BRIDLES

Riding bridles are snaffle, curb, or curb and snaffle. The plain snaffle is used on race horses, some hunters, and ponies; the curb alone in cavalry and police service and by stockmen; the curb and snaffle on either gaited or walk-trot-canter saddle horses, some hunters, and polo ponies.

A special hunting snaffle, with double rein, one of which is run through a ring martingale, is most commonly used on hunters.

REVIEW

1. Why do we presume that horses were ridden before they were driven?
2. What were the steps in the evolution of the wheeled vehicle?
3. Why does a wheeled vehicle require less traction than a stone boat?
4. What is the effect of rubber tires on draft?
5. Why are axle arms pitched?
6. Why are wheels dished?
7. How are vehicles classified? Give an example of each class.
8. What are the three classes of harness and the essential features of each?
9. What are the chief differences in the three types of saddles and the " seats " with which they are ridden?
10. Name the types of riding bridles and the uses of each.

CHAPTER XVIII

MARKETS AND SHOWS

The horse show serves a manifold purpose. It entertains the public, furnishes high-class sport for exhibitors, stimulates interest in horses and equestrianism, promotes the horse breeding industry by affording the best means of advertising, and, most important of all, it establishes ideals or standards for the guidance of breeders.

Classes of Show Horses.—Show horses are classified into market and breeding divisions. In the market division the classes are made up on the basis of type, primarily, the horses of each type being classified either according to weight, height, or performance and further into singles, pairs, threes, fours, sixes, and so on. Age, sex, and breed are not as a rule considered in the market classification. Any class may in addition have special requirements, as " performance only to count " or " conformation 40 per cent., performance 60 per cent."

Breeding classes are made up on the basis of age, duplicated for each sex and in connection with each breed. In addition there are usually classes for get of sire, produce of dam, groups either bred or owned by exhibitor, and specials.

Fitting horses for the show ring consists in schooling them for a creditable performance and feeding and grooming them into the condition and bloom in which they make the best appearance. All show horses, of whatever type, should be fat in some degree.

Showing.—Breeding classes are shown " in hand " either with lead bridle or on the lunge rein, in the case of stallions; to halter frequently, in the case of mares. Trotters and pacers are usually shown beside a pony, while drafters and heavy harness horses are shown by runners on foot.

Market classes are shown in harness or under saddle, as the case may be. An exception is made in the case of drafters, which are shown to halter as well as in harness. Harness horses

296

should be put to appropriate vehicles; appointments may or may not count, as indicated in the class requirements. Harness and saddle horses should be either driven or ridden well into the corners of the ring, in order to go as much of the route as possible straight away.

Exhibitors are at all times subject to the direction of the ring master, who acts under the instructions of the judges. Contestants, not in the short leet or disqualified for any reason, are dismissed from the ring or " given the gate."

HORSE MARKETS

Commerce is the interchange of commodities, and the market is the medium for this. The exchange takes place between the producer on the one hand and the consumer on the other, market values being determined by the balance maintained between the amount produced and the amount consumed. Consumption being fixed, over-production bears or depresses the market while under-production will bring about an increase in market values. With a given amount produced, excessive consumption bulls or increases market values, while a decrease in the demand from the consumer will have an opposite effect on values.

The demand of the consumer not only determines market values, but also the character of the product for which the top price can be secured. Therefore, while both the producer and the consumer are concerned in maintaining the strength of the market and with the character of the product involved, it is the consumer who really rules. This is a most important fact for the horse breeder to realize.

The Breeder and the Market.—Unfortunately there is a difference between horse breeding and the production of market horses. Too many breeders operate independently or in total ignorance of market conditions and requirements. Their ideal of a market horse is both single and selfish and does not comprehend type or class distinction. It is not unusual to find an owner sacrificing a colt which has some real outcome in a market class for which the demand is strong but of which the owner knows nothing, while trying to secure his price for one of whose value he has either an erroneous or exaggerated notion. " Picked out of the bushes " means bought cheaply from an obscure owner who had no conception of the horse's ultimate value. It represents the practice of buyers who measure their profits by the ignorance, in horse matters, of those from whom they buy.

With the exception of drafters, the horse breeder receives a smaller percentage of the price his colt eventually brings than in the case of any other live stock product. It is true that most farmers are not equipped with time or facilities to properly school or train high-class saddle, show, or race horses, the expense of which is usually worth about as much as the original cost of the green horse, but they frequently do not receive full value for their product in the rough, to which they are justly entitled.

In order to produce salable colts and to realize full value for them, the breeder must keep himself well informed as to the character of the horses that are topping the markets. And the horse that brought the high price years ago may not be the best seller to-day, since market demand is continually undergoing some modification which should be taken into account by the producer, if he is to be successful. Furthermore, the breeder should be able to see, in prospect, into just what his colt is capable of developing.

A knowledge of dealers, conditions of sale, and other essentials also aids materially in negotiating a satisfactory sale.

The particular class desired will of course depend upon the purpose for which the horse is purchased. It is important, however, that the requirements of some definite class shall be met, as those horses which are off type or misfits constitute the remnant stock of the horse market for which the lowest price and least profit are realized.

First-handedness.—Service in the city usually draws the line between first- and second-handedness. Marked evidence of a horse's being second-handed consists of the blemishes and minor unsoundnesses which come as a result of wear and tear, such as puffs, sprung knees, and cocked ankles. The dealer in buying first-hand country horses prefers that they should be untrimmed in any way.

Sex.—As a rule geldings outsell mares on account of their more general usefulness throughout the season and also in view of the possibility of mares being in foal. Spring farm trade may demand mares.

The Origin of Market Classes.—The origin of market classes is based on utility. Horses are required to perform a certain kind of service, and it is determined that those of certain definite features are better adapted to do this particular line of work than horses of any other sort. Thus, demand takes the form of specific requirements by the consumer, and there are created distinct market classes. Some of the classes are more or less arbitrary as to name and requirements, so that on different markets it is not always easy to distinguish between them. The major divisions, however, can be differentiated on the broad basis of type.

Market horses are, first of all, either classified or unclassified (see chapter on the Classes of Horses).

Sales are either public or private. Public sales are conducted by auctioneers and dealers; private sales by private owners and dealers. Sales, whether public or private, are usually followed as soon as possible by a transference of the horse to the buyer, who is allowed two days in which to give the horse fair examination and trial, at the end of which time, if the horse is not returned, the sale is considered complete. "Two days" is the rule most strictly abided by, but under certain conditions this may be extended to ten days or even two weeks, if so stated.

Letters or evidence bearing upon a contract may complete it in law, so that when horses are bought by correspondence the letters and documents act as a part of the contract.

When any defects or unsoundnesses, otherwise apparent, are purposely covered up or hidden in any way, and discovered after the sale, the buyer has redress. The measure of damages he can recover is *the difference between the price paid by him and the price he receives upon selling the horse in an open market.*

Auctioneers are usually licensed as such and are legally bound to conduct their sales under certain conditions.

Conditions of Sale.—The buyer should familiarize himself with the conditions of sale. In all cases horses must be as represented, but in catalogues or bills the owner's statement below the description of a horse is not to be taken as a part of the contract or guarantee. As a rule, age, height, weight, and speed are not guaranteed in these sales.

Sales are usually for cash, subject to the terms set forth in catalogues and bills and specified at the opening of the sale by the auctioneer.

The owner is the only responsible party in sales. The auctioneer is an intermediate party acting as the owner's agent or representative, but he is also a protection to the buyer, as he can hold the seller to any statements he may make concerning the conditions under which the horse is sold.

In most markets horses previously sold may be run through the sale like any other horses in order to give it life, color, and encouragement, and this is not considered an unlawful practice.

Sales Ring Warranty.—In Chicago, the largest horse market in America, horses are sold under five different guarantees of soundness, viz. :

1. *Sound.*—The horse meets all requirements of soundness; comparatively rare.

2. *Serviceably Sound.*—Unsound in some respect, which does not interfere with his fitness for the particular service for which sold.

3. *Sound to Wind and Work.*—The horse's wind is good and he will work, but he is otherwise unsound.

4. *Worker Only.*—True to work; all other conditions are to the eye of the buyer.

5. *At the Halter.*—Carrying with it no warrant or guarantee whatever.

Often horses sold at the halter are those that have been sold under previous guarantee and turned back, or sold to adjust some dispute or difficulty.

With all Faults.—When a horse is sold " with all faults " the seller is relieved from all liability.

Private Sales.—It is often desirable for intending purchasers to buy from private owners or dealers, under conditions which permit of more thorough examination.

How to Buy a Horse.—There is probably nothing about the

purchase of which there is so much suspicion and misgiving as a horse, yet there *are* horses sold on their merits and at prices which they are well worth. It may be further stated that there is nothing else in the purchase of which the buyer expects so much for so little. There probably always will be gyp dealers, but the only excuse for their existence is the credulity, ignorance, short-sightedness, and narrow policy of buyers. These traits of character constitute the business assets of the illegitimate seller.

On the other hand, much has been accomplished in an effort to put the horse business on a sound basis, where dealers stake their reputation on their sales the same as is done with pianos, real estate, diamonds, or any commodity of trade. One does not hesitate to pay a premium for a watch, a hat, or even a bottle of milk, which is the product of a house or firm with a reputation for furnishing full value in their goods. Yet a horse dealer is charged with unfairness and even chicanery, in many cases, if he charges much more than the cost of the raw material after having " made " the horses and sold them with a guarantee which protects the buyer from even the inevitable. This is done at the risk of the seller, who hazards many things for which he is in no way responsible, even should they occur. Another source of difficulty is the indiscriminate manner in which advice is accepted. The coachman, the town liveryman, the village blacksmith, Uncle Hiram, and all the others are regarded as the wise ones, whose conflicting opinions must be accorded more consideration than the claims of the perfectly respectable citizen whose own business prosperity depends upon the horses he sells making good all he claims for them.

It is a ridiculous situation. Any person who cares sufficiently for a horse to use him intelligently and with satisfaction should be competent to buy one. He should be able to determine, by trial, whether or not the horse meets the buyer's requirements; and if he is, temporarily at least, sound of eyes, wind, and limb. If there is any question in regard to an obscure unsoundness, the services of a veterinarian should be employed to settle that point. If one does not feel qualified to make his own selection, but finds it necessary to seek advice, he should go direct to the dealer—only reputable ones to be considered—admit his ignorance, state his requirements, and put himself, without any reservation, in the dealer's hands. It should not be difficult to find a dealer who would measure up to a responsibility of this kind. But he will charge, in the price of the horse, a reasonable fee for telling the truth about things of which the buyer is free to confess he knows little or nothing. For such advice the buyer can well afford to pay. If, however, he places no faith in the dealer, nor credits him with any conscience, but he and his advising friends proceed to bluff their way to a satisfactory purchase, they are tempting fate—and the dealer.

Avoid all go-betweens who are " in the deal " for a profit. If it is a harness or saddle horse that is to be bought, do the dealer the honor to eliminate the coachman from the transaction. It is astonishing how gentlemen who consider themselves so thoroughly competent to manage their own affairs that they resent the least suggestion on most matters, make their coachmen the absolute masters of the situation in all affairs pertaining to their stables. This is one of the most difficult and aggravating propositions with which the square-dealing horse seller has to contend, and has much to do with keeping the price of horses high. If some " direct to the consumer " method of conducting the horse business were permitted by buyers, it would be much to the mutual benefit of all concerned.

When buying green horses in the country, or whenever the buyer has no recourse but to rely on his own ingenuity in making a selection, some system should be followed. It is important that the horse be inspected in the stable. Note the condition of his stall; this is the place to detect such vices as kicking, cribbing, and weaving. Consider how he stands on his feet and the manner in which he backs out on the floor. The first few steps taken after standing will often reveal what the next few will quickly obscure. Watch him harnessed, put to, and driven out. Here again and here only many disagreeable traits may be discovered. Try him out in whatever way desired. Never buy a horse " hot," *i.e.,* warmed up. It may be more convenient to have a horse or a pair brought round for inspection, but there are a number of conditions of unsoundness that a horse may be warmed out of. Examine the eyes with a shadow cast on them; note the relative size of the two front feet; then wind him and work him to see how he goes.

The company plan of selling stallions may or may not be a perfectly legitimate transaction. It has its advantages and disadvantages to both buyers and sellers. It frequently happens that ten or twelve mare owners in a community would prefer taking a share or two of company stock to owning a stallion outright. To them the company plan renders available the services of a valuable stallion of which they would otherwise be deprived. If they simply subscribe for their own stock and take no further part in the deal, they may expect the expense of organizing the company and selling the horse to them to be included in his cost price. Yet if a good selection is made, each subscriber may receive good value, allowing for his own time saved. When, however, the company plan is adopted as a means of unloading a counterfeit stallion for which there is no sale at the firm's stables, the horse being shipped to the town selected, accompanied by a smooth salesman abundantly supplied with cash with which to mix among prospective subscribers and finally put through a sale, it should be condemned.

The company plan of *buying* is preferable to the company *selling* plan. Let the organization of the company be instigated and perfected by those interested, and one or more of the members be delegated to go direct to the seller's headquarters, make a selection, and pay cash. Otherwise the cost of the same stallion will be about 20 per cent more, if sold on the company plan and the cost of the sale added to his price.

REVIEW

1. What is a market, and how are market classes and values determined?
2. What is the importance of market information to the breeder and feeder?
3. Explain the creation of market classes.
4. What is a second-handed horse?
5. What are the usual conditions of sale?
6. Name six "don'ts" to observe in buying a horse.
7. Is the company plan of selling stallions commendable?
8. How are show horses classified?
9. Of what does fitting for show consist?
10. How are the different classes of horses shown?

CHAPTER XIX

TRANSPORTATION

RACE and show horses and also market horses for sale, which are shipped long distances, as from the Middle West to the Eastern markets, are usually carried by express, while individual horses or even a carload, shipped to or from local points, ordinarily go by freight.

Express Cars.—The express companies furnish either horse cars fitted with adjustable stall partitions which accommodate from twelve to sixteen horses standing four abreast lengthwise of the car (Fig. 166); or large, loose horse cars open about one-fourth the way down from the top and accommodating twenty-eight head with sufficient space to permit of their moving about and picking mates. The former type of car is used most by stallion importers, while the latter is preferred by the shippers of market geldings.

For freight shipment open stock cars are found to be less draughty and afford better ventilation than closed box cars. Experienced shippers of the highest class of horses declare they have less sickness subsequent to shipment, even in winter, in the open car. Horses are much less likely to contract colds if continuously exposed to low temperatures than if chilled, even slightly, after a period of overheating, and the danger of infection is always inverse to the amount of fresh air available. Most stock cars built nowadays are equipped with double coil springs to insure easy riding whether loaded heavy or light, a rigid steel underframe to prevent sagging, shock-absorbing draw-bars, rounded edges, countersunk bolt-heads and nuts in the interior, and are even of steel construction (Fig. 167).

It is further advised, on good authority, to turn horses loose in the car, even if but one or two are to go. They are less liable to be thrown than if tied, ride much more comfortably, some instinctively lying down as soon as they enter a well-bedded car, and they come off the car at the end of the trip in much better shape.

304

The more common practice, however, is to cross tie and even tie from above, allowing but little play. It usually matters not whether the horse is headed or backed to the locomotive, as a car rarely arrives in the same direction in which it was started,

Fig. 166.—Express horse car partitioned into stalls, four groups of four stalls each lengthwise of the car.

unless on a short, straight run. If a mixed car of stock is shipped, necessitating the partitioning of the car, such partitions should be very substantial in both material and construction. Horses have been seriously injured and permanently blemished by being thrown through or against frail or makeshift partitions.

Freight tariffs are not uniform the country over, but the following one is fairly typical:

A carload is billed at a minimum of 20,000 pounds; single horses or less than a carload at 5000 pounds for one mare or gelding; 3000 pounds for each additional head. Stallions are rated at 7000 pounds straight, whether alone or in a mixed car of stock other than horses, although a stallion shipped in a full carload of horses only is not discriminated against.

Care During Shipment.—Shipments of horses come under the federal law requiring all stock to be unloaded, fed, and watered every twenty-eight hours; this time may be extended to thirty-six hours if so agreed between the shipper and carrier

FIG. 167.—Stock car for shipping horses.

beforehand. Less than a carload, accompanied by an attendant who feeds and waters them, are not subject to this law. Most carloads of horses are shipped unattended, as a man can do little to either prevent or overcome trouble in the car *en route.*

Horses are best prepared for shipment by a good fill of timothy hay and only a moderate ration of soft feed. They require little if any feed *en route* within a twenty-eight-hour limit, a small amount of hay to pick over being sufficient. The Pennsylvania Railroad is eliminating the hay racks from its latest featured stock car, on the ground that hay is unnecessary with the operation of the twenty-eight-hour unloading law, that much of it is usually wasted, and that the racks take up valuable head room and, becoming loose or broken, as they frequently do, are a constant source of danger to the heads and eyes of horses.

Race and show horses are frequently covered from tip to toe, hoods, blankets, and bandages being provided to protect them from possible draughts. Unless accustomed to much clothing, horses so covered are liable to become overheated and not ship so well as others that are but lightly blanketed or perhaps not covered at all. The closeness of the quarters insures against a very low temperature if there are many horses in the car. Bandages rolled low around the coronets to protect from tramping,

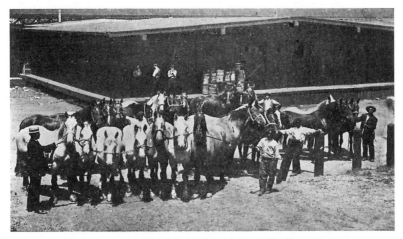

Fig. 168.—Just off the car from the West.

pads about the eyes and poll, and knee pads are often provided as an extra precaution.

Injury During Shipment.—The chief injury to horses in transit consists of bruises at the point of the hocks. There is little difficulty occasioned by horses getting down in the car, and if they do get down they usually experience little trouble in getting up on their feet again unless old or crippled, as is often the case in the second-hand horse trade.

The well-nigh inevitable influenza or shipping fever, so-called, could probably be controlled to a certain extent if thorough disinfection of cars were insisted upon.

Some high-strung, nervous horses are subject to car fits, as they are called, a form of hysteria resulting from the excitement and perhaps the cramped position which causes extreme discomfort. They will sometimes rear, pitch, and throw themselves to such an extent as to make it necessary to stop the train and remove them from the car in order to prevent them from doing serious damage to themselves or mates. Much travel will sometimes enable them to overcome the difficulty, while in other cases it simply aggravates their condition (Fig. 168).

REVIEW

1. When are horses shipped by express and when by freight?
2. Describe the express cars furnished to horse shippers.
3. What type of freight cars are best for horse shipments and why?
4. Should horses be tied or turned loose during shipment?
5. How are horses best prepared and cared for during shipment?

CHAPTER XX

THE MULE

THE importance of the mule as a factor in American agriculture justifies a consideration of his production and use in a general discussion of Horse Husbandry.

The mule conforms to the definition of a hybrid in that his sire is of one species, *Equus asinus,* and his dam is of another species, *Equus caballus,* the common ancestor within the genus being so remote as to render the hybrids sterile.

Mule breeding was practiced by the ancients, and in some countries they are depended upon almost altogether for work. The inverse cross, which produces a *hinny,* is more difficult to accomplish, the hybrid being smaller and less useful as a rule, although it is contended by some that hinnies cannot be distinguished from mules.

Mules have always been bred most extensively in semi-tropical regions, the line being quite sharply drawn between the production of mules and draft horses.

Classes of Mules.—An extended classification of mules is given, but they are all bred for essentially two purposes,—work in the fields and in the mines. Farm or plantation mules, or sugar and cotton mules, as the market classes them, are bred chiefly from well-bred mares of so-called hot blood and are therefore rangy, fine, and snappy movers. The Southerner regards it as no desecration to mate good saddle or trotting bred mares with a jack, and some extremely breedy mules are the result (Fig. 169).

The mine demand, which is of necessity for a draftier, bigger boned mule (Fig. 170), is met by mating the smaller, smoother class of draft mares with big-boned jacks. Mine mules work both on the surface and down in the mines. The latter range in height according to the veins in which they are to work. The little 12-hand pitters are much in demand and bring a price out of proportion to their size.

309

As Draft Animals.—Mules are not a success for heavy draft work on city streets, as they do not have either the weight or circumference of foot to give them a good hold on pavements. Furthermore, it is the experience of teamsters that a mule pulls by a direct forward push instead of by the lift with which draft horses start their load. This, too, is conducive to slipping. Some light pairs of mules do well in light delivery service, and their feet withstand the battering of the pavements especially well

Fig. 169.—Representing the Kentucky standard of mule excellence. Their size, rangy, smooth form, quality, breediness, and temperament are such as are required of the highest class sugar mule.

on account of a very thick, strong wall and sole, and their peculiar shape, which prevents both a contraction of heels and dropping of sole.

The Mule's Advantages.—The mule has some distinct advantages over the horse for some kinds of work. They may be enumerated as follows:

He stands hot weather better and is less susceptible to digestive disorders and founder, it being customary to feed mules from troughs, where they may take their fill, like cattle. A mule takes better care of himself in the hands of an incompetent driver than a horse does, accepting his lot more philosophically, being naturally more of a plodder and therefore more steady and less fretful.

On account of the peculiar form and structure of the mule's foot, he is less subject to foot lameness and the ordinary injurious effects of shoeing than is the horse, which is more commonly incapacitated for work on this account than any other. Lame-

Fig. 170.—A rugged pair of more drafty form and ample bone, representative of the best grade sought for mine use.

ness in a mule is most often due to spavins and ringbones, but he will get along with a spavin which would practically put a horse out of business. Mules are almost invariably good walkers. Stabling requirements for mules are much less elaborate than for horses, double stalls, with or without bales, or even pens in which a number are turned loose, being all that is needed. Age and infirmities seem to count less against mules, and as a rule an old or second-hand pair will outsell horses of equal merit.

Mules are subject to a general prejudice which militates against them in all but limited parts of this country, and on account of this it is difficult to secure competent drivers for them.

The mule is usually more sagacious than the horse, and is scarcely less responsive to proper treatment, yet the idea prevails that whatever service is gotten out of him must be knocked out, the black-snake whip and gag bit being considered essential features of mule team appointments.

Fig. 171.—A Kentucky jack of the size, substance, and shape desired for mule breeding.

Mare mules outsell horse mules on account of their smoother turned bodies and the fact that they are more easily kept in condition.

The Jack.—Jack stock breeders distinguish between the type of jack best adapted to mating with jennies for the production of jack breeding stock and the stamp of jack best suited to mating with mares for the production of mule hybrids.

The Standard of Excellence.—The jack most desired for

mule breeding is at least 16 hands high. The more weight and substance he has the better. He is long and wide in form, having good-sized, well-shaped head and ears, straight legs of ample bone, and well-shaped feet of good size and texture (Fig. 171). Black with light points is the color most favored, not only for appearance sake, but because the get of such a jack out of mares of any or all colors have proven most uniformly of good colors. He should also be stylish.

The native jack, so-called, although but a few generations removed from imported stock, has the reputation of getting a higher class of mules than the imported jacks themselves. Of the imported breeds, the Catalonian, Poitou, Maltese, Andalusian, Majorcan and Italian, the former is most popular.

Fig. 172.—The right stamp of mares as attested by their produce.

The Mare.—The mule is believed to take after the sire in the matter of head, ears, bone, and foot, while its stature and form of body, especially, are derived chiefly from the dam. There are many exceptions to this rule, however. Mares of good size and shape, black, bay, brown, or chestnut in color, and with a dash of hot blood, are best adapted to the production of mules (Fig. 172).

REVIEW

1. What is a mule? a hinny?
2. What are the two general classes of mules and how is each produced?
3. What can be said in favor of using mules instead of horses for farm work?
4. What type and breeding of jack is most desired for breeding mules?
5. What sort of mares make the most satisfactory dams of mules?

CHAPTER XXI

THE MOTOR AS A FACTOR

THE force of the foregoing statements concerning the profit-able production and use of horses will be influenced by one's conception of the future status of the horse. To this end the motor must be reckoned with. At no time in history has the horse been subjected to such keen competition for place and favor as at the present.

The motor is such an important factor as to require considera-tion in any discussion of equine affairs. The view-point, how-ever, should be fair and logical, not obscured by such sentiment or enthusiasm as characterizes a partisan review of either side of the question. There are ardent motorists who would have the horse annihilated for all time, while some riders and drivers would legislate the same end for all motordom; yet neither of these positions is warranted by the facts.

Other Factors.—History is but repeating itself, apparently, as in the case of the invention of gunpowder; the advent of canals and, later, railroads; the adoption of the cable and the trolley on street railways; and the past popularity of the bicycle; each of which in turn threatened to supplant horses in their different fields.

Advantages of the Motor.—An analysis of the situation at present concedes to the motor three distinct advantages over the horse: Speed, endurance, especially in hot weather, and vogue. Whenever the miles covered or the time consumed is the sole consideration it is reasonable to suppose that the motor will be shown the preference. So it is in the case of the doctor or the sales solicitor, men whose earning capacity is limited by the facility with which they can get about; likewise the travelling public and society folk have become so accustomed to a minimum time allowance for making trains or keeping engagements that they could hardly be expected to dispense with the taxicab or limousine. Suburban deliveries are made much more expedi-

314

tiously by auto when they entail long, straight-away runs with few stops; and the moving of large loads to a distant distributing point can be more quickly and cheaply done by the big motor trucks even than by railroad freight.

Advantages of the Horse.—For the about-town delivery of many small parcels, each one to a different house, requiring almost continuous starts and stops, with frequent runs in and out of short streets, the auto deliveries are more costly and less efficient. Horses have their routes, and lend their assistance in anticipating stops and starts or even turning round themselves and waiting round the corner while their driver resorts to a short cut across lots.

Wherever much time is spent in standing or waiting the advantage is with the horse-drawn vehicle on account of the smaller investment represented and the less depreciation involved.

Cost of Feed and of Gasoline.—Clever motor salesmen have taken advantage of the abnormally high cost of horse feeds for the past few years in their calculations of the relative economy of horse-drawn and motor vehicles. But with feed inclining again to a normal level, while the cost of gasoline is advancing at such a rate as to threaten automatically to check the patronage of the motor, unless other fuel or motive power is resorted to, there is little weight in such arguments.

A Motor Age.—There is every evidence of this being a motor age; the motor idea is conspicuous in our mode of dress; it predominates in our conversation. Whereas the small boy of past generations straddled the broomstick or harnessed two overturned chairs and played horse, he now turns his ingenuity to the construction and operation of racing pushmobiles of the latest type and full equipment; patrons of the remnant counters demand that the goods purchased by them shall be delivered by auto, in case the firm is so derelict as to still retain some antiquated specimens of the genus Equus in their delivery service. All this is fully appreciated by those engaged in the business of catering to public patronage, and it is played upon in every possible way by the auto salesman.

Vogue gives to the automobile, however, a much less stable advantage over the horse than does its greater efficiency in long, fast runs. Popular favor is self-limiting, and the stronger the wave of general popularity the harder the brakes will set. The pacemakers of fashion are the ultra-exclusive set; as soon as a fad which they have started gains sufficient momentum to reach the butcher, the baker, and so on, it is considered common and is dropped by the very ones who first became sponsors for it, and their example is invariably followed (Fig. 173). The remarkable increase in the number of cars used each season, together with the great variety of individuals enlisting in the ranks of

Fig. 173.—Park horse to victoria, correctly appointed. An equipage with an individuality which can never become common.

the motorists, suggest that we are rapidly approaching the crest of the wave.

The horse markets, shows, park drives, and bridle paths offer substantial evidence that the horse is being gradually reinstated, not in his former capacity perhaps, because the automobile has modified uses and customs, but in greater favor than ever, so far as some types are concerned. If the activities of the motor road monopolists were properly regulated, both as to the construction and use of roads, a preference for the horse would be shown by many drivers who have been forced off the road by fear of fallen horses and collisions.

With the present vogue abated, the motor will become, no doubt, a cold business proposition, which facilitates affairs in such a multitude of ways as to be indispensable, like the telephone.

Supplements to the Horse in Service.—The roadster, the touring car, and the limousine have all added so much to our possibilities in their respective fields that they must be included in every completely equipped establishment, but there is nothing to render them incompatible with the horse in a kindred relationship. The commercial truck, also, performs so many lines of service so much more acceptably than the horse ever can, that its supremacy within limits cannot be denied. Yet in this the motor is supplementing, not supplanting, the horse in service.

Demand for Saddle Horses.—It may seem like overdrawn optimism to attribute to the automobile any advantages accruing to the horse, but such is not difficult of demonstration. The motor car has been a most important factor in the prevalent country life movement. Distances are so contracted by its use as to place the country within easy access of many who could not otherwise enjoy it. The country without a horse is like a library without books. Fox hunting is becoming the sport of a greater number of people in this country each season, partly, at least, on account of the rapid transit facilities offered by the automobiles.

There are more people riding to-day on doctors' prescriptions than ever before. The convenience of the auto has removed the necessity for even a physiological amount of exercise, which must be compensated for in some other way. Thus, while no doubt depressing the market for coach and road horses, the automobile has furnished a boom to the saddle horse trade.

There is a sentimental side to the subject under discussion. Motor possibilities have left horses, except those in the commercial field, chiefly in the hands of people who want them because they are horses, with the result that they are in their highest estate, a condition most satisfactory to them and most gratifying to those interested in their well-being (Fig. 174). No one who cares for horses regrets either the substitution of the taxicab for the horse-drawn hansom or four-wheeler, nor the transference of the ordinary livery patronage to the garage. He who rides only for the thrill would confer a favor on horse kind by devoting himself to aëronautics.

Better Breeding of Horses.—Finally there is an economic significance to the whole situation. Competition stimulates to best efforts. Now the consumers of horses are discriminating; demand is for horses of the highest type. It has been observed that after an experience in buying and maintaining automobiles

FIG. 174.—Motor advantages enjoyed by the horse.

in service one becomes more appreciative of horse values and more liberal in his allowance for cost. The result will be more intelligent and systematic breeding for a definite purpose, with consequently less failures, and, finally, a more liberal profit to him who meets the demand of those who can afford to discriminate and pay well for what they require.

Prices of Horses Not Reduced.—The extent to which the horse market has actually been influenced by the increasing patronage of the motor vehicle is shown by the following statement from the *Farmer's Advocate:*

" The average price of the different classes of horses on the Chicago market in 1912 was as follows:

Draft horses	$210	Bussers and trammers	$175
Carriage pairs	473	Saddlers	195
Drivers	177	Southern chunks	97
General purposes	160		

" In all but two classes, viz., carriage pairs and drivers, these averages are the highest on record; even carriage horses and drivers sold high."

Under-production may be assigned by some as the cause of normal prices being so well sustained, and it may be so in the case of harness horses; but if the business of the stallion importers, the number of entries at the shows, and the general awakening of interest in draft horse affairs are any criterion, there is more draft horse breeding at this time than ever before.

REVIEW

1. What other factors have in the past threatened to supplant the horse as in the present case of the motor?
2. What are the undisputed advantages of the motor car in commercial service?
3. What advantages must be conceded to the horse in commercial service?
4. Why may the present vogue of the automobile be expected to abate?
5. What classes of horses have felt most keenly the competition with the motor car?
6. What classes owe their increased demand in part, at least, to the motor car?
7. How has the adoption of the motor vehicle improved the welfare of some horses?
8. Will the motor vehicle supplant or supplement the horse in service?
9. What will be its probable effect on the horse breeding industry?
10. To what extent has the common use of the motor affected the horse market?

INDEX